# Ideology and Political Choice

CHATHAM HOUSE STUDIES IN POLITICAL THINKING
SERIES EDITOR: George J. Graham, Jr.
*Vanderbilt University*

# Ideology and Political Choice

## THE SEARCH FOR FREEDOM, JUSTICE, AND VIRTUE

### Vernon Van Dyke
*University of Iowa*

Chatham House Publishers, Inc.
Chatham, New Jersey

IDEOLOGY AND POLITICAL CHOICE
The Search for Freedom, Justice, and Virtue

Chatham House Publishers, Inc.
Box One, Chatham, New Jersey 07928

*Publisher:* Edward Artinian
*Production Supervisor:* Katharine Miller
*Cover Design:* Lawrence Ratzkin
*Composition:* Bang, Motley, Olufsen
*Printing and Binding:* R.R. Donnelley & Sons Company

LIBRARY OF CONGRESS CATALOGING IN PUBLICATION DATA

Van Dyke, Vernon, 1912–
    Ideology and political choice : the search for freedom, justice, and virtue / Vernon Van Dyke
        p.   cm. — (Chatham House studies in political thinking)
    Includes bibliographical references and index.
    ISBN 1-56643-017-8
    1. Political science—United States. 2. Right and left (Political science) 3. Ideology—United States. 4. Liberalism—United States. 5. Conservatism—United States. I. Title II. Series.
JA84.U5V36   1995
320.5'0973—dc20                                          94-36870
                                                             CIP

Manufactured in the United States of America
        10  9  8  7  6  5  4  3  2  1

# Contents

# Chapter 1

# Introduction

THIS BOOK is about political ideologies—current political ideologies in the United States. It is designed to help you choose the ideology you want to endorse and, even more, to help you marshal good reasons for your choice. By the same token, it is designed to help you decide what ideologies to oppose, in whole or in part, and why. Your most likely choice is between some kind of liberalism and some kind of conservatism, but other possibilities exist.

In choosing among ideologies, you will be choosing among action-oriented theories. A political ideology is a guide to political action. It helps you decide what to support, what to oppose, and why. It consists of a set of ideas and principles relating to the purposes to pursue in political life and the methods to employ; that is, relating to ends and means. Thus an ideology requires and reflects a choice among values and decisions about the relative emphasis to give to them; and it requires a choice among political strategies. If you have a well-thought-out political ideology, you are in a position to appraise the appeals of political candidates and officeholders, and in a position to become a candidate and officeholder yourself.

A political ideology is not only a guide to political action, it is also a help in explaining. If you want to know why people or political parties favor one course of action and oppose another, knowledge of their ideology will give you a major part of the answer. Of course, ideologies tend to be general rather than particular in the guidance they give and the explanations they provide, so they may not help much with the finer points, but nevertheless they are likely to be helpful in explaining the larger patterns of behavior.

In addition to guiding and explaining, ideologies provide a basis for justifying or condemning a course of political action. Values (both goal values and instrumental values) are at the heart of ideologies. That is, ideas about good and bad, right and wrong, the desirable and the undesirable, are at their heart. So are ideas about the efficacy and morality of different strategies. Those who adhere to a given ideology are obviously taking the view that the ends and means it recommends are justifiable; others, adhering to a different ideology or bringing different standards of judgment to bear, do not need to agree. Nazism and communism are both ideologies that once got support, but they led to monstrous wrongs. A number of other ideologies contribute to the good, though in varying degrees. This book should put you in a better position to make judgments on such matters.

Note that I am speaking of choices among political ideologies, not choices among political parties. To be sure, most Democrats take stands of a "liberal" sort and most Republicans take stands of a "conservative" sort, but some liberals are Republicans and some conservatives are Democrats. Further, just as voters sometimes split the ticket, voting for some candidates of each major party, so they can be "liberal" on some issues and "conservative" on others.

The definition of *ideology* that I advance (ideology as action-oriented theory) is widely but not universally accepted. The most likely alternative is to treat ideology as a doctrine or dogma and to treat the adherents of an ideology as doctrinaire or dogmatic ideologues, more likely to be fanatical than reasonable. Nazism and communism are ideologies of this sort, but few ideologies are so extreme. In a sense, all ideologies are substitutes for thought, and they get condemned for this reason; but they do not deserve the condemnation. They are substitutes for thought in about the same way as the Ten Commandments are substitutes for thought.

If you accept "Thou shalt not kill" as a rule, you have a guide to behavior and do not need to start out anew to think through the question of murder every time you encounter someone you do not like. Like the Ten Commandments, a political ideology is a convenience and a time-saver, giving you a head start in considering issues that arise. Whether an ideology is a doctrine or dogma is a matter of degree. As long as you are willing to reconsider your ideology when occasion arises, recognizing that you might be wrong, you can reasonably claim that you are not doctrinaire, dogmatic, or fanatical. Reasoned analysis, not blind faith, is what we want.

No matter what those who write about ideologies do, the probability is that they will be accused of bias, and the accusation may have merit. I see in my dictionary the statement that the most pernicious kind of bias consists in falsely supposing that you have none. So, to give you an opportunity either to praise or to discount my judgments, let me say that I regard myself as a progressive liberal. If this is bias, so be it. To me, however, the word *bias* connotes ignorant, unthinking, unreasonable prejudice, and if I am guilty of this at all, I hope that my guilt is minimal. Like the editor of the *New Republic,* I think of my political views as those that a reasonable, intelligent person would take, but then I have to confront the fact that some other reasonable, intelligent persons adopt views that differ from mine. In treating the various positions, my effort is to be objective, and I assume that you would want me to be objective; but the meaning of that word calls for comment. You would not want me to avoid all appraisals, for that would make the book a dull recital of facts. Neither would you want me to rig the analysis somehow so as to make all ideologies appear to be equally attractive. After all, ideologies do have consequences—good and bad consequences for different sets of people—and learning about these consequences is an important purpose of the book. What objectivity requires, as I see it, is not the avoidance of judgment but fairness and reasonableness in selecting the questions to take up and in considering the evidence and arguments relating to them. I hope to be objective in this sense.

I have said that your most likely choices are between some kind of liberalism and some kind of conservatism. The contents gives a fuller list of the possible choices. The book starts out with a chapter on the British background, for that background is surprisingly relevant to American thought and practice. To a remarkable extent, current debates in the United States are reruns of debates that occurred in Britain in the nineteenth century. Next come four chapters on progressive liberalism—one focusing on Franklin D. Roosevelt and the New Deal, two focusing on Lyndon Johnson and the Great Society, and one offering a summary characterization. Governmental activism is a central feature of progressive liberalism—activism aimed mainly at giving worth to liberty and making opportunity equal and effective.

The next two chapters concern *libertarianism* and theory identified with *public choice,* which provide sharp contrasts with progressive liberalism. Libertarians are hostile to government. They are hostile mainly because they think that what happens in a society—in a collectivity—is too complicated to be managed deliberately; our knowledge is too limited. The bigger the collectivity, the greater the problem. Better keep government limited or minimal and leave affairs in the hands of individual persons to the maximum possible extent. Adam Smith, a classical liberal, first advanced the idea of an invisible hand that coordinates the activities of selfish persons so that, inadvertently, the public good gets served, but the idea fits well with modern libertarianism. Give people liberty, defined simply as the absence of governmental restraint, and wonders will be achieved. As I have noted, progressive liberals want people to have liberty too, but they are not satisfied with the kind of liberty that permits the big fish to eat the little ones. If liberty is to have worth, people must be in a position to take advantage of it. So progressive liberals want to use government as an instrument in making liberty worthwhile.

Theorists of *public choice* dwell on one theme: that the dominant concern of political leaders and all those employed by government (in truth, the dominant concern of people generally) is with their own selfish interests, not with the promotion of the public good. And since government turns out to be mainly a means by which officeholders and bureaucrats promote their own selfish interests, we should be distrustful of it and should restrict its role as narrowly as possible.

Next come chapters on five kinds of conservatism, kinds that I call conservative, economic, social, progressive, and neo-. Yes, I speak of both conservative and progressive conservatism. Conservative conservatives stress tradition and the wisdom of our ancestors and want us to be cautious and prudent about change. Economic conservatives say that their paramount concern is with prosperity and that the way to achieve it is to maximize liberty (defined as the absence of governmental restraint), keeping taxes low and governmental regulations sparse. Social conservatives emphasize the moral and the religious, claiming a transcendental source for their conception of the moral and putting their emphasis on such issues as abortion, the treatment of homosexual persons, and prayer in the schools. Progressive conservatives are like progressive liberals in wanting to enhance the well-being of the poor but are like the economic conservatives in wanting to do it by reducing taxes and the role of government. Neoconservatives are also eclectic, sharing some of the concerns of progressive liberals and some of the concerns of both the economic and social conservatives.

I wish I could provide you with some general, overarching definition of *liberal* and *conservative,* but I cannot. The problem stems in large part from the fact that classical and progressive liberalism differ so sharply from each other. A person who is *liberal* in the classical sense has more in common with the economic conservatives (with Ronald Reagan as their paragon) than with progressive liberals. The problem also stems from the fact that some who call themselves conservative, particularly progressive conservatives, have more in common with progressive liberals than, say, with those whom I call conservative conservatives. It's a muddle, but we have to work with the meanings that the words have historically acquired.

As is implicit in the above, the book reflects the fact that ideologies are identified mainly on the basis of the stands taken on domestic issues. Neoconservatism comes close to being an exception, for special alarm about the menace of communism and the former Soviet Union has been one of its central features. But the generalization is that people united ideologically on domestic issues tend to divide on foreign policy issues, which also means that people who are divided on domestic matters may find themselves united when they look abroad. Support exists for isolationism, for an emphasis on the national interest, for the promotion of human rights and/or democracy in the world, and for efforts to strengthen the United Nations and the rule of law. And debate over the choice is accompanied by a good deal of scorn for those who take the wrong position. Ideological positions on foreign policy issues come up in chapter 14.

The ideological lineup described in this book has not always existed and may not endure. Progressive liberalism dominated American life almost unchallenged for several decades after the Great Depression, few calling themselves conservative. As recently as 1976 Gertrude Himmelfarb declared that "the label conservatism has been so thoroughly vitiated that it is hopeless to try to rehabilitate it." Then came Ronald Reagan, doing what Himmelfarb had regarded as hopeless. With help from others, he made conservatism a popular label. Moreover, he heaped scorn on the "L-word," making "tax and spend" its regular modifier; and he did this so successfully that people who thought of themselves as liberal became hesitant to admit it. The result is that political leaders who proclaim their liberalism have become about as scarce as admitted conservatives were in the years after World War II.

While Reagan was in the White House the different kinds of conservatives were starry-eyed and full of zeal, confident that the future belonged to them. Then came Bush, whom conservatives disowned largely because he raised taxes and signed a "quota" bill; then also came the collapse of communism and the breakup of the Soviet Union, depriving the various kinds of conservatives of a basis for their coalition. Now the conservatives are in disarray. They can still disparage government and call for lower taxes and fewer regulations, but their unity now seems to depend more on attacking the Clintons on questions of character and personal behavior.

So, what next? If conservatism is in disarray, is liberalism resurgent, or is it so vitiated that it is beyond rehabilitation? In a sense, this is the subject of the final chapter: how to classify President Clinton and his administration. Clinton denies that he is a liberal, and he follows some policies that do not fit with progressive liberalism, stealing some of the thunder of conservatives in the process. At the same time, most of his policies and most of his rhetoric do fit. Among other things, he repeatedly expresses the hope that people will develop their God-given talents to the fullest. Reagan would endorse the hope, but, stressing self-reliance, he would only offer three cheers for those who try. Clinton wants to use government to help people achieve the goal, which is vintage liberalism. One of the suggestions is that the combination of attitudes espoused by Clinton should be described as *neoliberalism*.

In the final chapter I compare the conceptions of liberalism and conservatism developed in this book with conceptions associated with public opinion polling. And I offer some observations on the reasons for ideological disagreements.

Enjoy the book.

# Chapter 2

# The British Background

THE CENTRAL ISSUE in the ideological struggles in Britain a century and more ago was the same as the central issue in the United States today. It concerns relationships between government and the individual. What responsibilities should each have? What roles should each play? For what kinds of purposes and to what extent should government intervene in economic, social, and cultural life? Conversely, in what connections should government stand back, leaving people on their own? Why? And what kind of role, if any, should people have in resolving these and other public issues; that is, how democratic should government be?

The classical liberals of nineteenth-century Britain had answers to these questions that, oddly enough, provide a background for later chapters in this book on libertarianism and one of the varieties of American conservatism. And the "new" liberals who came forward in Britain toward the end of the nineteenth century had answers that provide a background for the later chapters on progressive liberalism in the United States.

## A Preview

I start with a preview. The basic concern of classical liberals was with the individual, and more particularly with the freedom or liberty of the individual. As classical liberals saw it, certain governmental arrangements and policies were the principal enemy of freedom in both political and economic life. The arrangements in question were those that gave extensive if not absolute power to the Crown, and the policies in question were those relating to civil liberties, mercantilism, and political participation.

The changed arrangements that the liberals sought with respect to the Crown were designed to curb its powers. The liberals were skeptical about universal suffrage, but sought representative government of a sort and the rule of law—including an independent parliament and an independent judiciary. Government should rest on the consent of the governed, or at least some of the governed. More particularly, there should be no taxation without representation.

The changed policies that the liberals sought with respect to civil liberties are suggested by the Bill of Rights in the Constitution of the United States. People should have freedom of religion, speech, press, and assembly. They should be free from arbitrary searches and seizures and entitled to due process of law and equality before the law.

In the economic realm, classical liberals sought to reduce the role of government, calling for the repeal of mercantilist regulations that limited both domestic and international trade and commerce. They took the private ownership of property for granted, believed that people are the best judges of their own interests, and accepted the pursuit of self-interest as the basic motive in economic life. People should be self-reliant.

Underlying the liberal stance was an assumption concerning the definition of freedom: freedom is what exists in the absence of coercion or restraint, actual or threatened. A person not coerced or restrained has unlimited freedom. Liberals were especially sensitive to coercion or restraint exercised by government. Also underlying the stance was the assumption that in the main, people can be counted on to be rational and tolerant and that progress is both desirable and a reasonable expectation.

These beliefs provided a basis for great progress, but they brought out problems. One of them is suggested by the observation that freedom for the wolf means death for the sheep. More generally, it is suggested by the possibility that an exercise of freedom by one person might encroach on the rights or damage the interests of another. The other problem—a related problem—is suggested by the possibility that, defined negatively as the absence of coercion or restraint, freedom might be a mockery. The problem is illustrated by thinking of the rich person and the pauper, both free to choose between going to a hotel or sleeping under a bridge.

The wolf/sheep problem was of course not new. Some people had always sought to advance their interests with scant regard for the interests of others and perhaps at the expense of others. Some had always started out in life with more advantages than others. There had always been inequalities. To some classical liberals this was fully acceptable, and, stressing liberty and the imperatives of self-reliance, they became social Darwinists—the political and intellectual forebears of today's libertarians and of many of today's conservatives. If some got rich while others had difficulty keeping themselves alive, so be it. Others became uncomfortable with this attitude and began seeking governmental restrictions on wolflike behavior and governmental programs for protecting the sheep and promoting their well-being.

The second problem was more difficult—the problem that freedom, defined as the absence of coercion or restraint, might be a mockery. Even if the rich man was not like a wolf and even if the pauper was not like a sheep, was the pauper really free to go to a hotel? The argument was that a negative conception of freedom was not enough —that freedom should be conceived in a positive way as what exists in the presence of an effective opportunity to choose. No choice, no freedom—or at least no freedom that was meaningful or worthwhile. The greater the range of choices, the greater the freedom. Freedom, then, was a power, and the main enemy of freedom was no longer royal absolutism and governmental interventionism but all those circumstances, in both the public and the private realm, that limited the capacity and the opportunity to choose among different imaginable courses of action. Freedom—worthwhile freedom—was to be achieved not by restricting the role of government but by expanding it—by using government as an active instrument in changing the circumstances that limited the choices of so many people.

Those taking this line, opposing the social Darwinists, are known as "new" liberals and are the political and intellectual forebears of today's progressive liberals in the United States. They won out in Britain near the turn of the century, the extension of the franchise having enhanced their power.

My purpose now is to elaborate on the above themes.

## The Focus on the Individual

Classical liberals took it for granted that the focus should be on the individual. They might have thought in terms of families, communities, economic classes, or nations, but instead, without arguing the case, they put the individual at center stage. In doing this they tended to conjure up an imaginary original state of nature in which, in the absence of government, all men were endowed—equally endowed —with natural liberties or rights.

Thomas Hobbes (d. 1679) was one of those who appealed to the idea of a state of nature. He assumed that in this state every man not only enjoyed unlimited liberty but also was driven by an insatiable lust for power, bringing on a war of all against all and making life "solitary, nasty, brutish, and short." Needing protection for life and property, men therefore made a social contract, establishing government. They thus forswore certain of their liberties but retained the rest; and protecting the rest against arbitrary government became a major concern.

The focus on the individual was not inevitable. It would have been easy to imagine a state of nature in which the individual was a member of a family, either dependent or a source of support for other family members according to age and circumstance. The prime concern might thus have been for the well-being of the family rather than of the individual considered alone. And this collectivist orientation might have been extended to a clan or community, individuals being required to safeguard and promote its interests. After all, no one is an island. The well-being of everyone depends on the social structure —on institutions and rules both old and new. Individuals who succeed do so not simply on the basis of their own industry and talents but also on the basis of the social system that provides opportunities and rewards. And the prime concern might have been for preserving and improving the social structure and the general welfare of people within it.

But Hobbes and many others chose not to take this approach. They were not entirely unmindful of the group, joining, for example, in accepting the need for national defense. But still they were mainly individualists.

## Constitutional Government and Civil Rights

The British started limiting the power of the monarch by wringing the Magna Carta from King John in 1215, and they took subsequent steps (most notably in the Glorious Revolution of 1688) that I will not attempt to summarize here—steps adding to the powers of Parliament and the courts and eventually making the monarch more a symbol than a wielder of governmental power. In the nineteenth and twentieth centuries they took successive steps toward universal adult suffrage.

The counterpart in the United States was the constitutional emphasis on checks and balances and the separation of powers, as well as the gradual extension of the suffrage.

Among the classical liberals, John Stuart Mill (d. 1873) gave fullest expression to the emphasis on the personal liberty of the individual, *On Liberty* being his best-known work. His general theme was that government should leave people alone, provided they do not harm others. He held that since we do not know beyond doubt what is desirable and undesirable, people should be allowed to argue the question freely, neither government nor society imposing any restraint on speech or press. Further, in their own lives people should be free to decide for themselves what to do and what not to do—free to experiment—provided always that they respect the right of others to do the same, inflicting no harm on them.

Several statements by Mill reflect these attitudes. "The only freedom that deserves the name," he said, "is that of pursuing our own good in our own way, so long as we do not attempt to deprive others of theirs, or impede their efforts to obtain it" (Mill 1975, 14). His guiding principle was that

> ... the sole end for which mankind are warranted, individually or collectively, in interfering with the liberty of action of any of their number, is self-protection. That the only purpose for which power can be rightfully exercised over any member of a civilised community, against his will, is to prevent harm to others. His own good, either physical or moral, is not a sufficient warrant .... (p. 10)

Mill went on to say that the required hands-off policy relates only to "human beings in the maturity of their faculties." Further, he assumed a state of civilization that is sufficiently advanced to make people "capable of being improved by free and equal discussion."

Mill insisted especially on freedom of the press: "If all mankind minus one were of one opinion, and only one person were of the contrary opinion, mankind would be no more justified in silencing that one person, than he, if he had the power, would be justified in silencing mankind" (p. 18).

## Economic Freedom

Adam Smith (d. 1790) was the major early liberal spokesman for economic freedom for the individual, especially in *The Wealth of Nations*. He wrote at a time when government followed mercantilist policies, interfering extensively in economic life: creating monopolies, regulating the uses of capital and labor, granting trading privileges and rights to specific persons and companies, restricting the importation and exportation of goods, and insisting on laws concerning succession that limited the purchase and sale of land. Such policies showed no trust in a free market and conceded little freedom to entrepreneurs. And the situation was made all the worse by incredibly low standards of honesty and competence in government, leading to erratic and arbitrary differentiation.

In measured and reasoned terms, Smith spoke against most of the government's economic policies, which he regarded as absurd. He thought that if all people could have liberty and could confidently expect, based on law, that they would enjoy the fruits of their labor, these conditions alone would be sufficient to make the economy flourish. In more modern terms, he believed that the establishment of a free market was the path to prosperity.

> The natural effort of every individual to better his own condition, when suffered to exert itself with freedom and security, is so powerful a principle, that it is alone, and without any assistance, not only capable of carrying on the society to wealth and prosperity, but of surmounting a hundred impertinent obstructions with which the folly of human laws too often encumbers its operations. (Smith 1976, 2:49–50)

Smith did not expect that people in a free market would strive benevolently to serve the public good. Instead, he urged the importance of self-interest as the main motivation in economic life and the main force making for progress. He acknowledged that people are in constant need of help from others, but believed that the best way to get it is to show them that the desired action is in their self-interest. "It is not from the benevolence of the butcher, the brewer, or the baker that we expect our dinner, but from their regard for their own interest. We address ourselves, not to their humanity but to their self-love, and never talk to them of our own necessities but of their own advantages" (2:18).

Smith acknowledged pitfalls in a policy appealing to self-interest. His caustic view was that "people of the same trade seldom meet together, even for merriment and diversion, but the conversation ends in a conspiracy against the public, or in some contrivance to raise prices." But he trusted to competition to protect the public good. Given competition, he held that the individual, by pursuing his own interest, "frequently promotes that of society more effectually than when he really intends to promote it." He is "led by an invisible hand to promote an end which was no part of his intention" (1, 47).

## Laissez Faire?

The views described above suggest a policy of *laissez faire* for government, and the policies of nineteenth-century Britain did go in that direction. "Nineteenth century England may be said to have come closer to experiencing an age of *laissez faire* than any other society in the last five hundred years of world history" (Taylor 1971, 64). Many of the mercantilist restrictions on the market, including the Corn Laws and the Navigation Acts, were repealed. A substantial degree of freedom was established, in both international and domestic commerce. But the acceptance of *laissez faire* was not doctrinaire. Neither Adam Smith nor any other English economist preached it as absolute dogma.

Instead of swinging fully to *laissez faire,* the government in London enacted some interventionist measures while repealing others. It was responding to the wolf/sheep problem mentioned earlier, and to the problem that freedom defined negatively might be worthless. In 1833 Parliament adopted a child labor law and a few years later prohibited the employment of women and children in the underground workings of collieries. At various times it adopted legislation having to do with sanitation and health in places of employment, and well before the end of the century the principle was established that one of government's major concerns was the regulation of the conditions of labor.

In the 1830s the government in London started extending support for education, and in 1870 it more clearly laid the foundation for a national system of state-supported elementary education. In 1840 it assumed powers of supervision and inspection over the railways. In 1848 it adopted a Public Health Act, and in 1867 it accepted responsibility for a system of medical care for the poor. Enough measures of these sorts were enacted that some trace the beginning of the welfare state to the Victorian era.

Adam Smith and John Stuart Mill are among those who, although supporting *laissez faire,* also called for many departures from it. So numerous were Smith's departures that in 1989 Adam Meyerson, who edits *Policy Review* for the conservative Heritage Foundation, wrote an article entitled "Adam Smith's Welfare State. Generous Government is Consistent with a Market Economy." As Meyerson says, Smith's *Wealth of Nations* makes a case for

> a number of government programs, among them universal public education, public health measures against contagious diseases, safety regulations such as the obligation to construct fire walls, and labor regulations protecting workmen against fraudulent payment by em-

ployers. Smith saw no contradiction between his general opposition to economic regulation and his support for safety regulation as well as programs providing opportunity for the less fortunate.

Smith named various duties of government here and there through his writing and then emphasized three main duties when he gave explicit consideration to the problem. The first, he said, is "that of protecting society from the violence and invasion of other independent societies"—that is, of providing for national defense. The second is "that of protecting, as far as possible, every member of the society from the injustice or oppression of every other member of it, or the duty of establishing an exact administration of justice." And the third is "that of erecting and maintaining those public institutions and those public works, which, though they may not be in the highest degree advantageous to a great society, are, however, of such a nature, that the profit could never repay the expence to any individual or small number of individuals"—for example, those "facilitating the commerce of the society, and ... promoting the instruction of the people" (Smith 1976, 2:213, 231, 244).

These duties of government are potentially extensive. Governments facing great foreign danger or war have sometimes virtually taken over the national economy. Similarly, governments seeking to protect people from injustice and oppression have taken on a vast range of functions, and so have governments seeking to erect and maintain public institutions and public works that are unattractive to private enterprise. Support for public education, the administration of rules designed to protect people from injury by others, and the construction and maintenance of the economic infrastructure—highways, bridges, airports, and ports—are major activities of government. Meyerson's conclusion on this point is that "Smith offers an intellectual framework for a generous and compassionate government consistent with a competitive market economy."

It goes without saying that Smith conceded a taxing power to government. In the light of contemporary right-wing demands that taxation be at a flat rate, it is more important to note that Smith explicitly recommended that taxation be progressive and therefore redistributive: "The subjects of every state ought to contribute towards the support of the government, as nearly as possible, in proportion to their respective abilities; that is, in proportion to the revenue they respectively enjoy under the protection of the state" (Smith 1976, 2:350).

Moderation with respect to *laissez faire* should not be surprising.

Even those convinced that it is the best strategy for achieving prosperity might also want to pursue or promote other values for which a different strategy would be better. Adam Smith himself took the view that "defence is of much more importance than opulence," and on this basis said that the navigation act—a gross departure from *laissez faire*—was "perhaps the wisest of all the commercial regulations of England" (Smith 1976, 1:487). Along this same line, it is plausible that those attaching importance to education or health care would conclude that *laissez faire* was hardly the most promising strategy to pursue.

Like Adam Smith, John Stuart Mill took the view that people have obligations toward each other and that government has certain rights of intervention. "Everyone who receives the protection of society," he said, "owes a return for the benefit." Not only should they refrain from harming others, but they should also bear their share "of the labors and sacrifices incurred for defending the society or its members from injury and molestation," and society is justified in enforcing this rule (Mill 1975, 70).

In harmony with this principle, Mill assigned extensive rights and duties to government, coming close to the endorsement of socialism in his later years. He held that taxes should be redistributive, imposed only on people with incomes above the subsistence level and progressive when levied on gifts and inheritances. Further, according to Mill, government may own certain utilities, including gas, water, and railways; it may take responsibility for "a number of services of 'general convenience' ranging from paving, lighting, and cleaning of streets to subsidizing scientific research, running the Post Office, and building lighthouses," and it should care for people who are unable to care for themselves, a potentially huge undertaking. Government should give people a legal entitlement to public assistance, making dependence on private charity unnecessary.

In addition, Mill held that trade is "a social act" and that the conduct of the trader "comes within the jurisdiction of society"; government is not infringing the principle of individual liberty if it prohibits the adulteration of products or imposes sanitary precautions. "Leaving people to themselves is always better, *caeteris paribus,* than controlling them; but that they may be legitimately controlled for these ends is in principle undeniable." Government is free to impose restrictions on dealers in liquor, since they have an interest in promoting intemperance, a real evil, and it is not a violation of liberty if government permits a couple to marry only if they can show that they have the means of supporting a family.

It was to Mill a "self-evident axiom" that government is free to require everyone to be educated up to a certain standard, although not necessarily in public schools. Moreover, the state is bound "to maintain a vigilant control" over the exercise of any power that one person has over another.

Mill spoke of the "many positive acts for the benefit of others" that people may rightfully be compelled to perform, and he was willing to require people to bear their share of the "labours and sacrifices incurred for defending the society or its members from injury and molestation." Moreover, his proviso concerning the prevention of harm to others opens the way to far-ranging governmental action relating to what we now call externalities—a subject that I treat later.

Although Mill stated his principles in such a way that they seemingly preclude arbitrary differentiation among persons, he did not explicitly deal with the question of equal and nondiscriminatory treatment, with one exception. The exception related to women, as in his book on *The Subjection of Women.* Wives, he said, "should have the same rights, and should receive the protection of law in the same manner, as all other persons." At the time he championed the principle, it was revolutionary.

In sum, while both Adam Smith and John Stuart Mill endorsed *laissez faire,* they did not regard it as a strict rule. They contemplated numerous sorts of governmental intervention in economic and social life.

## Social Darwinism

Although Smith, Mill, and others accepted and recommended departures from *laissez faire,* not all liberals did. A few took an extreme stand, characterized by the statement that what they sought was a night-watchman state, a minimal state. The permanent head of the British Treasury at mid-century provides an illustration. He deplored what he regarded as a "bolstering and cockering system" under which he thought people had grown worse rather than better. He classified dependence on government as a "moral disease." With respect to the Irish famine, "he seems to have believed that [it] was God's judgment on an undeserving and indolent people that showed too little self-reliance," and he thought that the calamity "must not be too much mitigated." "Death by starvation was a painful but necessary 'discipline' essential to secure a greater good" (Greenleaf 1983, 2:44).

Similarly, *The Economist* endorsed *laissez faire* or minimal government in language that has close parallels in libertarian journals today. If the state attempts to provide for the welfare of the people, *The Economist* held, it assumes a responsibility unwisely. One of the effects will be to "promote the helplessness of the masses," for they will come "to rely on government and take no care for themselves." It was a mistake for government to limit the hours of work or to assume any responsibility for the water supply or urban sanitation. It should not support education or research, nor should it have laws concerning patents and copyrights. If the system of self-interest did not lead to the general welfare, no system of government could accomplish it (Greenleaf 1983, 2:45–47).

Goldsmith put this line of thought in verse:

> How small, of all that human hearts endure,
> That part which laws or kings can cause or cure,
> Still to ourselves in every place consign'd,
> Our own felicity we make or find ....

Herbert Spencer was the outstanding champion of such attitudes. In fact, the idea of social Darwinism—the survival of the fittest—is associated above all with him. "Each individual," he held, "ought to receive the benefit and the evils of his own nature and consequent conduct: neither being prevented from having whatever good his actions normally bring to him, nor allowed to shoulder off on to other persons whatever ill is brought to him by his actions" (Spencer 1898, 2:17).

The "true function of the state," as Spencer saw it, is to protect people against aggressions, external and internal. If government tries to do more, it will be unable to foresee the consequences, and the high probability is that it will botch the job or somehow do more harm than good. Government should not support an educational system, operate a postal service, provide a sewage system, or control the currency. Least of all should it tax one person for the benefit of another. "Coercive philanthropy" is intolerable. "If, without an option, a man has to labour for a society (through the payment of taxes) then, to the degree that he has to do this, he is a slave."

> The poverty of the incapable, the distresses that come upon the imprudent, the starvation of the idle, and those shoulderings aside of the weak by the strong, which leave so many 'in shallows and in miseries,' are the decrees of a large, far-seeing benevolence.... It seems hard that widows and orphans should be left to struggle for life or death. Nevertheless, when regarded not separately, but in con-

nection with the interests of universal humanity, these harsh fatalities are seen to be full of the highest beneficence—the same beneficence which brings to early graves the children of diseased parents, and singles out the low-spirited, the intemperate, and the debilitated as the victims of an epidemic. (Greenleaf 1983, 2:76–77)

It was the natural order of things that society should be rid of "unhealthy, imbecile, slow, vacillating, faithless members." The Poor Laws, giving succor to failures, were indefensible. Do-gooders, "in their eagerness to prevent the really salutary sufferings that surround us," ended up inflicting on society "a continually increasing curse."

Suppose two societies [said Spencer], otherwise equal, in one of which the superior are allowed to retain, for their own benefit and the benefit of their offspring, the entire proceeds of their labour; but in the other of which the superior have taken from them part of these proceeds for the benefit of the inferior and their offspring. Evidently the superior will thrive and multiply more in the first than in the second.... The ultimate result of shielding men from the effects of their folly is to fill the world with fools. (Greenleaf 1983, 2:79)

Note the assumption of social Darwinists that people fully deserve whatever happens to them. If they suffer misfortune, it is a result of their own folly. If they strike it rich, it is a result of their own industry and shrewdness. Spencer showed no concern for the fact that the circumstances into which people are born may have a profound effect on their fate; more generally, he showed no concern for equality of opportunity. Neither did he seem aware of the fact that the free market sometimes works in inequitable ways, throwing willing and able people out of work through no fault of their own or failing to provide jobs for them in the first place. If widows and orphans suffered and died, so be it, for society would then be rid of the unfit; and tacitly Spencer was willing to apply the same rule to babies, children, the handicapped, the sickly, and the elderly, for those who did not take care of themselves should suffer the consequences. Dependency and poverty were signs of personal deficiency with natural consequences that were in the long run benign. The devil take the hindmost.

## New Liberalism

Social Darwinism did not carry the day in Britain. On the contrary, as the years passed through the nineteenth century, more and more changes occurred going in the opposite direction—toward more active governmental efforts aimed at social amelioration.

Several factors produced the change. First was an increasing sensitivity to poverty and squalor. In particular, a study of conditions in East London drew attention to the fact that approximately a third of the families were living at or below the subsistence level, and the presumption had to be that approximately the same situation existed throughout the realm.

Second (and more important), the view came to be widely accepted that, to a large extent, the poor were poor more for social reasons than because of their personal shortcomings. The problem was systemic and impersonal. Unemployment was to be explained by deficiencies in the free market; recessions and depressions threw able and willing workers out of work. One-third of the paupers were children, one-tenth were mentally ill, and half were infirm or aged—people who could not be expected to provide for themselves. Herbert Spencer could argue, of course, that parents rather than the government should take care of children and that if people failed to provide for their old age it was their own fault, but not everyone accepted such arguments as realistic.

A third consideration was philosophic, relating to the definition of freedom. Here T.H. Green led the way in holding that instead of viewing freedom as what exists in the absence of coercion or restraint, we should view it as the presence of a power. The person who has to sleep under a bridge because he lacks the money to rent a room is not free. "When we speak of freedom ... we mean a positive power or capacity of doing or enjoying something worth doing or enjoying...." The growth of a society in freedom, Green held, is to be measured "by the greater power on the part of the citizens as a body to make the most and best of themselves." Freedom is "the liberation of the powers of all men equally for contributions to the common good" (Green 1906, 3:371–72).

Green did not need to link his revised conception of freedom so closely with the promotion of the common good, for it is obvious that freedom as it is widely understood might be exercised in antisocial ways. Isaiah Berlin has advanced an affirmative conception of freedom that is less restrictive. To him freedom "is the opportunity to act ... the possibility of action." It exists in the absence of obstacles to possible choices and activities (Berlin 1970, xxxix, xlii). The possibilities of action open to a person who is poor, uneducated, or sick are obviously limited, which (according to Berlin's definition) means that the freedom of such persons is limited. The "new" liberals wanted governmental action to reduce the limits on freedom imposed by such conditions.

Note a possible source of confusion about the definition of freedom. Earlier in this chapter I in effect accept a negative definition of freedom—that freedom is what exists in the absence of coercion or restraint. Although accepting this definition, I also point out that when freedom is defined in this negative way, it may be without worth, raising the question whether government should adopt policies designed to give it worth. Green and Berlin, in contrast, reject the negative definition and adopt a positive one: freedom should be said to exist only in the presence of a capacity or a power to exercise it. Although the two definitions differ, they may call for precisely the same sorts of governmental policies.

The fourth major factor giving rise to the new liberalism was the need of the Liberal Party in Britain to meet the competition of other parties. I elaborate on this point below.

The result, beginning in the 1890s, was the accentuation of an already existing trend toward political and social reform, measures being enacted relating to subjects ranging from the establishment of public baths to the adoption of universal manhood suffrage. A surge of reform measures followed a Liberal electoral victory in 1906. Anticipating Lyndon Johnson by more than fifty years, Lloyd George called his "People's Budget" of 1909 a "War Budget."

> It is for raising money to wage implacable war against poverty and squalidness. I cannot help believing that before this generation has passed away, we shall have advanced a great step towards that good time when poverty, wretchedness and the human degradation which always follow in its camp will be as remote to the people of this country as the wolves which once infested its forests. (Cross 1963, 102)

The Liberal legislative program included measures providing for land reform, minimum wages, the protection of children, limits on the hours of work in coal mines, unemployment exchanges, old age pensions, and health and unemployment insurance. The pensions and the payments in connection with health and unemployment insurance were modest, but significant precedents were established. Moreover, the terms of political debate were shifted and sharpened. Given the objective of eliminating poverty, ignorance, and disease, as one of the Liberal leaders put it, it was necessary to attack "excessive inequity in the distribution of wealth." "Liberalism had to recognize that the great divide in society was between rich and poor and that its task was to narrow this gulf by political action" (Pearson and Williams 1984, 60). Thus the liberals took up a modest form of egalitarianism. Note that the objective was to "narrow this gulf," not to eliminate it. The liberals were not levelers.

Different authors trace the beginning of the welfare state to different periods, one of them being the decade of liberal reforms in Britain prior to the outbreak of World War I. The principle followed was the opposite of social Darwinism, reflecting the view that "it is the duty of government to do whatever is conducive to the welfare of the governed" (Greenleaf 1983, 1:126).

The shift in liberal concerns, it should be noted, can be viewed in a different light. The early liberals were overwhelmingly concerned with the production of wealth. To be sure, some of them showed concern for distribution in calling for relief for the indigent. Hobbes, for example, took the view that the indigent "ought not to be left to the Charity of private persons; but to be provided for, (as far as the necessities of Nature require), by the Lawes of the Common-wealth." And Locke declared that "charity gives every man a title to so much out of another's plenty as will keep him from extream want, where he has no means to subsist otherwise" (Moon 1988, 86–76). But Adam Smith neglected the subject, showing no concern for poverty. In contrast, the new liberals at the turn of the century preoccupied themselves with poverty and therefore with the problem of the distribution of wealth. And the new liberals thus accepted the possibility that horrified the social Darwinists—that what is done in the name of a more equitable distribution may have an adverse effect on production.

The principles of the new liberalism persisted through both world wars. A resolution of the Liberal Assembly of 1942 declared: "The four social evils that beset the people are ignorance, squalor, idleness and want. The Liberal party is determined to use the power of the State to do whatever is necessary to overcome those evils."

The Beveridge report of the World War II period, calling for the use of government to secure everyone against certain hazards of life from the cradle to the grave, had no connection with the Liberal Party but nevertheless reflected its principles. Beveridge joined the party some time after issuing his report. He saw want as "a needless scandal due to not taking the trouble to prevent it" (Freeden 1986, 366–68).

## A National Consensus?

The explanation that I give above of the shift of the Liberals to a positive conception of liberty includes a reference to the need to meet competition from other parties. It is now time to focus on that aspect of the matter.

From the early nineteenth century, two main strands of thought existed within the Conservative (Tory) Party, a strand calling for minimal government and a strand calling for benevolent paternalism (Greenleaf 1983, 2:193). The first of these strands came to be associated with social Darwinism and the negative conception of liberty, and the second came to be associated with Tory humanitarianism and the positive conception of liberty.

Through the last half of the nineteenth century and beyond, the second strand was dominant. The assumption was that the operations of the free market did not adequately serve the interests of a significant portion of the population, especially the working class, and that government should step in lest those neglected be alienated and become a threat to social equilibrium and stability. Not that class distinctions needed to be erased; conservatism was associated with a belief in hierarchy. But an aristocratic idea of *noblesse oblige* prevailed, implying that the lord of the manor had a duty to look after the poor. Norman Barry expands on this idea, saying that, according to conservatives:

> A property right is not an unlimited right to do what one will with what is rightfully one's own; it is a right limited by the needs of the community. Thus, the owners of lands and estates are understood to be carriers of a tradition; they have positive duties to maintain that tradition. The "duties" of property are never precisely defined in conservatism (perhaps they never can be), but they would include charitable obligations, public service, and the exercise of the political arts on behalf of the general good rather than for specific interest groups. (Barry 1987, 91)

Note the reference to the concern of the British conservatives for community. They sought to preserve "a harmonious, organic society, in which each of a complex hierarchy of ranks would receive its due share of the protection and support of the state."

As a guardian of the nation, Benjamin Disraeli reflected these views. In his eyes, "the objects of Toryism are maintenance of the old institutions of the country, preservation of the Empire, and elevation of the condition of the people" (Kirk 1953, 243). He took it for granted that the Conservative Party should "support all those measures, the object of which is to elevate the moral and social condition of the Working Classes, by lessening their hours of toil—by improving their means of health—and by cultivating their intelligence." And Disraeli championed social reform measures accordingly. His policies led to the Tory claim that "we have been in the forefront of the battle to help the people of this country to raise themselves, more than a generation before the word *Socialism* was coined" (Greenleaf 1983, 2:202, 208).

Disraeli's successor, Lord Salisbury, was suspicious of democracy and inclined to view efforts to gain working-class support through social reform as bribery, but he nevertheless "accepted the practical need to integrate the working classes into the social whole by reforming their living conditions." And he was attentive to the needs of the middle class (Pearson and Williams 1984, 84–85). Joseph Chamberlain, who followed in the Conservative leadership, even chided the Liberals for "failing to see that social reform was the question that must dominate contemporary politics." "Government," he said, "is the organised expression of the wishes and wants of the people, and under these circumstances let us cease to regard it with suspicion" (Greenleaf 1983, 2:227). He was willing that his program should be described as sounding the death knell of the *laissez-faire* system.

Faced with such competition from the Tories, it is not surprising that the liberals became champions of social reform. Moreover, in 1886 the Liberal Party split, largely over the question of home rule for Ireland, losing the support of the Whigs and of many radicals. And this made the party more than ever dependent on working-class votes—at the very time the trade unions were moving toward the establishment of the Labour Party with its socialist challenge. The future of the party thus seemed to depend on shifting away from an emphasis on "natural liberties" and toward an emphasis on enhancing liberty, affirmatively conceived, through social reform. With this partisan interest reinforcing the three considerations already mentioned, the shift occurred.

The above account indicates that the principles of ameliorative, humanitarian reform were not the exclusive preserve of the Liberal Party. Instead, for approximately a century, these principles were widely shared. Thus Norman Barry speaks of a consensus in Britain on economic and social policy after World War II—a consensus that he summarizes as follows:

> the near universal agreement on a positive role for the state in creating full employment, a structure of collectivised welfare services, the gradual implementation of social policies designed to bring about a

greater measure of equality than would occur as a consequence of unhampered market processes, the setting of targets of economic growth, and a significant measure of economic planning. The consensus view was that these aims were compatible with personal liberty, the rule of law, and the maintenance of a large private enterprise market economy.... (Barry 1979, 3)

Similarly, writing in 1958, Richard Titmuss points out that in the preceding decade Conservative and Labor governments alike had "claimed the maintenance of 'the Welfare State' as an article of faith." About the same time a Liberal group in England "urged that Liberalism repudiate any antithesis between liberty and welfare, regarding them rather as complementary means to the same basic end: the creation of opportunities for men and women to become self-directing, responsible persons" (Greenleaf 1983, 2:180).

Although a substantial consensus existed in the post–World War II years, a social Darwinist strand of thought—a libertarian strand —persisted in the Conservative Party, and that strand became the dominant one when Margaret Thatcher became the party leader in 1975.

The increasing concern of the British government for welfare necessarily had implications for its role in taxing and spending. Jeff Lipkis's figures are that government spending as a percentage of the GNP went up from 9 percent in 1870 to 52 percent in 1979, when Thatcher came to power. Lipkis cites these figures in explaining what he regards as Britain's decline (Lipkis 1991, 37).

## Reprise

A statement by A. V. Dicey—whether it expresses his own view or the view that some liberals take—provides a basis for a reprise: "Every person is in the main and as a general rule the best judge of his own happiness. Hence legislation should aim at the removal of all those restrictions on the free action of an individual which are not necessary for securing the like freedom on the part of his neighbors" (Dicey 1962, 146). I take it for granted that the restrictions to be removed are governmental.

Reactions to Dicey's statement can well depend on the underlying assumptions accepted. If you assume that liberty automatically exists in the absence of coercion or restraint, you are well on your way to the position that Dicey describes. Conversely, if, following Isaiah Berlin, you regard liberty as a power ("the opportunity to act ... the possibility of action"), you must go on to ask whether the removal of governmental restrictions will automatically provide it.

Suppose now that, taking the second view of liberty, you go on to argue that government, to give worth to liberty, must take affirmative measures to open up opportunities. For example, it should seek actively to reduce or eliminate poverty and should promote education. Perhaps it should even take on the role of employer of last resort.

Most of the active measures that government can adopt to give worth to liberty cost money, and the money has to come ultimately from taxes, which means that government becomes redistributive. It takes from the better off in order to help others overcome obstacles that they confront—poverty, illiteracy, ill health, and so on. But in taking taxes from the better off, government reduces their effective powers. Thus the liberty of some (conceived as a power) is reduced in order that the liberty of others can be increased. The question whether this is justifiable comes up again and again throughout this book.

## Reason, Tolerance, and Progress

Two related assumptions that pervade liberalism (both classical and "new") remain to be noted. One is that human beings are reasonable—capable of rationally deciding on the good and rationally choosing a strategy for pursuing it. Nothing about liberalism suggests any special concern for failings such as incompetence or greed or depravity that might produce change for the worse rather than change for the better.

The second assumption is that change is to be sought and welcomed. The attitude shows up in the writings of John Stuart Mill. He deplored "the despotism of custom" as a "hindrance to human advancement," and he equated "the spirit of liberty" with the spirit of "progress or improvement." These characteristics carried over to the new liberalism and continue today, showing up in those who resemble either the classical or the "new" liberals. More specifically, they show up in the attitudes of both the economic conservatives and the progressive liberals of today. The difference is that today's progressive liberals, like the "new" liberals of Britain, are readier to use government to bring about change and thus are sometimes thought of as "social engineers," whereas the economic conservatives look to the operation of the free market to bring about change in a way that they regard as natural. Conservative conservatives are resistant to change, fearing that it will be for the worse rather than for the better.

The above implies that the classical liberals were optimists, and not only about the invisible hand. Implicitly they believed that reasonableness could be expected to prevail and that progress of many sorts is possible. The common statement is that they believed in the perfectibility of man, which is an unfortunate hyperbole but which indicates the direction in which thoughts ran. The classical conservatives, forbears of those whom I call conservative conservatives, were more pessimistic, believing that the human tendency toward sin and depravity is so strong that our emphasis should be on conserving the gains of the past and on skepticism about change.

# Chapter 3

# Progressive Liberalism: The New Deal

L IBERALISM WAS the dominant ideology of American political life from the time of the New Deal into the 1970s, and Louis Hartz, writing on *The Liberal Tradition in America,* had good reason to say that it was dominant long before, even when the term itself was not much used. Then came Ronald Reagan, making liberalism a label that most political leaders want to avoid.

The question is why. What has liberalism stood for? What conditions and arguments once gave it such great popularity and then made it a millstone? What are its prospects?

Answers to these questions are to be derived in part from the writings of commentators and academic theorists but even more from the historical record itself. In this chapter I focus on the period of the New Deal, and in the following two chapters on the period of the Great Society.

## The Great Depression

The Great Depression produced the conditions that brought deliberate, self-conscious liberalism to the fore, making it the dominant creed. The depression was severe. Except in agriculture, which faced chronic problems, the 1920s were years of economic growth and optimism, production and productivity reaching unprecedented levels, but in the summer of 1929 unemployment began to increase and output to decrease, and in October the stock market crashed.

Rapid decline then set in. By 1933 the GNP was at about 70 percent of its 1929 level; approximately 13 million people were unemployed—one worker in four—and many others were working reduced hours. In addition, most of those who sought to enter the workforce during these years, mainly young people, were unable to find jobs. Lacking savings to fall back on, millions became destitute. Large numbers were homeless. Businesses began to fail, and those that kept going faced either outright losses or reduced profits. Many municipalities and even some of the states were unable to pay their civil servants and teachers, meet other bills, or service their debts. By the time Roosevelt was inaugurated as president in 1933, the banks of the country were either closed or paralyzed, and financial life was at a standstill.

The psychological aspects of the depression were also severe. Some of the unemployed, of course, managed to get back on a payroll, but many were without work for so long that they gave up hope. And even those who had jobs were likely to be living in straitened circumstances, unable to count on the future with confidence and depressed by the misfortune they saw around them. Despair was widespread.

## Laissez Faire?

Earlier in American history, state governments would presumably have stepped in to combat a depression. Through the middle of the nineteenth century they were major stimulants of economic growth. In this period "the public official replaced the individual enterpriser as the key figure in the release of capitalist energy; the public treasury, rather than private saving, became the major source of venture capital; and community purpose outweighed personal ambition in the selection of large goals for local economies." Important innovations generally depended on mixed enterprises, government everywhere taking on "the role put on it by the people, that of planner, promoter, investor, and regulator." Pennsylvania, for example, had by 1844 put public directors on the boards of 250 mixed corporations.

As time passed, the states tended to defer more to private enterprise, but they did not entirely renounce a role in economic life. Along with municipal and local governments, they continued to regulate businesses in many ways for the protection of consumers; and they began to offer tax breaks and other special inducements to private businesses to influence their choice of sites for new offices and plants.

Further, through the nineteenth century the general rule was that local governments and states provided for the indigent. Then in the first few decades of the twentieth century, the states tended to take on a broader responsibility for welfare. For example, between 1911 and 1920 forty states adopted legislation granting aid to widowed mothers (or other caretakers) of dependent children, and six more joined them by the early 1930s. Between 1911 and 1913, twenty-one states set up insurance programs providing for workmen's compensation. Between 1923 and 1931 seventeen adopted old age pension programs—although with payments that were small.

The point of this recital is that those who think of the American historical record in terms of rugged individualism and *laissez faire* are not entirely correct. State and local governments, at least, had records of extensive intervention in economic life. Thus it is not surprising that when the depression struck in 1929, many of the state governments provided relief, and some of them expanded their public works programs to provide jobs. Nevertheless, state efforts to overcome the depression were meager in relation to the needs, for the problem was obviously national in origin and scope.

The economic role of the federal government had been increasing, but was still limited. In the early days of the Republic, the government in Washington did relatively little to promote economic development. It expanded its role during the Civil War, but did not shift self-consciously to the principle of activism in economic affairs—this despite a statement by Lincoln that seemed to accept the principle. Lincoln said (and Franklin Roosevelt later quoted the statement) that "the legitimate object of government is to do for the people what needs to be done but which they cannot by individual effort do at all or so well, for themselves" (*Public Papers*, 5:524). Lincoln also said that the "leading object" of government should be "to elevate the condition of men—to lift artificial weights from all shoulders; to clear the paths of laudable pursuit for all; to afford all an unfettered start, and a fair chance in the race of life." These principles help to explain the Emancipation Proclamation, but Lincoln did little else to implement them.

Federal activity increased in the last half of the century. Congress made land grants that contributed to education and the building of railways; it expanded its regulatory activities by establishing the Interstate Commerce Commission and adopting antitrust legislation. Important as these actions were, however, the role of the federal government in economic life remained limited.

Herbert Croly bewailed the situation in *The Promise of American Life*, published in 1909. He was not satisfied with the stress on rugged individualism and on the states. Instead, he wanted the stress to be on the nation as a whole, and therefore on the federal government. Moreover, he looked to the federal government for reforms. The national promise, he held, was of "moral and social amelioration." For this purpose, reliance on the individual guided by self-interest was unwise, for the individual was not an "inevitable public benefactor." In fact, Croly held, "confidence in individual freedom has resulted in a morally and socially undesirable distribution of wealth."

The solution, Croly argued, was "vigorous national action for the achievement of a national purpose.... The nation has to have a will and a policy...." And it was up to the central government to shape the will and adopt the policy. In his view, the will and the policy should aim, through taxation, at an improved distribution of wealth.

It is uncertain how much influence Croly's work had, but during the decade after he wrote, the role of the federal government expanded. A constitutional amendment made a progressive federal income tax possible. The federal government established a Children's Bureau and adopted regulatory legislation relating to pure food and drugs, trusts, and the eight-hour day. It adopted a Federal Farm Loan Act, established the Federal Trade Commission and the Federal Reserve system, and expanded its support for education. And in connection with fighting World War I it exercised extensive powers to bring about economic mobilization.

These measures marked an expansion of the role of the federal government, but the emphasis on the states and their rights remained strong. And the restoration of "normalcy" under Harding and Coolidge meant, among other things, a less active federal government.

Given this background, Hoover's stance, when the Great Depression struck, was not surprising. Hoover should not be identified with *laissez faire*. In fact, writing after he had left the presidency, he said that *laissez faire* had been "dead in America for generations." He accepted the need for the regulation of business, noting with obvious approval that "we have devised and enforced thousands of regulations in prevention of economic domination or abuse of our liberties." He declared that "the humanism of our system demands the protection of the suffering and the unfortunate," and he described himself as a "strong advocate of expansion of useful public works in hard times" (Hoover 1934, 51–52).

But at the same time Hoover wanted "the least regulation that will preserve equality of opportunity and liberty itself"—"the minimum necessary to attain true public ends." He wanted protection for the unfortunate to come from the lowest possible level: neighbors should assume the responsibility, then the local community, then the state government, and only as a last resort the federal government (Hoover 1934, 106, 159; 1972, 68). The issue, he said, was not whether people should be allowed to go hungry or cold; instead, it was how hunger and cold should be prevented. He pledged that if the voluntary agencies of the country together with the local and state governments failed to prevent hunger and suffering, he would "ask the aid of every resource of the Federal Government." But he had faith that the need for this would not arise (Myers 1934, 54, 57).

As to public works, Hoover rejected the assumption that government could do better than private enterprise in creating employment, and he was therefore reluctant to raise taxes or to borrow. "Economic depression," he told Congress in 1930, "cannot be cured by legislative action or executive pronouncement. Economic wounds must be healed by the action of the cells of the economic body." He repeated President Cleveland's statement that "though the people support the Government, the Government should not support the people" (Myers 1934, 1:429–30, 497, 578). Later he asserted that "no nation ... has been able to squander itself into prosperity" (Hoover 1934, 126). He rebuffed suggestions that the federal government involve itself in unemployment insurance, holding that "the moment the Government enters into this field it invariably degenerates into the dole," and the net result would be "to endow the slacker" (Myers 1934, 579).

Underlying these views was an opposition to centralization and to bureaucracy. Not only welfare activities but everything else should be conducted at the lowest practicable level. This is the principle of *subsidiarity*. Hoover granted that he had not invented the concept "rugged individualism," but said that he would be proud had he done so. And his resistance to governmental action increased the farther removed it was from the level of the individual. He saw in bureaucracy "three implacable spirits—self-perpetuation, expansion, and an incessant demand for more power." And when he witnessed "the vast concentration of political and economic authority" in the hands of his successor, Roosevelt, he objected vigorously as a matter of principle.

Like the statements quoted above, Hoover's record in office was mixed. He endorsed the Agricultural Marketing Act of 1929, the Smoot-Hawley tariff of 1930 (a kind of governmental intervention in economic life that economists generally condemn), and the establishment of the Reconstruction Finance Corporation (RFC), which loaned money, mainly to banks. He claimed in 1931 that federal expenditures to reduce unemployment had trebled, and he subsequently backed other measures to increase governmental spending, such as the Emergency Relief and Construction Act of 1932 . But in the eyes of most of the people, his efforts to combat the depression were not adequate.

In the light of Hoover's view that "economic depression cannot be cured by legislative action or executive pronouncement," it is ironic that, according to Milton Friedman, the government was to blame for the seriousness of the depression. The governmental agency at fault, according to Friedman, was the Federal Reserve Board. Friedman is a monetarist, believing that government can regulate economic life by regulating the quantity of money in circulation, and he thinks that the Federal Reserve Board reacted in precisely the wrong way to the problems that began to appear in 1929, converting "what otherwise would have been a moderate contraction into a major catastrophe" (Friedman 1962, 38, 45–50).

## Roosevelt's Stance

In 1932 the voters showed their discontent by rejecting Hoover and electing Roosevelt. They clearly wanted a more active federal government, and Roosevelt was willing to give it to them. As governor of New York he had already suggested a public philosophy that differed sharply from Hoover's. "What is the State? " he asked. And he answered that "it is the duly constituted representative of an organized society of human beings, created by them for their mutual protection and well-being." Later, in a campaign speech, he rejected rugged individualism. Responsible heads of finance and industry, he said, must be prepared to sacrifice private advantage where necessary for the general advantage, and government may properly apply restraint to those who decline to join in achieving ends recognized as being for the public welfare (*Public Papers*, 1:754–55).

As to "immediate relief," Roosevelt's first principle was that "the Nation, this national Government, if you like, owes a positive duty that no citizen shall be permitted to starve.... While the immediate responsibility for relief rests ... with local public and private charity, in so far as these are inadequate the States must carry the burden, and whenever the States themselves are unable adequately to do so the Federal Government owes the positive duty of stepping into the breach." Moreover, in addition to providing emergency relief, "the Federal Government must provide temporary work wherever that is possible" (*Public Papers*, 1:851). Later Roosevelt pointed out that the depression was nationwide, caused by conditions that were not local but national, and he said that "the Federal Government is the only governmental agency with sufficient power and credit to meet this situation" (*Public Papers*, 4:20). He spoke of plans that "build from the bottom up and not from the top down, that put their faith once more in the forgotten man at the bottom of the economic pyramid" *(Public Papers*, 1:625, 648).

Given this outlook, Roosevelt called for a New Deal—"a

changed concept of the duty and responsibility of Government toward economic life." "Modern society, acting through its Government, owes the definite obligation to prevent the starvation or the dire want of any of its fellow men and women who try to maintain themselves but cannot" (*Public Papers,* 1:782, 788). The "deeper purpose" of government, he said, "is to assist as many of its citizens as possible, especially those who need it most" (*Public Papers,* 5:636). One of the duties of government, he held, is to care for "those of its citizens who find themselves the victims of such adverse circumstance as makes them unable to obtain even the necessities for mere existence without the aid of others" (*Public Papers,* 1:632).

Roosevelt spoke of using government not only to combat the existing depression but also to ward off future depressions, and he endorsed economic planning to this end. He viewed government as a means of protecting and enriching a "shared common life."

At the same time, Roosevelt had broader, reformist goals. He endorsed a "philosophy that strives for something new, ... social justice through social action." This philosophy, he said, "calls definitely, plainly, for the reduction of poverty.... We mean the reduction of the causes of poverty.... We have got beyond the point in modern civilization of merely trying to fight an epidemic of disease by taking care of the victims after they are stricken. We do that; but we do more. We seek to prevent it; and the attack on poverty is not very unlike the attack on disease." He saw "one-third of a nation ill-housed, ill-clad, ill-nourished," and he said that "a new idea has come to dominate thought about government, the idea that the resources of the nation can be made to produce a far higher standard of living for the masses of the people if only government is intelligent and energetic in giving the right direction to economic life" (*Public Papers,* 6:360–61).

Near the end of his life and his presidency, Roosevelt declared that "true individual freedom cannot exist without economic security and independence," and he claimed that "we have accepted, so to speak, a second Bill of Rights under which a new basis of security and prosperity can be established for all—regardless of station, race, or creed." The second Bill of Rights, as he conceived it, contained provisions similar to those later included in the international Covenant on Economic, Social, and Cultural Rights: the right to a useful and remunerative job; the right to earn enough to cover the costs of adequate food, clothing, and recreation; the right of every farmer to raise and sell his products at a return that provides a decent living; the right of every businessman to freedom from unfair competition and domination by monopolies; the right of every family to a decent home; the right to adequate medical care; the right to adequate protection from the economic fears of old age, sickness, accident, and unemployment; and the right to a good education.

Roosevelt's attitude toward the budget and toward taxes was not entirely consistent with his expansive view of the role of government. His view when he moved into the White House was that government "costs too much." He had endorsed the platform of his party calling for a 25 percent reduction in the cost of the federal government, and he sought a balanced budget. In a campaign speech of 1936 he was proud to claim that his administration had "created a tax structure to yield revenues adequate to pay the cost of this war against depression in this generation and not in the next." Not until World War II came along did federal spending reach levels that brought unemployment substantially to an end. At the same time, Roosevelt declared that a state that was unwilling by governmental action to tackle new problems was headed for decline and ultimate death. He gave his support to the principle of a progressive income tax, considering taxation according to ability to pay as "the only American principle."

## New Deal Legislation

Roosevelt sponsored legislation that reflected his principles. He used government to provide relief, promote recovery, and regulate private enterprise for the public good. Some of his measures promoted two or three of these purposes at once.

Programs aimed at relief provided for jobs and doles. New Deal measures in the early years included both the Civil Works Administration and the Public Works Administration—names that suggest their nature and purpose. Doles were offered through state governments that got federal grants-in-aid. In less than a year, aid of one sort or another reached 28 million people—more than a fifth of the population of the country.

Roosevelt was uncomfortable with the part of the program providing doles.

> The lessons of history [he said in 1935], confirmed by the evidence immediately before me, show conclusively that continued dependence upon relief induces a spiritual and moral disintegration fundamentally destructive to the national fibre. To dole out relief in this way is to administer a narcotic, a subtle destroyer of the human spirit. It is inimical to the dictates of sound policy.... Work must be found for able-bodied but destitute workers. (*Public Papers*, 4:19)

Nevertheless, even though money for doles stopped coming from Washington, state and local governments continued their programs, extending support to more than 4 million families per year from 1936 to 1940. Federal programs to reduce distress by providing jobs continued.

In continuing to sponsor programs designed to provide jobs while objecting to the dole, Roosevelt anticipated a problem that has plagued welfare programs ever since. Belief in the work ethic is powerful. Able-bodied adults should earn their own living. But if the economic system (the private sector) does not provide jobs, what should be done? The Judeo-Christian tradition, humanitarian principles, and fear that the destitute will turn to crime all call for action, but what kind of action? If the government is unwilling to provide relief in cash or in kind, the only alternative is for it to become the employer of last resort. The New Deal put the emphasis on jobs, provided by the government if necessary, but it did not entirely avoid (still less, kill off) the dole.

In fact, the Social Security Act of 1935 included programs, subsequently expanded, making the dole (cash payments to relieve distress) a permanent feature of governmental policy. These were programs for the elderly, for dependent children, for the blind, and for maternal and child welfare. In one form or another these programs all continue. Those serving people who are not expected to be able to earn their own living arouse little controversy, but ADC (Aid to Dependent Children), which later developed into AFDC (Aid to Families with Dependent Children), is in a different category.

In the early years many local officials sought to extend ADC benefits only to "deserving" mothers, which means that they sought to exclude the divorced and the unwed. In any event, in the early years of ADC divorce and unwed motherhood were much less common than they have since become. Stable, two-parent families were the accepted and almost unchallenged ideal. The work ethic was strong, and seemed to be in no danger, permitting the assumption that any aid given would be temporary. Nothing about the situation made it seem imperative to impose conditions on aid designed to prevent the development of long-term dependency.

But times changed. Divorce and unwed motherhood became more and more common, including unwed motherhood on the part of teenage girls. Many of the unwed mothers, especially those still in their teens, found it difficult to become self-supporting and began accepting dependency as a way of life. Among those accepting dependency, blacks came to be disproportionately represented. The upshot is that ADC/AFDC is identified with the undermining of family values and the work ethic, and with whatever feelings race arouses. As we see abundantly in the following chapters it has become a much criticized and unpopular program, regarded by many as "America's most serious social-policy error."

In addition to providing in different ways for doles, the New Deal, through the Social Security Act of 1935, provided for two programs based on the insurance principle—an old age and survivors insurance program and an unemployment insurance program. Both of them depended on contributions (taxes) paid by workers and employers, building up funds (or at least credits) on which to draw later for pensions and unemployment insurance. The old age and survivors insurance program, administered directly by the federal government, has become so important to so many that it is what people ordinarily mean when they speak of "social security." It has eliminated destitution among the elderly. The unemployment insurance program is administered by state governments aided by grants from Washington.

Roosevelt sought not only to provide relief but also to stimulate economic recovery, both in industry and in agriculture. The problem was that, at least with respect to industry, he did not know how to do it, and his advisers sought to steer him in different directions. One of them, Rexford Guy Tugwell, later identified five theories concerning the most promising lines of action: (1) reliance on business and thus on private enterprise, government reducing regulatory interference and seeking to restore business confidence; (2) reliance on action relating to the quantity of money in circulation and the price of gold; (3) the stimulation of demand for products by measures to increase the purchasing power of consumers; (4) fiscal action, relating to interest rates and federal taxing and spending; and (5) "balance—the equalizing of income among mutually supporting groups" (Tugwell 1958, 184). The first of these theories would now presumably classify as libertarianism, the second as monetarism, and the third and fourth together as Keynesianism.

The situation illustrates the point that problems sometimes become political issues mainly because of a lack of reliable knowledge. Given reliable knowledge of how to reach a desired goal, the reason for political controversy is reduced or eliminated. Lacking reliable knowledge, the choice of a course of action is likely to involve different guesses by different people (probably reflecting different sets of values and interests) and then perhaps a power struggle to determine whose guess will be followed.

Roosevelt did not make a clear choice. His legislative program was eclectic, not reflecting any one coherent theory. The most flamboyant of his measures was the National Industrial Recovery Act, providing the legislative basis for the National Recovery Administration (NRA). The NRA sought to bring those involved in related kinds of economic activity into agreement on the rules governing both cooperative and competitive relationships. In other words, the NRA sponsored what amounted to cartels or trusts, or what is sometimes called a corporatist approach to economic life; it involved if not a rejection then a severe modification of the free market system. Rather than reduce "social rigidities," which Mancur Olson cites as the leading cause of the decline of nations, it added to them. Whether the NRA did more to stimulate than to impede recovery is still debated. The Supreme Court declared it unconstitutional in 1935.

For agriculture, the counterpart of the NRA was the AAA (the Agricultural Adjustment Administration), which built on a program that Hoover had launched and which, much modified, continues today. Roosevelt also continued the Reconstruction Finance Corporation, established by Hoover, and by 1937 it had made loans to more than 6,000 banks.

In addition, New Deal legislative measures included a number of others aimed in varying degrees at recovery and/or regulation: acts relating to the banking system—providing, among other things, for the Federal Deposit Insurance Corporation; an act setting up the Home Owners Loan Corporation, designed to facilitate homeownership; a Farm Credit Act; an act relating to the stock market, establishing the Securities and Exchange Commission (SEC); the National Labor Relations Act (to which Roosevelt was indifferent almost to the moment of enactment) requiring management to accept trade unions and engage in collective bargaining; a Fair Labor Standards (Wage and Hour) Act; a Communications Act, establishing the Federal Communications Commission; a Railroad Retirement Act, providing a pension system for railway workers; a Public Utilities Holding Company Act; an act relating to the interstate shipment of oil and gas; acts providing for rural electrification and soil conservation; and an act aimed at developing the resources of the Tennessee valley, establishing the TVA.

## Roosevelt's Ideology

Both Hoover and Roosevelt described themselves as *liberals,* but they obviously gave the word different meanings. Although neither cited the British tradition, what Hoover had in mind can be described as a variant of classical British liberalism, and what Roosevelt had in mind can be described as a variant of the "new" liberalism of Lloyd George.

Describing the Democratic Party as "the bearer of liberalism" in the 1932 campaign, Roosevelt was explicit in identifying liberalism with a view of "the Government's duty in matters affecting economic and social life," but he did not describe the view succinctly. What he did was to reject the view of the "party of Toryism"—the view that "a favored few" should be helped in the hope that some of their prosperity would trickle down. That, he said, was not and never would be the theory of the Democratic Party. He wanted "real progress, real justice, ... real equality for all of our citizens, great and small" (*Public Papers*, 1:648–49).

In 1941, in an introduction to a volume of his *Public Papers*, Roosevelt made a fuller statement concerning his ideology, reflecting his conception of the experience of countries with representative governments (*Public Papers*, 7:xxix–xxx). In such countries, he said, "there are usually two general schools of political belief—liberal and conservative" differing in several respects. He identified the liberal party with the extension of the suffrage to as many people as possible and thus with the belief that government should be in the hands of the many rather than in the hands of the few. He also identified the liberal party with the belief that

> as new conditions and problems arise beyond the power of men and women to meet as individuals, it becomes the duty of Government itself to find new remedies with which to meet them. The liberal party insists that the Government has the definite duty to use all its power and resources to meet new social problems with new social controls—to insure to the average person the right to his own economic and political life, liberty, and the pursuit of happiness.

It is in this connection that Roosevelt quoted Lincoln as saying that the legitimate object of government is to do for people what needs to be done when they cannot do it, at all or as well, for themselves.

In Roosevelt's eyes "the conservative party" takes opposite positions, believing that "in the long run, individual initiative and private philanthropy can take care of all situations."

The true liberal, Roosevelt said, does not claim that his remedies are perfect, but he is willing "to start with something less than perfect in this imperfect world." The conservative, in contrast, believes that governmental action is unnecessary and that perfection can be obtained more readily and more quickly through private initiative.

Earlier Roosevelt had said that "in our generation a new idea has come to dominate thought about government, the idea that the resources of the nation can be made to produce a far higher standard of living for the masses of the people if only government is intelligent and energetic in giving the right direction to economic life." He considered that idea "wholly justified," and implicitly he claimed it for liberalism.

Thus Roosevelt rejected the idea that that government is best that governs least. The counterpart is that he rejected the assumption that private initiatives, whether by entrepreneurs or philanthropists, can alone provide adequately for the general welfare. He saw a need for an activist and interventionist government—a government that would actively strive to make it possible for people to have better lives. He emphasized a concern for the "forgotten man"—for those rendered jobless and destitute by the depression—but this emphasis probably reflected the circumstances he confronted more than the nature of liberalism. He called for governmental leadership and guidance in economic and social life even in normal times as a means of promoting economic security and enhancing the general well-being.

Robert Nisbet speaks of a "notable reversal of values in the United States during the New Deal" and goes on to say that "the central value of contemporary American liberalism is not freedom but equality; equality defined as redistribution of property" (Nisbet 1988, 62). It is true that Roosevelt at times spoke of equality—I quote him above as looking forward to "real equality for all our citizens, great and small." It is also true that Roosevelt sought to alleviate distress in various ways, which can be construed as narrowing the gap between the rich and the poor. Further, he was hostile to "the acquisition of wealth which, through excessive profits, creates undue private power ... over public affairs ...."

At the same time, Roosevelt said that "... we do not destroy ambition, nor do we seek to divide our wealth into equal shares.... We continue to recognize the greater ability of some to earn more than others" (*Public Papers*, 4:17). He was not a leveler. It is totally wrong to say that "equality defined as the redistribution of property" was his "central value" (Graham 1971, 37–38, 42–43). The better argument is that his concern was for freedom, as indicated by his stress on the four freedoms during World War II: freedom of speech, freedom of religion, freedom from want, and freedom from fear. Among other things, he wanted to give worth to freedom by making jobs and food available.

Roosevelt was not even egalitarian in the sense of upholding the requirement of the Fourteenth Amendment concerning equal treat-ment. He regarded the depression as the problem, and he was unwilling to dilute or jeopardize his program for economic recovery and reform by taking on problems associated with race. Had he done so, he would surely have lost the support and cooperation of a number of the states, especially in the South, and he would have lost the support of a number of the members of the House and Senate. Thus he satisfied himself with meager gestures—mainly a requirement that skilled black craftsmen be hired on a proportionate basis in certain PWA projects, and later an executive order prohibiting discrimination because of race, creed, color, or national origin in defense industries. His wife, Eleanor, added another meager gesture in reacting to the refusal of the Daughters of the American Revolution (DAR) to allow a black singer to give a concert in Constitution Hall: she arranged to stage the concert at the Lincoln Memorial.

These various gestures were enough to win substantial black support for the Democratic Party, but the fact that blacks would reward such meager efforts testifies mainly to the extent of their plight. Roosevelt permitted discrimination against blacks in the armed forces to continue. And he did little to promote the equal treatment of women.

The depression convinced almost everyone of the shortcomings of the free market, and the numerous reform measures included in the New Deal testified to the fact that Roosevelt was sensitive to them. In sponsoring the TVA, moreover, he sponsored a measure that is easily classified as socialist. But in general he sought to maintain a capitalist, free-market system—regulated and limited by government more than in earlier times, to be sure, but a free-market system nevertheless. In fact, it is plausible to contend, as some do, that Roosevelt's achievements were essentially conservative in that they took the country through the depression without drastic, fundamental change.

Hubert Humphrey described the major contribution of the New Deal in other terms:

> More than anything else, the New Deal was a change in the scope of public responsibility, particularly in the spheres of economic and social action.... The New Deal made liberalism a positive force for the betterment of the human condition; it saw freedom as more than the absence of restraint. Freedom was characterized by a better life, better homes, better education. Government was to be more than the protector and the regulator, it was to be a partner, a constructive force, in improving the nation and helping the individual. (Humphrey 1970, ix–x)

Directly or indirectly, Humphrey had clearly been influenced by T.H. Green. Negative freedom (freedom conceived as the absence of restraint) was not enough. Freedom must be conceived as a positive capacity. To be significant, it must have worth.

# Chapter 4

# Progressive Liberalism: The Great Society and Welfare

L IKE THE NEW DEAL, the Great Society program of Lyndon Johnson helped to define the current conception of liberalism, and it probably did even more than the New Deal to shape current attitudes. Some features of the program are still sources of strength for liberalism, and others give ammunition to critics.

I divide the treatment of the Great Society program into two chapters. The main object in this chapter is to describe the primarily economic parts of the program—those having to do with welfare and well-being. Features relating to equal treatment—mainly to discrimination based on race and sex—are the subject of the next chapter. First in this chapter, however, I want to take note of the hegemony of liberalism in the years before the Johnson administration.

## The End of Ideology

During the first several decades after World War II a substantial degree of ideological consensus prevailed, at least through the broad center of the political spectrum. Lionel Trilling was correct in saying that "in the United States at this time [1950] liberalism is not only the dominant but even the sole intellectual tradition. For it is the plain fact that nowadays there are no conservative or reactionary ideas in general circulation." There were "impulses" toward conservatism and even toward reaction, but the impulses were not being expressed in ideas. According to another writer, the consensus called for an activist government—"a positive state"—and for internationalism in foreign policy. Moreover, the consensus prevailed not only in the United States but in other countries as well:

> Virtually every Western leader of republican conviction, whether nominally Social Democratic, Christian Democratic, plain Democratic, or even high Tory, believed government had a major function to perform in the economy, as stabilizer, as planner of public investment, as guarantor of high employment, as arena of social bargaining, and as custodian of a benign welfare state. (Kuttner 1991, 16)

True, some dissenting notes were heard. The Republican platform of 1952, for example, charged that successive Democratic administrations had sought "unceasingly to achieve their goal of national socialism," and the platform of 1956 pledged a reversal of the "20-year Democratic philosophy calling for more and more power in Washington." But the 1956 platform also called for expanding the old age and unemployment insurance programs and expressed the determination of the party "that our government remain warmly responsive to the urgent social and economic problems of our people."

Although Eisenhower vetoed bills for the construction of public works in depressed areas, he accepted an extension of social security to cover workers suffering from disabilities, and in the decade of his presidency the number of persons employed in administering social security more than doubled. Well before the end of his administration it could simply be assumed that the regulatory and welfare measures of the New Deal were normal features of the political system, the only question being whether to extend them. Moreover, Eisenhower supported federal activism in new areas: he approved legislation that gave the federal government a major role in developing the interstate highway system, and he approved the extension of federal functions provided for in the National Defense Education Act.

It might be recalled too that Eisenhower appointed Earl Warren as Chief Justice of the Supreme Court and that Warren soon led the Court in its watershed judgment (*Brown v. Board of Education*, 1954) outlawing segregation in the schools—a judgment that Eisenhower was soon obliged to enforce at Little Rock. Eisenhower later described his appointment of Warren as a mistake; and he regretted the need to enforce the Court's decision. Nevertheless, he did it, and in doing it he got widespread support. The irony is that, however unintentionally, Eisenhower pushed liberalism farther toward governmental activism on the racial issue than Roosevelt himself had dared to go. Moreover, the decisions of the Warren Court and the events at Little Rock surely helped to stimulate the civil rights movement of the 1960s that did so much to drive the federal government toward change.

A substantial degree of consensus likewise prevailed in the realm of foreign policy: the Soviet Union was the adversary, and the prescription was "containment." Except at the left and right extremes of the political spectrum, the Truman Doctrine, the Marshall Plan, the conclusion of the North Atlantic Treaty, and the organization of NATO all got general support, as did intervention against communist aggression in Korea.

The principal source of controversy was on the question of communism as a domestic danger, and even more on the question what to do about it. Senator Joe McCarthy brought the controversy to a head, claiming that Democrats and liberals had allowed communists to infiltrate the Department of State and other federal agencies. Although his claims had some basis in fact, they were wildly exaggerated. I deal with this question in chapter 14.

By the middle of the 1950s McCarthy had been discredited, and anticommunist fears and fervors had subsided. John F. Kennedy, elected in 1960, brought progressive liberalism to the fore again. He signed the Manpower Development and Training Act in 1962 and took the first steps toward what became the Great Society program, sponsoring a bill concerning civil rights and initiating studies looking toward a war on poverty.

Lyndon Johnson took over where Kennedy left off, extending the role of government in a major way, as I discuss more fully in the next section. Barry Goldwater, the Republican candidate in the election of 1964, demanded a rollback of federal powers, but ended up contributing to their enlargement because he was so roundly defeated. Thus Johnson could proceed with his Great Society program, and Nixon could accept and even extend it. Nixon sponsored the enactment of a few Great Society measures that had failed to make it through Congress before Johnson's term came to an end. And he initiated proposals himself that were in the spirit of the New Deal and Great Society. Not until the later 1970s, and more especially the election of Ronald Reagan in 1980, was the New Deal paradigm finally repudiated.

## Expanded New Deal Programs

Lyndon Johnson spoke of the Great Society without listing the potential sources of greatness; and he spoke of a war on poverty without specifying what legislative measures and policies should be regarded as aspects of the war.

Two of the programs identified with the Great Society and the war on poverty are actually New Deal programs that, for varying reasons, have taken on much more importance than they once had: social security and AFDC. I focus on these programs first and then deal with other programs that are more fully identified with Johnson.

### SOCIAL SECURITY

As noted in the preceding chapter, the Social Security Act of 1935 provided for a number of programs, including an old age insurance program. That one program soon achieved such importance that references to "social security" have come to be references to it alone. Limited in its application at first, the program now covers virtually everyone who is or has been on a payroll and, in addition, any dependents who survive them. At the end of 1992 benefit payments were going to more than 41 million persons, or to approximately one person in six.

The system operates on the insurance principle, premiums taking the form of taxes paid by workers and their employers. Theoretically the premiums go into a trust fund (not into a separate piggy bank for each worker), and when the worker retires, the appropriate social security payment comes out of the fund. Actually, the taxes collected as premiums go toward meeting general governmental costs, including the costs of current social security payments. In effect, money is transferred from current taxpayers to current recipients of social security.

As already indicated, social security has come to cover a far higher proportion of workers than it did originally, and the program has expanded in other ways. More women are in the workforce. People are tending to retire earlier and to live longer, increasing the number of years during which benefits are paid. Congress has from time to time increased the base income to which the social security tax applies (bringing it to $57,600 in 1993), increased the tax itself, and increased the benefits. In 1972 it linked the benefits to the consumer price index, meaning that they go up automatically as that index rises. The total costs of social security (Old Age Survivors and Disability Insurance [OASDI]) have risen from $784 million in 1950 to $152 billion in 1980 to $352 billion in 1990. In other words, social security has become a major charge on the federal budget. Currently, however, the social security tax produces not only enough revenue to provide for the benefits but also a surplus that the federal government spends for other purposes.

The general guiding principle in connection with social security is that benefits received should be proportionate to the taxes paid in, but some redistribution occurs. One kind of redistribution is disappearing—the payment of benefits to those who retired during the early years of the program that were disproportionate to the taxes they had paid in. The redistribution is now mainly from one period of a person's life to another, and from those who die young to those who live longer. But some redistribution also occurs from the more to the less affluent workers, and from all others to single-earner married couples (Meyer and Wolff 1993, 20–21). In 1974, while Nixon was president, Congress adopted a Supplemental Security Income program (SSI) that is redistributive in that it draws on general tax funds to supplement benefits for those aged and disabled persons whose employment records leave them with especially low levels of support; but only a small portion of those on social security are also receiving SSI benefits.

As we see in the later chapters, libertarians and the more reactionary conservatives deplore the whole arrangement and would like, if they could, to get the government entirely out of the social security business. Their argument is that people should assume responsibility for their own fate and fortunes, implying (among other things) that government should not tax them in order to provide for them in old age. They should decide for themselves how to use their money. But the program is so popular throughout the country that it is relatively safe from attack.

The program is popular for good reasons. Despite the argument of libertarians and others, the fact is that before social security many people reached retirement age with little or nothing to live on. Perhaps they made so little money during their working years that they could scarcely meet their day-to-day needs, let alone put money aside. Perhaps they were simply improvident. Perhaps they encountered a misfortune that ate up their savings. And when they became too old to work, the question was what to do. Until the social security program began, the answer was to let them be dependent on their children or on local charity, private or public; and libertarians and some conservatives still tend to regard this as the best policy. But many children were in poverty too, and local charitable organizations were often poorly financed, in which case the indigent elderly faced lives of destitution, indignity, and perhaps exploitation.

It is from this kind of fate that social security saves them. Because of social security and Medicare (to be described below), poverty among the elderly has been drastically reduced. Absolute poverty (utter destitution) has disappeared. And since benefits go to all—that is, to all who have ever worked and to their dependents—they are not stigmatizing. Most of the beneficiaries rightly feel that they are simply getting back the money they have paid in. The system has faced problems, but they appear to be solved for many years to come, and the indications are that the system is administered efficiently.

### Aid to Families with Dependent Children

Like social security, the AFDC program dates back to the Social Security Act of 1935. That act provided for Aid to Dependent Children (ADC)—dependent ordinarily on the mother, the father being dead, absent, or disabled. In 1950 Congress amended the act to permit coverage of the mother or any other needy adult who takes care of the child, and subsequent amendments require the states to offer aid to two-parent families that are needy because of the unemployment of one of the parents.

The states fix the level of the benefits, and the amounts vary widely, ranging in 1992 from $120 for a family of three in Mississippi to $923 in Alaska. The average monthly benefit was $388, which (after accounting for inflation) was 40 percent less than the average provided in 1970. In nine states the combined AFDC and food stamp benefit came to less than 60 percent of the poverty level. In the median state, the benefits were 70 percent of that level. In no state did the benefits come up to the poverty level (*Green Book* 1993, 615, 655–58). A few women have managed to collect multiple benefits by using more than one name, but the idea of the "welfare queen" should be dismissed as a fiction. The program is redistributive in that the money comes out of general tax funds.

When people speak of the "welfare state," the likelihood is that they have in mind the whole range of programs, including social security and Medicare, aimed directly at the enhancement of welfare. But when they speak of a person as "going on welfare" or "being on welfare," the likelihood is that they simply have AFDC in mind. Or they might also be thinking of other programs based on a means test, such as food stamps.

As with social security, the numbers helped by ADC/AFDC, and the costs, have greatly increased. In 1950 ADC was going to fewer than a million persons, but by 1992 the number had risen to 13.6 million. More than 9 million of the 13 million were children. Total costs have grown accordingly, rising to $22.2 billion in 1992. Looked at in absolute terms, this is a lot of money. Relatively, however, it is a tiny fraction of the GDP (less than 0.4 percent), and less than 4 percent of total federal welfare spending.

Various circumstances have led to the increase in the numbers and the costs. Especially from the 1960s on, people have been more conscious of their rights and more inclined to take advantage of them. Thus a higher proportion of those eligible have tended to apply. The numbers applying, too, have varied depending on whether administrative policies confront the potential applicant with hassles or facilitate enrollment. The biggest surge in enrollment coincided with the great migration of blacks from the South into the central cities of the North, where many of them were unable to support themselves. Further, the state of the economy plays a role: the higher the rate of unemployment, the greater the number of applicants.

Much more important, however, are changes relating to the family. Beginning in the 1960s, divorce and desertion became increasingly common, meaning in many cases that women with children were left in dire need. And beginning at about the same time, it became increasingly common for unmarried women, including teenage girls, to have babies and to get no support from the absent fathers. By the mid-1980s, more than half of the women on the AFDC roll were teenagers when they had their first baby. Further, teenage mothers were especially unlikely to have the education and skills necessary for earning a living, which means that the AFDC program was their salvation; and especially if they had a second baby, they were likely to be dependent indefinitely.

Different authors give startlingly different statistics concerning the length of time during which beneficiaries are on the AFDC roll, as elementary arithmetic permits them to do. Suppose that, in an eight-year period, eight beneficiaries are on AFDC one at a time for one year each and one is on for all eight years. This permits you to say that eight out of nine get benefits for only one year, at a relatively small per person cost. But it also permits you to say that half of those on the roll at any one time get benefits for all eight years. Those who want to promote a fair evaluation of AFDC presumably cite both kinds of figures, but those who want to load the case one way or the other can choose the figures that best suit their purpose.

The illustration suggests what apparently is the actual situation, complicated a little by the fact that some of those on AFDC for one spell go back on it for one or more later spells. Apparently about 30 percent are on the roll for less than two years and about 50 percent are on for less than four years. But about 65 percent of those on the roll at any one time are on for eight or more years (*Green Book* 1993, 714; Coughlin 1989, 108–10). To them, AFDC is a way of life.

Problems arise over eligibility rules, and adults involved are often cross-pressured. For long, many states withheld aid from two-parent families even if both parents were unemployed, which encouraged the breakup of the family: the unemployed husband could provide for his family (through AFDC) by deserting it, or the wife could qualify for AFDC by getting a divorce. Even now, regardless of the state of residence, a woman on welfare who takes a job may or may not gain. The job is likely to mean increased costs for travel to and from the workplace and perhaps for clothing and child care. At the same time, if her earnings go over a certain level, she loses her eligibility for AFDC; for long, she also lost her eligibility for Medicaid, but now she retains that eligibility during a transition period. In any event, it has been and still is quite possible that a woman who takes a job may be worse off than if she had stayed on welfare; that is, she may be in the so-called welfare trap.

AFDC is unpopular, at least with the middle and upper classes. It is associated with dependency and thus involves redistribution and the subversion of the work ethic. It is associated with unwed motherhood and single-parent households and thus goes counter to widely held moral and family values. It is associated with race and thus with whatever feelings race arouses. Not that the only beneficiaries are black. Far from it. Most of them are white. But blacks are disproportionately represented, and critics of AFDC capitalize deliberately on this fact.

The fact that AFDC is associated with dependency, unwed motherhood, and single-parent households leads easily to the conclusion that it causes them, and it may be among the causes. But if it was a controlling factor, or even a very significant factor, you would expect the size of the payments to make a difference. The problem in Alaska and California, where the benefits are relatively high, should be greater than the problem in Mississippi. But no such correlation exists. Furthermore, unwed motherhood and divorce have become more and more common at every socioeconomic level, not simply among the poor; and they have become more and more common in a number of other countries. Factors having nothing to do with AFDC have clearly been at work exacerbating the problems that it faces. At the same time, it is worth noting that unwed mothers of the middle and upper classes rarely become dependent on the taxpayers, while unwed mothers from the lower socioeconomic level commonly do; AFDC benefits, food stamps, and Medicaid save them from most of the penalties that unwed motherhood would otherwise involve. It may well play an enabling role—enabling the adult beneficiaries to get by without facing up to the irresponsibility of their behavior.

Tending to believe the worst about AFDC, the various sorts of conservatives are inclined to dwell on the view that the irresponsibility of the poor is the main problem. They are school dropouts, immoral, unwilling to forgo present pleasures for future gain. They are too choosy, willing to take a job only if it is "decent." They thus belong to an "underclass," living in a "culture of poverty."

No one can deny evidence lending some support to the view that poverty is due at least in part to the failings of the poor, but progressive liberals are more inclined to emphasize circumstances over which the poor have no control: their family background, wages so low that something like a fifth of all full-time workers end up below the poverty line, the plain lack of enough jobs to go around, or the lack of various kinds of opportunity.

The unpopularity of AFDC leads to various suggestions for change. Virtually everyone favors a crackdown on the absent father, some proposing to deny benefits to any woman who does not name him. A few propose to deny benefits to minors who have children. Many want to deny any increase in benefits if, after going on AFDC, a woman has additional children. Others want to reduce the number of children born to AFDC mothers by arranging for Medicaid to cover the cost of abortions. Clinton and many others propose to limit the number of years of eligibility for benefits.

In a somewhat different category are suggestions designed to encourage self-support. Think, for example, of the fact that, for long, a mother on AFDC got Medicaid, whereas a working mother whose wages were no higher than AFDC benefits did not. The Family Support Act of 1988 reduced this problem by assuring transitional Medicaid benefits for those shifting from AFDC to a job, and the earned income tax credit further alleviates the problem. But AFDC got a bad reputation well before these reforms were enacted.

I might note that some countries, France, for example, largely avoid the problem by emphasizing different values. From their point of view, children are an important national resource to be cherished and developed out of concern for the public interest. Such countries thus have child-support programs extending into homes at every socioeconomic level, and they manifest their concern for children in other ways.

## Food Stamps

Strictly speaking, the food stamp program should not be identified either with the New Deal or the Great Society, but it is nevertheless a significant feature of the welfare state. Congress introduced the program on a small scale in 1964 and then Nixon called for a vast expansion of it in 1969. Within five years, food stamps were being given out to all those on welfare, as well as to others who met a specified means test. In 1992 more than 25 million persons were receiving food stamps—almost one person out of every ten—at a cost to the federal government of $23 billion per year.

## Medicare and Medicaid

Unlike the programs described above, Medicare and Medicaid, established in 1965, were central features of Johnson's Great Society program. Medicare is administered by the federal government. It covers persons sixty-five and older, plus the disabled and those with end-stage renal disease. On the basis of an increased social security tax, it provides for hospital and related services and offers voluntary supplementary insurance financed in part by monthly premiums paid by participants, covering the services of physicians.

Medicaid, in contrast, is administered by the states, with the federal government paying at least half the cost. All the states except Arizona participate. Coverage varies from state to state, but in general it extends to indigent families with dependent children, to indigent pregnant women, and to all those receiving AFDC benefits or other cash welfare payments.

The costs associated with Medicare and Medicaid are high, and have grown at an alarming rate. Payments for Medicare went up from $7.6 billion in 1970 to $129 billion in 1992, and payments for Medicaid (by the federal and state governments combined) went up in the same period from $4.8 billion to $118 billion.

In addition to Medicare and Medicaid, the health-care system includes various other arrangements. Some of them are on a group basis, as when people buy health insurance from a private company, join a health maintenance organization (HMO), or get health care as a fringe benefit of employment. Members of an HMO buy care for a fixed fee, a major presumed advantage being that the HMO has an incentive to keep costs down while being compelled by competition to be effective in protecting and promoting the health of members.

Something like 35 million people are not covered by any of these arrangements and so are left to fend for themselves, the theoretical presumption being that they go to the doctor and hospital of their choice and then pay whatever bills follow.

Medicare and Medicaid produce different reactions. Libertarians and many economic conservatives deplore them for the same reasons they deplore social security. But most others, while perhaps condemning the "welfare state," seem to accept the view that an arrangement should exist assuring medical care to everyone. This belief is so widespread that virtually all those who aspire to election or reelection believe that they must favor, or appear to favor, some kind of reform so as to provide universal or nearly universal coverage.

When Medicaid is considered alone, it is not as popular as Medicare, at least with the middle and upper classes, for it serves only the poor. Moreover, race comes into the picture again, as it does with AFDC, for even though most of the poor are white, blacks are disproportionately represented. The middle class and middle-aged who lack health insurance themselves can ask why they should pay taxes to provide it for others, above all if they are inclined to think of the others, and especially the black poor, as members of a shiftless, undeserving underclass.

The problem of health care, like the problem of AFDC, comes up again in later chapters.

## Economic Opportunity

Lyndon Johnson declared "unconditional war on poverty in America." He did it in his first State of the Union message, before either he or his staff had fully analyzed the reasons for poverty or worked out a strategy for waging war against it. Presumably Johnson chose his words for their dramatic and challenging effect, but it is questionable whether the choice was wise. To speak in terms of war is to suggest an activity going on for a limited period, ending in victory, with no need for further action. If need persists, this shows that the war was lost or that its outcome was otherwise unsatisfactory.

But the elimination of poverty is not to be expected. Factors that are beyond control and that lead to poverty are always at work and will be at work for as far into the future as anyone can see. Further, although individual freedom and reliance on the free market are better than other systems at minimizing poverty, an unavoidable implication of freedom is that some will do badly, jeopardizing their own well-being and that of their dependents. Further, experience with the free market gives no basis for hope that it will provide jobs for all who want them or otherwise solve the problem of poverty. In speaking of a war on poverty, Johnson virtually invited Reagan's later comment that poverty had won, with the implication that liberals and Democrats had failed.

The heart of the war on poverty was presumably the Economic Opportunity Act of 1964, which established the Office of Economic

Opportunity (OEO) to administer or coordinate a number of programs, some of them existing already and some of them new. Among them were various employment and training programs targeted at minorities, low-income youth, and people on welfare: Head Start and Follow Through for young children; Upward Bound for high school students preparing for college; Volunteers in Service to America (Vista); Legal Services; Community Action, which carried a requirement of "maximum feasible participation" by the poor; and others.

The requirement of "maximum feasible participation" by the poor in the Community Action program was in effect a challenge to local elites—party elites and others—and so made the program unpopular with those elites. Similarly, the availability of legal services to the poor led some of them to initiate suits against local leaders and local governments, adding to the unpopularity. And it was difficult to tell how much good some of the other programs did, although the whole enterprise tended to focus attention on the problem of poverty and thus perhaps make remedial action more likely.

Of the various programs, Head Start has probably been the clearest success, although funding for it has been so low that, year after year, less than half of the potentially eligible children have been served. The other programs have likewise been starved, and some of them have gone out of existence. In the years when the budget of OEO was at its maximum, the average was about $1.7 billion. If all its money had gone directly to the poor, each poor person would have received about $50 to $70 per year. The war on poverty was starved by the needs of the war in Vietnam.

OEO was abolished in 1974. During the period of its activity, poverty was reduced, but the reduction was due more to the Civil Rights Act, social security, Medicare, Medicaid, AFDC, and food stamps than to the programs entrusted to OEO. "Declared but Never Fought" is suggested as the war's epitaph.

## Redistributive?

I have already mentioned the question of the redistributive nature of some of these programs, but should focus on the subject because critics tend to do so, usually denouncing "transfer payments."

Governmental taxing and spending necessarily involves some redistribution, and some of the features of the welfare state—AFDC, food stamps, Medicaid, SSI—accentuate the redistribution. But, according to Mancur Olson:

Most of the redistribution of government is not from upper-income
and middle-income people to low-income people. Most of the redistribution of income in fact is from middle-income people to other
middle-income people, or from the whole society to particular
groups of rich people, or from one group to another where the
groups are distinguished not by one being poor and the other being
rich, but only by the fact that some groups are organized and some
are not.... Most redistribution is not in fact redistribution to the
poor. (Olson 1984, 245)

Social security, for example, is redistributive, but (as noted earlier) the
redistribution is mainly from one period of a person's life to another
and from those who die young to those who are long-lived. It is not
mainly from the rich to the poor.

A substantial portion of the redistribution that occurs is accom-
plished through tax expenditures, which are made figuratively when a
person or firm is excused from paying a tax that would otherwise be
due. The best illustration stems from the wish of Congress to make it
easier for people to borrow money in order to buy a house. Long before Johnson became president, Congress made it easier by saying that
the income tax would not apply to the portion of the borrower's income that goes for interest on a mortgage.

The mortgage-interest exemption has the same effect as if the
government collected the tax and then gave the money back. If the
IRS did collect the money and then gave it back, it would be spending
far more than the federal government spends on AFDC. This means
that those in a good enough financial position to buy a house get more
help from the federal government than those in such dire poverty that
they cannot buy the basic necessities of life. The bigger the mortgage,
the more help people get. And they get still more help if they buy a
second house.

This bit of governmental generosity has not been especially controversial, and it is interesting to ask why. Part of the answer is that
governmental generosity to people with mortgages is not as obvious as
its generosity, say, to those on AFDC. No special appropriation is
made, and no administrative agency hands out money. House buyers
simply deduct the amount they pay in interest from the income on
which they pay a tax. The give-them-cash principle on which AFDC
operates makes the subsidy more conspicuous.

Another part of the answer has to do with socioeconomic class
and with bias. Commentators tend to take it for granted that
homeownership is good and ought to be encouraged, and they tend to

see buyers of houses as responsible middle- and upper-class persons like themselves, usually white, who live by the rules and deserve respect. They see no danger (and presumably there is in fact no danger) that the tax concession will undermine the work ethic. It may not even occur to them that the mortgage-interest exemption is a subsidy. In contrast, they have no comparable problem when considering welfare for the poor. A tax concession to the virtuous seems to be in a totally different category from a cash payment to the (undeserving?) poor.

Tax expenditures of all sorts came to a grand total of $310 billion in fiscal 1989, thus costing far more than all means-tested welfare programs combined.

## The Market

Progressive liberals do not put much stress on the market. Their tendency is simply to take it for granted. The presumption is that economic activity will occur within the framework of the market, property being privately owned and people producing, buying, selling, and consuming as they please. But the presumption in favor of the free market is not absolute. Every one of the programs described in this chapter addresses a need that, in liberal eyes, the market has failed to meet. Moreover, although this chapter has not stressed the fact, successive administrations since World War II have maintained the regulatory agencies set up under the New Deal, have added others, and have issued numerous regulations that by definition limit the operation of a free market. In other words, although progressive liberals assume the market, they also support policies that modify its operation and supplement what it does.

Subsequent chapters deal with the market more fully in connection with the analysis of libertarian and conservative thought.

## Johnson's Ideology

Proposing the war on poverty to Congress, Johnson assumed that poverty is not, or at least not simply, due to the failings of individuals. He implicitly denied that prosperity is to be identified entirely with virtue and poverty with indolence or vice. On the contrary, he assumed that poverty is caused at least in part by environmental circumstances that are open to change—environmental circumstances relating to opportunity. The gates of opportunity, he said, have been closed to one-fifth of the population. His war was not designed simply to support people, still less to make them dependent, but was a "struggle to give people a chance." It was "an effort to allow them to develop and use their capacities." The goal was "an America in which every citizen shares all the opportunities of his society, in which every man has a chance to advance his welfare to the limit of his capacities" (*Public Papers* 1963–64, 1:376). In other words, Johnson's purpose was to give worth to liberty and to promote equality of opportunity, and he obviously believed that government had a proper role to play in promoting these ends. These are central features of progressive liberalism, as I indicate more fully in chapter 6.

Johnson pursued these goals not only in the economic realm but also in the realm of civil liberties and equal treatment, which is the subject of the following chapter.

# Chapter 5

# Progressive Liberalism: Equal Treatment

G REAT SOCIETY LIBERALISM is identified with the problem of discrimination as much as with the problems of poverty and health care. It is especially identified with the problem of racial discrimination, and the attack on racial discrimination helped to spur and strengthen attacks on other kinds of discrimination too.

To identify Great Society liberalism with the problem of discrimination is to identify it with policies relating to membership in the community. Should some be excluded or relegated to second-class status? Why? Kenneth Karst puts it as a question of *belonging*—in a book entitled *Belonging to America* (1989). The liberal inclination is toward tolerance, toward the acceptance of differences, toward policies of inclusiveness. Let almost everyone *belong*.

An attack by government on discrimination necessarily involves an extension of its regulatory functions, which progressive liberals find acceptable. In fact they go on to ask for regulations serving additional purposes, most notably the protection of the environment.

These are the subjects of the chapter. But first a reminder concerning the need for action against racial discrimination.

## Jim Crow

It takes an act of imagination for members of the white majority to grasp the extent of the discrimination that blacks suffered after the Jim Crow system developed in the decades following the Civil War. Employers (almost all white) discriminated in their employment practices. Owners and managers of public accommodations (stores, restaurants, hotels, theaters, sports arenas, means of transportation, and other facilities serving the public) generally denied or somehow limited or regulated access by blacks. Those with houses to sell or rent did it on a racial basis. Segregation prevailed even in sports. Displays of contempt for blacks, and deliberate efforts to demean them, were common. Thus a white man might address a black man as "boy," and whites employed numerous other devices to keep blacks obsequious and "in their place."

Especially in the South, local and state governments required discrimination in the private realm and practiced it in the public realm. Louisiana, for example, required railways to carry blacks and whites in separate cars—a requirement that gave rise to the Supreme Court judgment in *Plessy* endorsing the "separate but equal" rule. State governments in the South generally denied blacks the vote, which was itself discriminatory and which left government free to engage in additional discrimination. Segregation was the rule in the schools, with blacks getting an inferior education. Whites alone decided what the law should be and whether and how it should be enforced. If government employed a black, it was in a menial capacity. In many jurisdictions, the police and sheriffs mistreated blacks with impunity; public prosecutors and courts denied them justice; and city councils and county commissioners neglected their interests. Blacks were barred from juries. Lynchings occurred, with no punishment for the guilty.

The other side of the coin was the preferential treatment of whites. Arbitrary discrimination against blacks meant arbitrary preference for whites. Moreover, discrimination and preference were based explicitly on race, questions about relative merit not being raised. The white community simply arrogated privilege to itself and condemned the black community to inferior status on a group basis. When whites endorsed equality of opportunity, the tacit understanding was that it was for whites only. And, for that matter, for men only.

Government itself followed policies of absolute preference—for example, admitting only whites to law schools and hiring only whites as teachers, firefighters, or police officers. A New Deal agency, the Federal Housing Administration, reinforced private preferential rules when it underwrote mortgages. Had the discrimination occurred only on a sporadic basis, as in the case of other ethnic minorities, it would have been bad enough; but it was pervasive, virtually inescapable.

The summary truth is that preferential treatment (for whites) and quotas (100 percent quotas) are vintage America. When neoconservative Norman Podhoretz says that "affirmative action and quotas represent the most radical assault yet on the traditional American ethos," he is obviously looking at the American ethos with one eye closed (Podhoretz 1993, 45).

Blacks and others protested discrimination and preferential treatment from the first, even when protest was futile. The federal Constitution and morality were both on their side. The Constitution provides that no state shall deny to any person the equal protection of the laws, and it was morally difficult to square Jim Crow either with the Christian doctrine of brotherhood or with the liberal doctrine of respect for the individual. But leading members of white communities and those who administered the law at local and state levels, especially in the South, tended to be racists, and anyone tempted to reject the system of discrimination and preference was under community pressures to stay in line.

The earliest significant breakthroughs came in the federal courts. Even though the judges in these courts were under a clearcut obligation to uphold the rule of equal treatment and even though their livelihood was secure against local prejudice, it took courage for them to go against the practices upheld by their friends and neighbors, but they tended increasingly to do it, their decisions culminating in the *Brown* case on school segregation. *Brown* repudiated the "separate but equal" doctrine of *Plessy* and declared the opposite: separate could not be equal.

In handing down *Brown,* the Supreme Court did not require that segregation be brought to an end immediately. It simply asked for "all deliberate speed," which, it turned out, permitted inaction; and discrimination continued outside the educational system as well, regardless of the letter and spirit of *Brown*. Resentments and guilt feelings therefore welled up. In 1955 in Montgomery, Alabama, black resentments led to a boycott of the bus system, which brought Martin Luther King to prominence, and later in other cities black resentments led to sit-ins, marches, and other demonstrations. The choice for whites was between continued hypocrisy and virtue; and, it became plain, the choice was also between greater fairness to blacks and greater social and political disorder.

## Racial Discrimination and the Problem of Redress

It was in this situation that Congress, urged on by Lyndon Johnson, enacted the Civil Rights Act of 1964 and the Voting Rights Act of 1965. And it was in this situation that the federal courts, including the

Supreme Court, supplemented *Brown* and earlier decisions with others that called for an end to racism in public life and for equal treatment. States' rights in this realm came substantially to an end.

The Civil Rights Act of 1964 prohibits racial discrimination in employment practices, public accommodations, and any program or activity receiving federal financial assistance. The terms are thus far reaching. Together with *Brown* and numerous other court decisions, the act has brought on a revolution in race relations—a revolution that is still incomplete but that has nevertheless gone far.

The problems were and remain formidable, relating not only to the termination of discrimination but also to the question of redress for blacks for the illegal and unconstitutional treatment that they had suffered. And the question of redress has its counterpart in the question whether whites should retain all the advantages gained under Jim Crow. After all, their position is roughly analogous to the position of the person who receives stolen goods. Most of those who speak up as progressive liberals tend to go in one direction in responding to the problems, and most of those who speak up on the conservative side tend to go in the other direction, but the division is not neat. Liberals and conservatives differ among themselves.

## EDUCATION

First consider the problem of implementing the *Brown* principles in elementary and secondary schools. In 1968, after years of delay, the Supreme Court finally became explicit about the nature and timing of the action required. It held that school boards had "an affirmative duty to take whatever steps might be necessary to convert to a unitary system in which racial discrimination would be eliminated root and branch," and they were to perform this duty not "with all deliberate speed," but "now." They were to "convert promptly to a system without a 'white' school and a 'Negro' school, but just schools" (*Green* v. *School Board,* 1968).

The Court thus said that school boards could not meet their obligations simply by revoking segregationist policies. They must do more: they must take affirmative action to undo the effects of illegal policies and bring about integration. What might be necessary to undo the effects was never studied as carefully as it might have been. But whatever else might be needed, the assumption was that black and white pupils should be in the same building and the same classes. On this basis, in many communities, busing became necessary so that the composition of the student body in each school would roughly reflect the composition of the population in the school district.

Busing turned out to be unpopular, not only with whites but also with many blacks. Moreover, a problem arises in that the composition of the population in many school districts is overwhelmingly white or overwhelmingly black, which means that the only way to achieve a mixing of the races is to redraw the boundary lines of school districts. A good argument can be made for this, based on the fact that the Constitution imposes the obligation of equal treatment on *states,* not on the separate school districts individually. But so far, the courts have required a redrawing of the boundaries of school districts only where it is clear that they were originally drawn with a racial intent. Thus in many communities de facto segregation continues.

As if to add to the problem, experience raises the question whether integration is of much significance if it is defined simply as placing white and black students under the same roof, where a kind of voluntary apartheid sometimes continues. Perhaps attention ought to be directed more at the quality of the education provided than at the composition of student bodies.

A problem of a different sort relating to education arises out of the principle cited above that conversion must occur "to a system without a 'white' school and a 'Negro' school, but just schools." At the elementary and high school levels, this has been interpreted to mean, as indicated above, that the racial composition of student bodies shall be roughly the same as the composition of the population of the school district. But how should the principle apply in institutions of higher education? In particular, how should it apply to the traditionally black colleges? If the composition of their student bodies must be made to reflect the composition of the population of the geographical area from which they draw students, they will become predominantly white, losing their historic character; and if they are obliged to merge with a white institution, they will disappear. Progressive liberals—and blacks—thus face a problem. Should blacks be free, if they wish, to maintain the distinctive character of the traditionally black colleges and universities? If so, how can this be reconciled with the requirement that primary and secondary schools be integrated?

Contradictory stands are being taken on this issue, and it is not clear that ideological preferences for "liberalism" or "conservatism" provide the explanation. Congress is willing to deal with black colleges on a separate basis. Many of them are struggling, with inadequate resources. Declaring that their current state is partly attributable to discriminatory governmental policies in the past and that remedial action is therefore required to ensure their continuation, Congress grants them financial aid.

### EMPLOYMENT PRACTICES

The problem of racial discrimination arises not only in the field of education but also with respect to employment practices. And here the influence of ideology is clearer. Not that anyone speaks up for racial discrimination, but people differ in their sensitivity to different kinds of interests. On the one hand, progressive liberals, seeking to give worth to liberty, are especially sensitive to the interests of minorities, and on the other hand, libertarians and economic conservatives, thinking of liberty as the absence of restraint, are especially sensitive to the interests of business firms and employers.

The difference shows up in the process of deciding what to count as prohibited racial discrimination. Little or no problem arises in principle, of course, about what is called "disparate treatment." If an employer deliberately and intentionally favors whites over blacks, everyone can agree that racial discrimination has occurred. Suppose, however, that an employer fixes a qualification for employment that appears to be racially neutral but that ends up screening out more blacks than whites. In other words, the apparently neutral qualification has what is called a "disparate impact."

This issue was fought out first in the courts. When the Supreme Court was dominated by justices regarded as "liberal," judgments concerning disparate impact tended to go against employers. For example, the Court once faced an employer's rule that, to be eligible for a job as janitor, applicants must have a high school education. The rule screened out black applicants disproportionately, and the employer could not show that a high school education was necessary to success on the job. Thus the Court held that the rule was racially discriminatory.

One of the implications of this decision was that an employer might be unintentionally guilty of discrimination; and this led to the argument that, to minimize the risk, employers would have to hire on a quota basis, without regard to merit, making sure that they hired enough blacks to keep clear of the law. Thus the expense of doing business would go up.

In the years following the decision referred to, the composition of the Court changed, justices regarded as conservative replacing justices regarded as liberal. The result was that the Court drastically narrowed down the possibility that a finding of guilt might be based on disparate impact. And that in turn led Congress, where progressive liberals were stronger, to pass a bill designed to restore the earlier situation. President Bush vetoed the bill, but after various adjustments in the wording he signed it a year later, only to be denounced for doing so by numerous conservative commentators who were primarily sensitive to the needs and interests of business.

## REDRESS

When discrimination occurs, the question of redress arises. None of the civil rights acts provides especially for it. In fact, the Civil Rights Act of 1964 creates a problem in that it seems to forbid all racial discrimination even when the purpose is remedial. But the courts do not always give words the meaning they seem to have; and, anyway, courts may sit in equity and provide redress to those whose constitutional rights have been violated.

Think of three kinds of situations: (1) the party guilty of discriminating and the victim are both known; (2) the guilty party is known, but not the victim, or at least not all of the victims; (3) a party that has never discriminated wants to help provide redress for discrimination by others.

Liberals and conservatives generally agree on the principles to apply to the first situation—a situation of "victim specificity." The guilty party must make amends. For example, employers who refuse to hire for racial reasons may be obliged to hire after all, perhaps with back pay from the time the discrimination occurred. Or monetary damages may have to be paid. The cases are easy because, in a formal sense, redress is based not on the race of the victims but on the fact that their rights were violated. Thus the question of "reverse discrimination" is avoided.

Unfortunately, the rule of "victim specificity" is narrow, not providing an adequate basis for justice. Think, for example, of acts of discrimination that occurred so long ago that witnesses and documents are no longer available. Everyone knows that such cases exist, but how can discrimination in a specific case be proved? And how practical would it be to have courts consider the hundreds of thousands, if not the millions, of cases that could properly be brought? Who would bear the costs?

Further, think of passive discrimination, which occurs when a policy of restricting jobs to whites is so well known that blacks do not apply. It is scarcely imaginable, for example, that a black would have applied to Governor George Wallace of Alabama for a teaching job while he was standing in the schoolhouse door to bar black children. But to hold that the absence of an application means the absence of discrimination is a mockery.

Liberals who take up this question generally argue that it is fine to give redress on the basis of "victim specificity" when possible, but that to limit redress to such cases is mainly to protect white gains and deny redress to blacks.

The second kind of situation is illustrated by a case involving the Detroit Edison Company (*Stamps v. Detroit Edison,* 1973). According to the federal district court that heard the case, the evidence was overwhelming that invidious racial discrimination permeated the company's employment practices. Discrimination was "deliberate and by design" in identifying the kinds of jobs for which blacks would be considered, in restricting their employment and promotion, and in calculating seniority. Nevertheless, the company denied that it engaged in discrimination, refusing, the court said, "to acknowledge the obvious."

Holding that the Civil Rights Act authorized it to issue a decree designed not only to prevent future discrimination but also to correct insofar as possible the effects of past discrimination, the court laid down goals and requirements for Detroit Edison in the future: "Subject to the availability of qualified applicants, the Company shall recruit and endeavor to hire black applicants for all positions within the Company on an accelerated basis with the goal of having a number of blacks employed by the Company at 30 percent of its total workforce." The court considered 30 percent a reasonable proportion in view of the fact that blacks constituted 44 percent of the available labor force in Detroit.

In certain employment categories, the court ordered the filling of vacancies by blacks and whites at a ratio of 2–1 until blacks held 25 percent of the jobs, and it ordered that every other promotion to the level of supervisor go to a black. It ordered back pay for specific victims who could be identified, restoring them to the economic position they would have enjoyed but for the discrimination. It ordered that those previously rebuffed for racial reasons should have "first opportunity" to apply for vacancies in high-opportunity jobs. And it ordered changes in the rules pertaining to seniority.

Note that, although the court called for redress for victims of discrimination who could be identified, it did not restrict itself to the principle of "victim specificity." In ordering ratio hiring it was providing redress for passive discrimination; and it was minimizing the chance that the Detroit Edison Company could find new and perhaps more subtle ways of continuing its policies of racial discrimination. The problem is that ratio hiring made it probable that blacks who had not suffered any discrimination would be hired to the exclusion of white applicants. Those hired were to be "qualified," but not necessarily the most highly qualified. This obviously goes counter to the ideal that hiring should be by merit. Not that the company had been hiring by merit in the past, for it clearly had not. It had been giving preferential treatment to whites regardless of merit. But still, a special problem is created when official policy accepts the possibility that a better-qualified person will be passed over so that a less-qualified person can be hired.

The principles that the court approved for Detroit Edison presumably hold for all other private employers, and a similar problem has come up again and again in other contexts. The Department of Justice has brought suits against trade unions for their racial practices, and it has taken dozens of city, county, and state governments to court. Police and fire departments have been notorious for recruiting whites on a preferential basis and discriminating against blacks and other minorities. And time after time the courts have called for ratio hiring. It is as if redress is going to the whole black community through the individuals who happen to get the jobs.

The third kind of situation involves a party that is not trying to compensate for its own past sins, if any, but simply wants to help provide redress for societal discrimination. Thus a college may adopt special measures to help struggling black students, or a medical school with a limited enrollment may admit some black applicants on a preferential basis. Or those recruiting on the basis of tests may engage in race norming, which means that those passing the test are put on different lists depending on race and the appointment may go to the person at the top of the preferred racial list, even if the top person on the other list had a higher score. Or a municipality may establish set-asides; for example, it may specify that at least 20 percent of the contracts made with private firms must go to firms under minority ownership.

I mention the above measures as measures of redress, designed to make up to the black community in some degree for the illegal discriminations of the past. An alternative is to say that, regardless of what has happened in the past, we want to create a society in which race becomes less and less significant; that is, we want to have a nonracial society, with blacks represented in something like the same proportion as whites in the various kinds of pursuits. To achieve this goal, the thought is, we are justified in adopting special measures to see to it that blacks have opportunities to develop and use their talents.

One implication of the preferential treatment of blacks is that whites are called on to accept a sacrifice. This is a hard fact and cannot be dismissed. To be sure, the sacrifice is limited. No one is fired so that a black can be hired; no one is deprived of what he or she already enjoys, even if it was gotten as a result of the system of discrimination and preference. But even if the sacrifice takes the form of a disappointed effort to get something new, it may be severe. The question is whether the promotion of the public good is enough to provide a justification.

President Johnson stated the principle that justifies the special measures and the expectation of sacrifice. He said that

> freedom is not enough.... You do not take a person who, for years, has been hobbled by chains and liberate him, bring him up to the starting line of a race and then say, "You are free to compete with all the others," and still believe that you have been completely fair.
>
> Thus it is not enough just to open the gates of opportunity. All our citizens must have the ability to walk through those gates.... We seek not just legal equity but human ability, not just equality as a right and a theory but equality as a fact and equality as a result. (*Public Papers* 1965, 2:636)

In asking for "equality as a result," Johnson gave ammunition to critics who, at least by innuendo, accuse him of seeking economic leveling, but the context makes it clear that what he sought was an effort to help blacks overcome the disadvantages imposed on them by generations of discrimination. He wanted opportunity to be effective for them. He wanted their liberty to have worth.

## The Voting Rights Act of 1965

Like the Civil Rights Act of 1964, the Voting Rights Act of 1965 has had consequences going in opposite directions. It forbids rules and arrangements whose purpose or effect is to deny or abridge the vote because of race, color, or membership in a minority-language group. It also fixes criteria for identifying communities with flagrant records of discrimination and requires such communities to get "preclearance" —either from the attorney general or from the federal district court in the District of Columbia—if they want to change their electoral arrangements.

Many communities have accepted blacks as voters without qualification. Many others, however, though required to allow blacks to vote, have tried to keep them from making significant political gains. One of the strategies is to switch from single- to multimember districts and then to use at-large elections so that whites can swamp the black vote. Another is to engage in racial gerrymandering. Still another is to transfer functions and powers away from offices that blacks succeed in winning.

To combat the first two of these strategies, blacks have time and again taken advantage of the "preclearance" requirement. The basic rule in this connection is that any changes in voting arrangements shall not have the purpose or effect of denying black voters a reasonable chance to elect officials in proportion to their number. Not that they are entitled to proportional representation, but that they shall not be denied opportunity. This means that those drawing the boundaries of electoral districts, for example, have no choice but to take race into account, and they may need to engage in a kind of reverse gerrymandering, perhaps with oddly shaped districts as the result.

The main obvious effect of the Voting Rights Act is that the number of blacks serving in political office has increased markedly. The total number of black elected officials went up from about 1,500 in 1970 to over 7,500 in 1992. And numerous blacks have come to serve in appointive offices as well.

## Equal Treatment for Nonracial Groups

I have dwelt on the problem of race because it was a central concern of Great Society liberalism. Lyndon Johnson did not take a comparable interest in discrimination based on other grounds, but what he did for blacks stimulated and strengthened action for groups identified by other characteristics.

### DISCRIMINATION BASED ON SEX

The Civil Rights Act of 1964, although aimed primarily to benefit blacks, also prohibits discrimination based on sex in places of public accommodation and in connection with employment. Various other pieces of legislation include comparable provisions—among them a measure adopted in 1972, when Nixon was president, specifying that no sex discrimination may occur in educational programs and activities supported by federal funds. Also in 1972 Congress adopted the Equal Rights Amendment, providing that "equality of rights under the law shall not be denied or abridged by the United States or by any state on account of sex." To become a part of the Constitution it needed to be ratified by thirty-six states, but it failed that test.

Attitudes toward governmental requirements of equal treatment for women do not fit neatly along ideological lines any more than attitudes toward race, but support is most likely to come from progressive liberals and opposition is most likely to come from social conservatives, to be described in chapter 11.

Several features of progressive liberalism suggest support for efforts to ban sex discrimination. Liberals are predisposed more than most conservatives to welcome change, at least when they can identify it with progress. They are predisposed toward activism on the part of government, looking to government to solve problems. And they attach more importance than many others to the idea of equality of opportunity, and give that idea a more extensive meaning. I discuss this last feature of liberalism in the next chapter. The identification of the movement for the equal treatment of women with liberalism is suggested by the practice of referring to it as a movement for "women's liberation."

I need not dwell on the fact that discrimination based on sex amounts to a denial of equal opportunity. The situation is suggested by historic provisions of the British common law, inherited and long applied by most American states. According to the common law, a woman, once she married, had no legal existence separate from her husband. Any property of a bride passed forthwith to the groom, and any earnings of a wife became the property of the husband. She had to live where he chose or be guilty of desertion. She could not sue or be sued, or make a will or a contract. This meant that she was unlikely to be able to borrow money in her own name. The common law even allowed the husband to take a switch to his wife, provided it was no bigger in diameter than his thumb.

Much of this discrimination went by the board long ago, but much persisted. Women were long denied the vote and, by extension, eligibility for public office. Like blacks, they were excluded from jury service. They were exempted from compulsory military service, and, if they volunteered, the assignments open to them were limited. In civilian life, some jobs were formally or informally earmarked for women and others for men, it being rare for women to enter certain professions at all or to rise to the top in any enterprise in which they became associated. The dominant view was that a woman's place was in the home, nurturing the husband and children, and perhaps participating in activities associated with the church and charitable organizations. In other words, equality of opportunity was denied in a major way.

Agitation against the discrimination began long ago, and extensive changes have been accepted. Some of the issues are about the same as those plaguing race relations—mainly issues about affirmative action and what it should include. Other issues are distinctive to the question of equal treatment of women. Should discrimination directed only against women who are pregnant count as sex discrimination? What kinds of clubs can be for men only and what kinds must also be open to women? What constitutes sexual harassment in the workplace? What should public policy be with respect to abortion? In what ways should the armed forces be permitted to differentiate between the sexes?

The wording of the last question is deliberate. No one in any position of leadership argues that the armed forces must always treat men and women in exactly the same way, for values in addition to equal and nondiscriminatory treatment need to be taken into account. For example, no one argues that the armed forces must assign men and women to the same barracks or the same toilet facilities indiscriminately. Rights of privacy are acknowledged that justify differentiation. Currently the big issue concerns the long-standing practice of excluding women from roles that might put them into combat.

This is an issue on which even many liberals waver. The general principle, however, is reasonably clear: the strong presumption of progressive liberalism is in favor of fair equality of opportunity. Approximately the same point can be expressed in different words: progressive liberalism favors individual liberty and wants to make sure that liberty has worth.

Abortion is not ordinarily debated in terms of equality of opportunity, but it might well be. Pregnancy automatically limits a woman's activities, and to prohibit abortion is to deny her any escape. Once she gives birth, her freedom is limited in other ways, although here she has a possible escape in the form of putting the child up for adoption. The problem is complicated by the fact that not only the woman's life but also the potential life of the fetus is involved. I choose those words carefully, not wanting to speak of the life of an "unborn child."

Legal and moral judgments are both potentially involved. The legal question is when a "person" or a "human being" comes into existence. The Fourteenth Amendment, for example, says that no state is to deny to any *person* the equal protection of the laws. The international Covenants on Human Rights say that these rights are for all *human beings*. To speak of an "unborn child" is to prejudice consideration of the issue, for the words suggest that a person or a human being is there waiting to be born, which is plausible in the later stages of gestation but wildly implausible in the early stages, when most abortions occur.

In *Roe* v. *Wade* the Supreme Court took the position that a *person* does not come into existence until a live birth occurs. Thus the zygote, the embryo, and the fetus have no claim to the equal protection of the laws. In contrast, the pregnant woman is a person with both rights and interests that she is entitled to promote and protect. The moral issues are essentially the same as the legal issues, and progressive liberals are likely to answer them in the same way.

I state the argument above in terms of the question when a *person* or a *human being* comes into existence. Even if it be assumed that the zygote, embryo, or fetus is a person, it does not necessarily follow that abortion is wrong and should be illegal. Callous as it may sound to say it, the organism in the womb is a parasite, sapping the energy of the woman, threatening her well-being and even endangering her life. Morality and law require people to take risks and make sacrifices for others, but the process of gestation involves more risk and sacrifice than we require in any other connection. To most progressive liberals this means that the acceptance of the burdens involved should be a matter of choice.

## Sexual Orientation

In private life we are free to discriminate as we please, for good or bad reasons. If you want to invite one person into your home, but not another, you are not accountable to anyone for your choice.

Public life is different, and public life includes not only governmental affairs but also private activities that, according to government, are affected by a public interest. Places of public accommodation, like stores and hotels, are in this category, and so are enterprises employing more than some minimum number of people.

Even in public life, discrimination is not always bad. When it is reasonable (based on acceptable grounds or appropriate standards), it is usually considered good. For example, we want presidents to be discriminating in the appointments that they make, choosing the better qualified and rejecting the others. In contrast, when discrimination is arbitrary, we condemn it. The rule is that we should treat people in the same way in the absence of good grounds for treating them differently.

As already indicated, most of the differentiation based on race or sex has come to be condemned as arbitrary discrimination. In a few situations, of course, race or sex may be what is called a bona fide occupational qualification (a bfoq); for example, it is all right to differentiate by sex in selecting models who are to display the new styles in a fashion show. But the general presumption is that race or sex is irrelevant in public affairs and therefore is not to be the basis for differentiation.

But how about sexual orientation? In connection with public affairs, is differentiation based on homosexuality reasonable or arbitrary? Through most of American history homosexual persons themselves did not raise the issue, thinking it prudent to remain "in the closet" and thus permitting liberal leaders and others to remain silent. Whether there was a liberal position on the issue is doubtful. But, stimulated and encouraged by the success of blacks and women in attacking discrimination, many homosexuals have come out of the closet and brought the issue to the fore, and they have many friends and allies. Now the question is inescapable: in what connections, if any, are there good grounds for the differential treatment of persons because they are gay or lesbian? The extent of liberal agreement is uncertain. Liberal principles, however, and their logical extension suggest the following.

We start with the fact that many people entertain prejudices about homosexuality. Sometimes the prejudices amount to strong antipathies, leading to "gay bashing" and even to murder. Sexual love between men and women is everywhere accepted as natural, associated with marriage and families, usually including children. In contrast, sexual love between members of the same sex is widely regarded as unnatural and perverse; it involves sodomy, which the Bible condemns and which many regard as immoral and disgusting. The assumption that homosexuality is perverse involves another assumption: that it is a matter of choice.

Many people accept these views, and go on to conclude that penalties ought to be imposed on those who choose to be homosexual: there should be no tolerance of those who flout the moral standards of the community and who conduct themselves in such a way as to undermine the family and lead young people astray. Such attitudes are widespread enough that as of 1961 the laws of all the states made sodomy a crime and the laws of twenty-four states still do. No state recognizes same-sex marriage as legal or permits same-sex persons who live together to adopt children. Until recently, the armed forces not only prohibited sodomy on the part of those in the service but sought to exclude homosexuals and discharged any who got in. A few organizations, such as the Boy Scouts, hold that homosexual persons are not acceptable as leaders, and discrimination against homosexuals who apply for teaching positions or who seek housing is not unusual. Political leaders, if they want to be elected or reelected, have to take the prejudice against homosexuals into account, and so may make decisions that are adjusted more to the political wind than to the dictates of reason.

How sound are views that condemn homosexual persons? Whether homosexuality is natural or a matter of choice is hotly debated, which means that the issue has not been resolved scientifically. No one has discovered in either men or women a genetic characteristic that determines sexual orientation. This makes it possible to hold that the orientation is a matter of choice. At the same time, homosexuals themselves claim overwhelmingly that they were born that way; it was God's choice, not theirs. They grant that some people seem able to swing either way, but they hold that this is the exception rather than the rule. The rule, they claim, is that homosexuality, like heterosexuality, is beyond the individual's control.

Public policy toward homosexuality can well turn on this issue. Those who believe that homosexuality is a matter of choice can say that this justifies measures to penalize those who make the wrong choice and to prevent them from influencing others. In contrast, those who believe that homosexuality is natural can hold that discrimination based on it is no more justified than discrimination based on other immutable characteristics such as race or sex itself. People born that way should not be condemned. Differentiation based on merit can occur, but not differentiation based on sexual orientation.

As to sodomy, at least three considerations need to be taken into account. In the first place, it is not confined to homosexuals. Some proportion of heterosexual couples practice it too—no one knows how large a proportion, but apparently it is substantial. The fact that a couple practices sodomy is of course unlikely to become known, but even if proof were somehow available, it is extremely unlikely that a responsible official would prosecute; and this raises the obvious question why, if sodomy is regarded as a private matter between a man and a woman, it comes under the purview of government if practiced by gays or lesbians.

What actually happens is that laws against sodomy are scarcely ever enforced. But they are sometimes used as a reason (an excuse?) for discrimination. For example, a police department looking for a new recruit and facing an applicant who admits to being a practicing homosexual can say that it is inappropriate to hire an admitted lawbreaker.

A second consideration is implied in the first. It is that rights of privacy surely exist with respect to sexual practices. What two persons do privately and willingly, harming no one else, can well be considered their own business, whatever their sex. In this respect an odd inversion exists in the attitudes of progressive liberals and many conservatives. In general, progressive liberals are inclined to endorse governmental activism, but they take an opposite stand where privacy is at stake. And many conservatives who in general oppose "big government" want government to play an interventionist role on various moral and cultural issues, including the issues raised by homosexuality.

A third consideration concerns the presumption that homosexual persons practice sodomy. The presumption is surely correct in most instances, and the arguments advanced above assume that it is correct. But some homosexual persons no doubt lead celibate lives, just as some heterosexual persons do, and those who think that homosexuality calls for penalties must therefore face the question whether a homosexual *orientation* is enough to bring on the penalties or whether the focus must not be on *conduct* instead. Holding that homosexuality is genetic and that sexual abstinence is a possibility, the liberal can go on to argue that if any penalties are imposed, they must be based on conduct and not simply on orientation. One specific implication is that the policy long followed by the armed forces of discharging personnel simply on the ground of a homosexual orientation is indefensible.

Whether homosexual marriages and adoptions should be permitted is a question that divides liberals just as it divides others. To permit marriages and adoptions, and to give a place of respect to families headed by lesbian mothers, is to deprive the traditional family of its place in the sun. As we see in later chapters, social conservatives and some others argue that it therefore tends to undermine the traditional family. But liberals should and do ask whether it is fair and just to homosexual persons, and whether it is good public policy, to deny legal status to homosexual marriage. To deny it is to deny a status and a mark of social acceptability that heterosexual persons enjoy without question. Further, it is to lose whatever influence the recognition of homosexual marriages might have in promoting stable, monogamous relationships. Especially in the light of the problem of AIDS, something is to be said for any public policy that might reduce promiscuity. It is not the case even with heterosexuals that marriage is necessarily connected with procreation.

A court decision in the state of New York has obliged the government there to recognize gay couples as families entitled to the protection of rent control, and a court in Minnesota has recognized a lesbian relationship in appointing one of the persons involved as the legal guardian of the other. In 1993 a court of appeal in Hawaii, facing the refusal of a lower court to recognize a homosexual marriage, did not explicitly reverse the decision, but required the lower court to give it further consideration in the light of the equal rights amendment included in the state constitution. Movement in the direction of giving legal status to homosexual marriages is thus occurring. Which leads to a question: would and should liberals give legal recognition to the marriage of almost any small set of persons who want to be joined in a family on a " 'til-death-do-us-part" basis?

As noted above, the policy of the Department of Defense has been to reject acknowledged homosexuals who sought to enlist and to discharge those who somehow got in and whose homosexuality became known. Soon after taking office, President Clinton moved to terminate this policy, proposing to allow acknowledged homosexuals to serve. He thus stirred up a hornets' nest. Support for the policy of exclusion is based mainly on considerations relating to cohesion and morale. The argument is that mutual respect, trust, and confidence are vital within a fighting force—that soldiers must ideally act on a one-for-all and all-for-one basis—and that the presence of homosexual persons in any unit will reduce the chance that this kind of *esprit* will develop. A malaise among those involved is anticipated especially where military personnel must share cramped quarters. The further argument is that, at least in many circumstances, service in the military is not a nine-to-five matter with people going their separate ways in off-duty hours, but involves twenty-four-hour-a-day membership in a community of mutual support. And the argument is also advanced that homosexual persons, unless they are open about their homosexuality, will be especially vulnerable to blackmail.

The counterargument is that negative attitudes toward homosexual persons are matters of prejudice not to be indulged in official policy: that homosexual persons are as much entitled to equal treatment as anyone else and prejudices based on homosexuality should be fought in the military, just like prejudices based on race. The rejoinder to this is that homosexuality implies a certain kind of conduct more surely than does race.

Homosexual persons have in fact been serving in the armed forces all along. In some cases it has led to problems, but in others it has proved acceptable, either because the homosexual persons remained "in the closet" or because, if their homosexuality became known, everyone involved winked at the fact.

The uneasy solution to the problem in the armed forces is that recruits will not be asked about their sexual orientation and will not be discharged simply because of homosexuality if it becomes known. But homosexual *conduct* will be a basis for discharge. Rules against sexual harassment, whether by heterosexuals or homosexuals, will surely stand.

An alternative framework for dealing with the question of homosexuality is suggested by the term *permissiveness:* if people engage in homosexual practices by mutual consent, doing no harm to others, their behavior is to be permitted. As we see later, various kinds of conservatives are inclined to condemn liberals for their *permissiveness,* that is, their refusal to insist that everyone uphold a prescribed set of standards. The accusation relates not only to homosexuality but to sexual activity in general. Not that liberals advocate premarital or extramarital sex or unwed motherhood, but they adjust to it. They may favor sex education in the schools, not limiting the teaching to the rule of abstinence outside of marriage. They may even be willing to make condoms available to high school students on demand.

## NATIONAL ORIGIN (LANGUAGE)

People respond differently to the presence of minority language groups. Some regard such groups as threats to the prevailing culture and therefore favor policies designed to get them into the melting pot, including policies that make it difficult for them to get along unless they take up English. In fact, a number of states have adopted "English only" legislation. Others are more likely to see minority-language groups as composed of persons who should be protected against discrimination and served with bilingual education and bilingual elections, thus allowed to decide for themselves about abandoning their own language and culture and joining the dominant community.

Progressive liberals are likely to be in the second category. As with other minorities, they see language minorities as composed of persons entitled to liberty (to a kind of liberty that is worthwhile) and to equal treatment. This is in the American tradition. Throughout American history, the general rule has been that each locality was free to choose its language of communication—free to choose the language in which school would be taught and the affairs of government conducted. A number of local communities operated in German for many years, but eventually decided of their own accord to switch to English. Pennsylvania came close to giving German equal status with English, but chose not to do so. At the federal level, we have never had a language formally designated as official. In effect, languages other than English have been killed off with kindness and not through oppression. Thus it is no accident that the Civil Rights Act of 1964 prohibited discrimination on the basis of "national origin" and that various other pieces of legislation have shown solicitude for the linguistic and cultural heritage of minority peoples.

## DISABILITY

Religion and age have not figured much in ideological struggles, and Lyndon Johnson did not concern himself with discrimination against those faced with disabilities, but in 1990 Congress enacted and President Bush signed an Americans with Disabilities Act (ADA). Even though adopted much later than the Great Society legislation, it is in the spirit of that legislation. Its aim is to assure fair equality of opportunity to people with disabilities. It seeks this by requiring employers and those providing public services to make reasonable accommodation to the disabled as long as they can do it without suffering undue hardship themselves and without imposing undue risk on others. For example, it is not enough to tell a paraplegic that he is free to walk up steps and stairs to get to the various offices of the courthouse.

The other side of the coin—the one at which economic conservatives look—is the regulation of business and the higher taxes and other costs that equal treatment for the disabled entails. The conservative complaint, as we see in chapter 10, is that the Americans with Disabilities Act goes too far in imposing burdens on business, threatening profitability.


## Multiculturalism

As we see in chapter 11, conservatives accuse liberals of giving rise to multiculturalism. One of the problems with the charge is that the term *multiculturalism* has more than one meaning. To some it simply calls for due respect to the cultural heritage of distinct ethnic groups— Mexican Americans, for example. The most prominent feature of multiculturalism, so conceived, is support for bilingual instruction in the schools. Not that anyone should be able to go through school in the United States without learning English but that the pupil's native tongue should be used in some degree during the transition period while English is being learned.

Others give *multiculturalism* a more drastic meaning. As Arthur Schlesinger says, "self-styled 'multiculturalists' are very often ethnocentric separatists who see little in the Western heritage beyond Western crimes." The Western tradition, in this view, is "inherently racist, sexist, 'classist,' hegemonic [and] irredeemably repressive.... Such animus toward Europe lay behind the well-known crusade against the Western-civilization course at Stanford ('Hey-hey, ho-ho, Western culture's got to go!')" (Schlesinger 1991, 72). Multiculturalism of this more extreme sort is especially associated with agitation on the part of blacks calling for greater emphasis on their African heritage.

Many liberals and others accept the mild form of multicultural-ism typified by bilingual instruction, although they are more likely to call it pluralism than multiculturalism. It fits with liberalism to follow policies compatible with the self-esteem of different ethnic groups and respectful of different traditions. And it fits to respect choices that individuals sometimes make to associate primarily with others who share their cultural heritage. Such policies as these do not imply the grant of any special political status, and if an ethnic or racial group is strong enough to get control of local government it runs into constitu-tional and legal restrictions on what it can do.

So far as I am aware, no leading liberal endorses multiculturalism in its more extreme form. Arthur Schlesinger, who has impeccable lib-eral credentials and who gives *multiculturalism* the more extreme defi-nition cited above, deplores it as an attack on the idea of "a common culture and a single society." This is an idea that he wants to preserve, and surely most liberals would join him in this view.

## The Environment

Concern for the environment did not figure significantly in the thoughts of Lyndon Johnson. Under Nixon, however, Congress adopted the National Environmental Policy Act, establishing the Envi-ronmental Protection Agency and making the protection of the envi-ronment an important federal concern. Measures to reduce pollution in the air and water were among those adopted. Later, in 1991, Bush signed a measure enlarging the role of the federal government in com-bating air pollution.

The fact that Nixon and Bush played prominent roles in promot-ing measures to protect the environment leads to a question whether environmentalism is to be identified especially with liberalism. But at least it is identified with a belief in activism on the part of government in attempting to solve problems. Conservatives, especially economic conservatives, tend to denounce environmental measures on the ground that they impose costs on private enterprise and make for "big government."

The preceding chapter and this one describe policies identified with progressive liberalism. They provide a basis for a general charac-terization of progressive liberalism, which is the objective of the next chapter.

# Chapter 6

# Progressive Liberalism:
# Its Nature

A UTHORS FIND IT EASIER to discuss liberalism than to define it. Relatively few offer definitions, and even fewer do it satisfactorily. It is difficult to resist the conclusion that most of those discussing liberalism do not know what they are talking about.

Stephen Holmes and Glenn Tinder are among the exceptions in that they offer definitions, but their definitions are ill suited to discussions of the kind of liberalism associated with the New Deal and the Great Society. In *The Anatomy of Antiliberalism*, Holmes chooses to address himself to the liberalism "that flourished from the middle of the seventeenth to the middle of the nineteenth century." And he goes on to describe it in terms of its "core practices": religious toleration, freedom of discussion, restrictions on police behavior, free elections, constitutional government, and so on (Holmes 1993, 3). He is thus primarily concerned with classical liberalism, not with the new liberalism that developed in Britain at the end of the nineteenth century or the progressive liberalism that developed in the United States in connection with the New Deal. And he presumably defines antiliberalism accordingly.

Glenn Tinder, reviewing the book by Holmes, defines liberalism as "the philosophy and practice of liberty understood not only as protection against undue interference with an individual's life, but also in terms of representative government, constitutionalism, rule of law, and other such institutions commonly found in the polities of North America and Western Europe" (Tinder 1993, 116). This is a perfectly good definition of one kind of liberalism, but not the kind that has prevailed in the United States since the time of the New Deal. Similarly, when Ronald Beiner says that "liberalism is principally a doctrine of the limitation of state power," he must have classical liberalism in mind, not the progressive liberalism of the United States (Beiner 1992, 26). And both Thomas Pangle and Georg Sørensen, writing on democracy, proceed as if all liberalism is classical liberalism (Pangle 1992, 131–59; Sørensen 1993, 5–6).

Critics of contemporary liberalism do not help much either, even if they define the term, for they tend to advance definitions that are obviously designed to make liberalism look bad. Thus William Kristol says, "By 'liberalism' I mean post-1960s liberalism: a movement committed in politics to further expansion of the welfare state, and in social matters to an agenda of individual autonomy and 'liberation'" (W. Kristol 1993, 33). And Irving Kristol, speaking of "the liberal ethos," says that it "aims simultaneously at political and social collectivism, on the one hand, and moral anarchy, on the other" (I. Kristol 1993b, 144). Others write as if liberalism is to be defined essentially in terms of the promotion of "big government," more spending, and higher taxes.

Supporters of liberalism do not always do much better. Thus George McGovern satisfies himself with the statement that "liberalism is the 'middle way' between the right-wing glorification of an unregulated market and the left-wing advocacy of full-scale government ownership and direction" (Barash 1992, 6).

I do not myself have an entirely satisfactory succinct definition, but I am most attracted to a statement by Philip Green that "central to liberalism [is] the notion of a social order in which individual liberty will be able to flourish equally for all to the limit of their capacities" regardless of the social group to which they belong (Green 1992, 324). And I am also attracted to the statement by Arthur Schlesinger that liberalism is "primarily concerned with the expansion and redistribution of political and economic opportunity" (Schlesinger 1990, 16).

The merit of the last two definitions becomes clearer as the analysis proceeds. The successive sections of the chapter dwell on principles relating to (1) the liberty of the individual; (2) equality, equal treatment, and equality of opportunity; (3) neutrality and tolerance; (4) the role of reason; (5) the usefulness of government; (6) the need for welfare; and (7) taxes. Then comes a brief acknowledgment of other underlying principles, such as the desirability of constitutional democracy, that do not provoke so much controversy.

## *Liberty*

Like the classical liberals of Britain, the progressive liberals of the

United States are concerned with the liberty of the individual. John Rawls illustrates the fact, in both *A Theory of Justice* (1971) and *Political Liberalism* (1993). The first of his two principles of justice is that "each person has an equal right to a fully adequate scheme of equal basic liberties which is compatible with a similar scheme of liberties for all" (Rawls 1993, 5, 291). And he identifies basic liberties as "freedom of thought and liberty of conscience; the political liberties and freedom of association, as well as the freedoms specified by the liberty and integrity of the person; and finally, the rights and liberties covered by the rule of law." Moreover, he says that "among the basic liberties ... is the right to hold and to have the exclusive use of personal property" (Rawls 1982, 5, 12; 1993, 291). It goes without saying that liberty is called for within the framework of a democratic society.

Stated in broad terms, as above, this aspect of Rawls's thought, and of progressive liberalism, is not controversial. Classical liberals, libertarians, and most kinds of conservatives also believe in individual liberty. But issues exist nevertheless.

The fundamental issue relates to the meaning or worth of liberty. To T. H. Green the question was one of meaning: As noted in chapter 2, he was dissatisfied with the negative view that freedom is what exists in the absence of external restraint, and he proposed instead that people should be considered free only to the degree that they have positive powers or capacities. He defined freedom as "a positive power or capacity of doing or enjoying something worth doing or enjoying...."

Rawls focuses not on the meaning of liberty but on its worth. He takes the negative definition for granted—that liberty consists of an absence of external restraint. But seeking "fair terms of cooperation" in a society, he wants to be sure that liberty has worth; and he holds that liberty has worth in proportion to the capacity of people to advance their ends. In the absence of a capacity to advance their ends, people are not free, at least not in any meaningful sense. The liberal conception of justice, he says, calls for "measures to ensure that all citizens have sufficient material means to make effective use of [their] basic rights" (1993, 157), and he wants "to maximize the worth to the least advantaged of the complete scheme of liberty shared by all" (1971, 204–5). The position fits with the idea that the pursuit of happiness should be a major human goal. It is difficult to imagine that happiness could be achieved by people who are taught to prize liberty but whose liberty lacks worth, leaving them unable to pursue their ends.

Others speak of the importance of self-actualization or self-fulfillment, wanting to create and maintain social conditions conducive to
it. Thus David Norton, championing what he calls "eudaimonism"
but what I would call progressive liberalism, says that "preferences
are right or wrong according as they contribute to or impede the individual's moral work of actualizing his or her worth in the world."

A mixture of these perspectives lies behind the response of President Johnson to the charge that the federal government had become a
menace to individual liberty. He denied it by asking a series of rhetorical questions. Is liberty reduced when we redeem the pledge made a
century ago in the Emancipation Proclamation? Is it reduced by
guarding people against destitution? Is it reduced by bringing electri-
city to farms? Is it reduced by abating pollution or by seeking knowledge relating to cancer and heart disease? Is it reduced by providing
school lunches or improving the safety of the airways?

Johnson might have done better to say explicitly that his aim was
to give worth to liberty, but the rhetorical questions aim at the same
point. "The truth is," he said, "far from crushing the individual, government at its best liberates him from the enslaving forces of his environment" (*Public Papers* 1963–64, 1:757).

Further, as noted at the end of chapter 4, Johnson described his
goal as "an America in which every citizen shares all the opportunities
of his society, in which every man has a chance to advance his welfare
to the limit of his capacities."And he later declared that "all our domestic programs and policies converge on a common set of aims: to
enrich the quality of American life; to provide a living place which liberates rather than constricts the human spirit; to give each of us the
opportunity to stretch his talents; and to permit all to share in the enterprise of our society" (*Public Papers* 1963–64, 1:376; 1966, 2:
1111).

Senator Hubert Humphrey, a champion of progressive liberalism, took a comparable view, similar to that of T.H. Green. I have
quoted Humphrey earlier, but repeat the quotation for emphasis and
convenience:

Positive liberty means that an externally unimpeded interest is capable of proceeding to its realization. In other words, positive liberty
embraces not only the removal of restraint but also the arrangement
of all factors so as to make accomplishment possible.... It is not
enough that both the rich and the poor may sleep under bridges....
The most ancient, persistent, and oppressive enemies of liberty are
not always external hindrances, whether physical or human, but are

poverty and ignorance, insecurity and fear.... It would be misleading to think that there is any clear line of demarcation between liberty and welfare. (Humphrey 1970, 88)

A contrast between progressive and classical liberals is clear; and the contrast sheds light on the current ideological conflict. Progressive liberals, wanting to make liberty meaningful or give it worth, assign a role to government. Libertarians and the various kinds of conservatives, holding that liberty exists automatically in the absence of external restraint, want to keep the role of government small if not to eliminate government entirely.

In comparison with the question of the meaning or worth of liberty, other issues relating to rights of liberty are not so portentous, but some of them should be recalled nevertheless. One concerns free speech. Mainly in the 1980s, a number of university administrations adopted speech codes making it a punishable offense to use language reflecting hatred, contempt, or disdain for members of a particular racial group. In the main, the codes were directed at whites who were hostile to blacks, the intent being to protect and promote racial harmony. The intent fitted well with liberalism, but the method came under overpowering attack, and the view came to prevail that racial harmony should not be sought at the expense of free speech.

Another issue concerns the relative emphasis on respect for civil rights and the protection of other public interests. Consider, for example, the statement attributed to Attorney General Janet Reno that "my highest priority has always been not to convict criminals but rather to protect their rights." Progressive liberals are likely to be sympathetic with the statement, perhaps giving it a ringing endorsement, whereas most sorts of conservatives are more likely to condemn it as insufficiently tough on crime.

Consider, too, the question whether the police should be free to establish checkpoints on streets and highways, stopping all drivers in an effort to reduce drunken driving or the trade in drugs. Liberals, emphasizing the right of law-abiding citizens to be free from police harassment, are likely to say that such checkpoints are not acceptable, whereas conservatives are somewhat more likely to hold that the public interest in repressing crime takes precedence.

A pregnant woman who uses "crack" raises a comparable problem. What stand does the pro-choice liberal take on the use of "crack" by a pregnant woman? Should the potential child be protected against the irresponsible mother? How?

A similar question arises about artistic freedom. During the Great

Society, Congress established the National Endowment for the Arts and the National Endowment for the Humanities, the object being to promote cultural development. Both endowments make grants to organizations and individuals—for example, to artists and writers. The question immediately arises, of course, how to go about selecting the recipients of the grants and how much freedom they should have in using funds provided by the taxpayers. Liberals and conservatives of all sorts generally agree that "peer review" must be involved in the selection process, but what if an artist or an author who receives an award produces art or writing that some regard as obscene, pornographic, blasphemous, or otherwise objectionable?

The liberal answer is likely to be that judgments usually differ on what is objectionable and that, in any event, people judged by their peers as worthy of awards must be given freedom to do what they will. In contrast, social conservatives (and perhaps others) regard it as intolerable that they, as taxpayers, have to support allegedly artistic or literary work that undermines values that they regard as precious.

## Equality

In calling for liberty, Rawls also speaks of equality: each person has an *equal* right to the most extensive scheme of *equal* basic liberties compatible with a similar scheme of liberties for all. An *equal* entitlement to basic liberties, then, is a fundamental feature of liberalism. At the same time, according to Rawls, "social and economic inequalities are permissible, provided they are (i) to the greatest expected benefit of the least advantaged, and (ii) attached to positions and offices open to all under conditions of fair equality of opportunity" (1993, 271).

What Rawls does here is to assign the burden of proof—the burden of justification. He accepts a presumption that equality is desirable and puts the burden of justification on those who support some kind of inequality. Among the questions that his position suggests are those relating to the distribution of income and influence, equal treatment, and equality of opportunity.

As to income, the Rawlsian proposition presents difficulties. Although saying that inequalities are to be to the *greatest* advantage of the least advantaged, Rawls says nothing about the question how to measure or predict relative advantage. If the average income of the top 1 percent of the population goes up by $50,000 (5 percent), what, according to Rawls, should happen to the average income of the bottom 1 percent?

Mancur Olson points to another difficulty. Suppose that an inequality benefits the second most disadvantaged without hurting the most disadvantaged (Rowley 1987, 201). Or suppose that an inequality benefits the most disadvantaged, but gives an even greater benefit to the second most disadvantaged. Or suppose it benefits society as a whole without hurting the most disadvantaged. It is scarcely plausible that all such inequalities should be ruled out.

In fact, in most of Rawls's references to equality and inequality, he drops the requirement that the *greatest* advantage go to the least advantaged. His imaginary starting point is one in which everyone has an equal share of all primary goods, including income and wealth, but he grants that organizational requirements and the need for economic efficiency make it unreasonable to stop at equal division. Inequalities are to be accepted so long as they "improve everyone's situation, including that of the least advantaged, provided these inequalities are consistent with equal liberty and fair equality of opportunity" (1993, 281). Obviously, a call for the improvement of the situation of the least advantaged is not the same as a requirement that the *greatest* benefit go to them.

Rawls also drops any reference to the *greatest* benefit in various other statements. For example, he says that his second principle, concerning equality and inequality, calls for "measures assuring to all citizens adequate all-purpose means to make effective use of their liberties and opportunities" (1993, 6). His point is that "below a certain level of material and social well-being, and of training and education, people simply cannot take part in society as citizens, much less as equal citizens" (1993, 166).

How great the gap may be between the rich and the poor Rawls does not say. The principle (the "constitutional essential") is that due weight should be given "to the idea of society as a fair system of cooperation between free and equal citizens," which leads to concern not only about the worth of liberty but also about the distribution of income and wealth. Paul Starr's position is that "in matters of income distribution and material well-being, the objective should be, above all, to eliminate poverty and maintain a minimum floor of decency to enable individuals to carry out their own life plans" (Starr 1991, 79).

As to the distribution of influence, it would be preposterous to contend that in politics people are entitled to equality, for some inevitably become more influential than others by virtue of their talent and industry. But what of differentials in influence that stem simply from money? Should the liberty of one person (in this case, the right to free speech) be permitted to be worth ten times more than the liberty of another simply because of differences in the amount of money spent?

In connection with federal elections, the Supreme Court has said yes. It approves limits on contributions to candidates, but not limits on spending by candidates. Its concern is with the possibility of corruption—the possibility that contributors may expect quid pro quos.

To Rawls, the Court's refusal to accept restrictions on spending is "profoundly dismaying." In his eyes the public financing of political campaigns, limits on contributions, and other regulations are all "essential to maintain the fair value of the political liberties." He wants to "keep political parties independent of large concentrations of private economic and social power." Rawls might also bewail a situation in which the costs of judicial proceedings go so high that the poor cannot get equal justice.

Questions about equality and inequality arise not only with respect to income but also with respect to both personal treatment and opportunity. Since the preceding chapter discusses equal treatment and discrimination, I do not pursue the subject here, but equality of opportunity calls for comment.

Almost everyone endorses equality of opportunity, but it is plain that they do not give the words the same meaning. Think of three definitions, progressively more sweeping. The first is that equality of opportunity is simply what exists in the absence of arbitrary discrimination. The second is that equality of opportunity is what exists not only in the absence of arbitrary discrimination but also in the absence of disadvantages or handicaps for which society is responsible. The third is that equality of opportunity is what exists in the absence of (1) arbitrary discrimination, (2) disadvantages or handicaps for which society is responsible, and (3) disadvantages or handicaps for which the individual is not responsible, such as birth in a poor family or with a physical handicap.

Apparently without giving the matter much thought, economic conservatives seem to take the first of the above meanings for granted, although what they are concerned with is not so much discrimination as what they regard as reverse discrimination; that is, they champion what they call equality of opportunity as against "quotas" and set-asides. But progressive liberals hold that the first definition, even when conceived more broadly, is too narrow. Perfect equality of opportunity in the full sense suggested by the second and third definitions is not achievable, but progressive liberals want to go in that direction. In some degree, as indicated in the preceding chapter, they want to undo the effects of earlier illegal discrimination and the corresponding earlier preferential treatment—to reduce the extent to which the advantages and disadvantages created by that discrimination and preferential treatment in the past are carried into the future. And they want to take measures to compensate for disadvantages that people suffer through no fault of their own. Public provision for education is the most obvious measure of this sort, but almost any sort of publicly provided benefit, like the use of roads and highways, can also be viewed as contributing to equality of opportunity for the poor: if all roads were toll roads, the poor would be at a disadvantage.

John Rawls advances a conception of equality of opportunity similar to the broader ones described above. He accepts what he calls the liberal principle and wants to go beyond it. According to him, the liberal principle is that "those with similar abilities and skills should have similar life chances. More specifically ... those who are at the same level of talent and ability, and have the same willingness to use them, should have the same prospects of success regardless of their initial place in the social system, that is, irrespective of the income class into which they are born" (Rawls 1971, 73). But to Rawls this principle does not go far enough, for it ignores "the arbitrary effects of the natural lottery." To mitigate these arbitrary effects, he urges a principle like the one referred to above: that "the advantages of persons with greater natural endowments [be] limited to those that further the good of the poorer sectors of society" (1971, 74). Note, however, the assumption that some kinds and degrees of inequality are justified. Those who say or assume that progressive liberals are economic levelers are wrong. Departures from equality are acceptable, given good reasons for them.

## Tolerance and Neutrality

Liberalism calls for tolerance and neutrality, but the proposition leads to problems. The necessity for tolerance goes with an emphasis on liberty. Given the various freedoms, people are bound to differ in their beliefs and in their behavior—in their choice of ends and means—and in the degree of success that they achieve; diversity is inevitable. To object to diversity is to reject liberty.

But tolerance and neutrality have to have limits, and it is not easy to say exactly what those limits are or should be. Anyone who believes in government cannot believe in unqualified tolerance or neutrality. Law is not neutral. The question is what kinds of moral rules or principles to incorporate in the law, and the act of incorporation means the abandonment of neutrality. Liberals have no more difficulty than anyone else with the idea that the moral rule "Thou shalt not kill" should also be a rule of law; and the same goes for a large number of other moral rules incorporated in the law. The statement that liberals want "the legal disestablishment of morality" is simply wrong (Gray 1992, 28).

Liberalism does, however, insist on neutrality on certain matters. For example, government is not to "establish" a religion. It is not to sponsor either religion in general or a particular church. This leads to controversy, such as the question of prayer in the public schools, but the official position (which is also a liberal position) is that freedom of religion includes freedom to reject religion and that government should do nothing that goes contrary to this principle. It must tolerate different bona fide religions and be neutral with respect to them; and it must be neutral as between believers and nonbelievers. Problems arise about the meaning of the rule, but liberals do not question the rule.

For Rawls, the main question relating to tolerance and neutrality concerns what he calls comprehensive religious, moral, or philosophical doctrines—doctrines in which all values and virtues, political and other, are more or less systematically ordered. His theme is that government must be tolerant of such "comprehensive doctrines" and neutral with respect to them, provided they are reasonable. It must avoid favoring one over any of the others. It must limit governmental action to areas within "the domain of the political" where the different comprehensive doctrines overlap.

The call for neutrality with respect to comprehensive doctrines presents problems. Suppose, for example, that a doctrine provides for human sacrifice or for slavery. Suppose that it provides for the strict subordination of women. Suppose that it calls for an end to liberal democracy and the establishment of an authoritarian regime of the sort that militant Islamic fundamentalists favor. Progressive liberals would surely refuse to be tolerant and neutral in the face of such doctrines.

Communists once presented progressive liberals and others with this kind of problem. Communists wanted to use democracy in order to destroy it. They claimed the benefit of the liberties that progressive liberalism upholds but planned to abolish those liberties and establish an authoritarian, totalitarian regime when and if they came to power. They thus presented a difficult problem, and liberals wavered. Some held that communists were entitled to their civil and political liberties along with everyone else and that, in any event, the propaganda battle against them could be conducted more effectively if they were allowed to operate legally and openly rather than in a clandestine way. Many conservatives were not so generous, favoring repressive action.

The general assumption underlying democratic politics is that participants who lose out now can try again later. But if defeat is going to be definitive, putting an end to democracy itself, the question is whether neutrality in the face of a threatening doctrine is still required. It can well be argued that "the present majority must not be allowed to deprive future majorities of the right to correct earlier mistakes" (Holmes 1991, 93). A provision of the International Covenant on Civil and Political Rights is in point. It specifies that "nothing in the present Covenant may be interpreted as implying for any State, group, or person any right to engage in any activity or perform any act aimed at the destruction of any of the rights and freedoms recognized herein. . . ." In other words, although diversity is to be expected and calls for tolerance, there is no obligation to be tolerant of the intolerant and no obligation to be neutral between those who would uphold democracy and those who would impose their own comprehensive religious, moral, or philosophical doctrines.

Currently within the United States the major struggles relating to tolerance and neutrality do not concern choices between comprehensive doctrines but rather choices about lesser issues such as abortion, sexual freedom (or license), and discrimination based on sex or sexual orientation. In this realm liberals are likely to stress their commitment both to liberty and to equal treatment, asking government to keep hands off or to intervene as these principles require. Liberals are torn over the question of governmental action against pornography. On the one hand, liberalism suggests freedom, including the freedom to indulge in pornography; on the other hand, it condemns attitudes and practices that inflict harm on others and deny them equal treatment. A liberal may thus call for governmental action against pornography on the ground that it robs women of their dignity and self-respect, demeaning and degrading them arbitrarily and placing them under a burden that men do not share.

One of the major criticisms of liberalism, both classical and progressive, is that in stressing individualism, and thus individual liberty, it gives inadequate attention to community. The appropriate response depends on the definition assumed. If *community* is defined in such a way that it exists only among those who share a comprehensive religious, moral, or philosophical doctrine, then liberalism is unwilling to have government foster and support it. This is on the assumption that those sharing a *comprehensive* doctrine would seek control over government so as to impose their doctrine on others. The situation is different, however, if *community* is given a less threatening meaning. After all, any group sharing a given set of values (conceptions of desirable ends and means) can be considered a community; and liberalism is for the most part indifferent to them. It leaves the way wide open for people to pursue the kinds of values that can be realized only through community, and, assuming general respect for democratic and constitutional procedures, it leaves the way wide open to communities to compete for influence and control in government. What liberalism does not tolerate is any attempt by one community to impose a comprehensive doctrine on others. More about this in chapter 11.

I should note that the charge that liberalism is neglectful of community has its counterpart in the charge that liberalism is collectivist, taxing some for the benefit of others and seeking to promote the public good instead of relying on the free market. Since the term *collectivism* is so fully identified with socialism and communism, it is inappropriate as applied to liberalism. It would be better to say that progressive liberalism is concerned with community in the sense of accepting the view that everyone has a degree of responsibility for the fate of others and for the community as a whole. It holds that we should all be concerned with creating and maintaining conditions that give worth to liberty and that promote effective equality of opportunity for all. Cooperation for the common good is itself a kind of communitarianism.

## The Role of Reason

Progressive liberals believe in reason and in the possibility of achieving progress through its use. Belief in reason, reasonableness, and rationality pervades the writing of Rawls concerning justice and liberalism. He does not get the principles of justice from a divine or any other authoritarian source, or from tradition. He does not appeal to natural law, nor does he look in any major way to coercion as a means of achieving and maintaining public order and achieving progress. Instead, he looks to the rational capacities of people. He assumes that liberals, regardless of their personal religious beliefs, should base public political arguments on secular considerations, such as respect for reason and fairness. This means that liberals do not argue from authority and that they must grant some uncertainty in the conclusions to which they think reason leads.

In contrast, libertarians and the various kinds of conservatives tend to appeal to authority, disparaging or rejecting reason as a basis for action. They appeal to natural law, to tradition, or to God or religion. Social conservatives especially denounce relativism and empiricism and charge that the liberal emphasis on reason leads to secular humanism, which they abhor.

To work out the principles of justice Rawls puts a group of people in an original position, behind a veil of ignorance concerning the implications of their decisions for themselves. Being reasonable and assuming that others are reasonable, they look for "fair terms of cooperation" in a society and expect people to abide by these terms on the basis of reciprocity. Moreover, they anticipate "the use of public reason in directing the legitimate exercise of political power in a constitutional regime."

Not that reasonable people always agree with each other. Far from it. Although implicitly granting that a comprehensive religious, moral, or philosophical doctrine may be unreasonable, Rawls also assumes that more than one can be reasonable. That is, he assumes diversity, disagreement. But he depends on reason to lead to principles that enable people to cooperate despite differences among them. His ideal is "a fair system of cooperation between reasonable and rational citizens regarded as free and equal" (1993, 103).

The emphasis on reason assumes autonomy as a value—the capacity of individuals to make up their own minds and decide for themselves what course of action to pursue. They may be guided by others in their decisions, but ought not to be slavish about it; if they follow others, they should be able to give good reasons for their choice.

The implications of the emphasis on reason and autonomy are far-reaching. The assumption is that men and women have a capacity for moral judgment, for distinguishing between good and bad, right and wrong. They are not so limited in their rational capacities, or so selfish or sinful or given to depravity, that they need to subordinate themselves to some authority beyond their control. They have a capacity for practical judgment, a capacity to choose policies that will shape the future in a desirable way. They are rational, honest, and reliable enough to justify deliberate efforts to achieve the good life. They can be what others sometimes disparagingly call "social engineers."

## The Usefulness of Government

The overarching issue between liberals and those to their right concerns the usefulness of government, especially the usefulness of the federal government. The most fundamental change that the New Deal made was an expansion of the role of the federal government. It would be a contradiction in terms for progressive liberals to think of the state as the enemy, but this is quite possible for a libertarian or for an economic conservative. Ronald Reagan set up the contrast sharply when he said that government is part of the problem, not part of the solution.

To progressive liberals, government is part of the solution. In their eyes the functions of government are pervasive and fundamental. The Preamble to the Constitution suggests this expectation, saying that we the people establish the Constitution "in order to form a more perfect Union, establish Justice, insure domestic Tranquility, provide for the common defense, promote the general Welfare, and secure the Blessings of Liberty to ourselves and our Posterity." Lincoln too suggested the almost limitless reach of government in saying, as indicated in chapter 3, that "the legitimate object of government is to do for the people what needs to be done but which they cannot by individual effort do at all or so well for themselves." As noted before, liberalism expects government to respect a realm of privacy, but apart from that it is inclined to look to government, including the federal government, as a useful instrument in attacking a wide range of problems.

Foremost among the problems is that of keeping the economy in high gear, the problem of avoiding depressions and promoting economic growth and progress. Like the libertarians and most conservatives, liberals want to rely predominantly on private enterprise and the market in this connection, but they are also inclined to assign an important role to government. History reinforces the inclination. Recall from chapter 3 that in the period before the Civil War state governments played a prominent part in supporting new economic enterprises, and in recent years they have been at it once again. David Osborne describes their activities:

> Over the past decade, they have created well over 100 public investment funds, to make loans to and investments in business. Half the states have set up public venture capital funds; others have invested public money in the creation of private financial institutions. At least 40 states have created programs to stimulate technological innovation, which now number at least 200.... A few states have even launched cooperative efforts with management and labor to revitalize regional industries. (Osborne 1988, 1)

The core solutions to problems of economic development, according to Osborne, are to be found not in *laissez faire* but in "new *partnerships* between the public and private sectors."

The curious feature of such developments at state and local levels is that governors who are Republican and who are usually thought of as conservative may be involved as well as governors who are Democratic and who are usually thought of as liberal. Ideological predilections do not appear to play a controlling role. At least, this is Osborne's view. His position is that the problems faced and the policies followed do not fit in the old categories and that what is developing, and what is needed, is a "new paradigm." But the developments reflect the view that state and local governments can be useful in promoting economic growth and development, and this fits with progressive liberalism more than with libertarianism or economic conservatism.

The activities of a number of central governments, including the federal government of the United States, lead progressive liberals to about the same conclusion on the usefulness of government. For example, in *Perpetual Innovation* (1989) Don Kash dwells on the role of the federal government where special circumstances overcome the opposition to federal action. The special circumstances relate to defense, health, and agriculture. It is accepted that national defense is the sphere of the federal government, and interest in health has been so strong and so general that leaders endorsing different ideologies have joined in arranging for the federal government to play an important role there. Similarly, farmers have been powerful enough politically that they have been able to command federal help.

In these areas, Kash points out, the federal government has acted in various ways: letting contracts, subsidizing research, and buying products. It has done this through various agencies, mainly the Department of Defense, the National Aeronautics and Space Administration (NASA), the National Science Foundation, the National Institutes of Health, and the Department of Agriculture. In part because of the activities of such agencies, the United States has come to lead the world in the aircraft industry, and it has a strong competitive position in microprocessors, pharmaceuticals, medicine, and agriculture. "The evidence is that where there is cooperation between the public and private sectors, the United States is competitive in the international marketplace."

Michael Borrus (1992, 79) advances a similar theme. He identifies the six industries that grew fastest in the United States from 1972 to 1988 and notes that five of them "were sponsored or sustained, directly or indirectly, by federal investment: computing equipment, semiconductors, optics, imaging technologies, and biological products." Lithographic services were the exception.

A number of governments in Europe and Eastern Asia are also heavily involved in efforts to promote economic development. "European governments spend from 5.5 percent (Italy) to 1.75 percent of the GNP aiding industry. If the United States had spent what Germany spends (2.5 percent of GNP), $140 billion would have gone to help United States industries in 1991" (Thurow 1992, 27). In two of the "Tigers" of Asia, South Korea and Singapore, the government has played a *dirigiste* role in economic development, and the Japanese government has played a comparable role.

I do not mean to argue that the case for governmental action on behalf of economic development is so fully established that it can be regarded as closed. I am impressed by Mancur Olson's statement that "there is probably no really strong and unambiguous relationship between the role of government and the level of economic performance that can be inferred from either the cross-sectional or historical experience of the developed democracies" (Olson 1984, 238). The argument simply is that progressive liberals—and some others—tend to see government as a useful instrument in stimulating and maintaining economic growth, and that at least some evidence supports their view.

According to the liberal perspective, government has a number of other functions in addition to those of the night watchman state. In many situations, as history has shown, employers have a bargaining advantage over workers, which has led liberals to support governmental intervention regulating labor-management relations. In many situations, producers and distributors have an advantage over consumers, which has led liberals to support governmental intervention to protect the consumers. In some situations private enterprisers, left to themselves, can establish monopolies or oligopolies, giving them unfair advantages and leading liberals to support governmental intervention. Historically, government has played a major role in education. Increasingly in recent decades, the federal government, under the influence of liberalism, has come to play a prominent role in promoting the arts. Liberals have led the way, as the preceding two chapters indicate, in expanding the role of the federal government in promoting welfare, broadly conceived to include social security and health care. And they have led the way in obtaining action to protect the environment.

Liberals see a major role for government too because of *externalities,* that is, because of the fact that a great many of the choices that people make have consequences for others. Neighbors gain if you beautify your property and lose if you let it run down. A municipality loses if the fertilizer that a farmer puts on a nearby field pollutes its water supply. Environmentalists are anguished if logging operations threaten the spotted owl with extinction. Many lose, even if only in a minor way, when automobiles pollute the atmosphere with exhaust and noise and contribute to congestion on the highway. Many lose, and fish and wildlife are threatened, if a chemical company dumps its wastes into a stream. The Chernobyl disaster illustrates that millions of people over a wide geographical area may face a life-threatening externality in the form of danger from a nuclear plant. An even greater disaster might come to the world if people follow practices that lead to a significant rise in the level of the oceans. And so on.

In some circumstances market forces keep the problem of externalities in check. For example, a business concern may reduce or eliminate practices that pollute the atmosphere or otherwise create costs for others lest it lose goodwill. It may need to eliminate certain practices in order to avoid suits for damages. But market forces are at least as likely to accentuate the problem, for profits can sometimes be made at other people's expense.

Harmful externalities are of course the main problem. People threatened may have no practical way of warding off the threat, and people actually harmed may have no practical way of obtaining redress. Even if the party creating the externality wants to compensate those harmed (for example, by exhaust from automobiles), there may be no practical way of doing so. Thus intervention by government may be a necessary feature of an attack on the problem. For example, government might prohibit the harmful action or impose regulations that minimize the harm. From the liberal perspective, handling the problem of externalities is an important function of government.

As liberals see it too, libertarians and most conservatives underplay the role of government in providing a basis for a free market. Liberals point out that government fixes the structure—the political, legal, and economic structure—within which everything happens, effectively making the "free" market dependent on government. Among other things, the market depends on government to maintain order, to keep property rights and civil rights secure, to provide the legal basis for contracts and their enforcement, and to uphold the principles of reason, honesty, integrity, and reciprocity. More broadly, the market depends on government to maintain a system of rules basic to stability and predictability in economic and social affairs. Where government is embryonic, impotent, arbitrary, or hopelessly inefficient or corrupt, the market does not have much chance. The field is open to charlatans and thugs.

I should not leave the impression that progressive liberals seek a role for government all down the line. As indicated earlier, there are areas where liberals want less government rather than more—for example, less governmental intrusion in a realm of privacy.

## *Welfare*

Progressive liberalism is identified with the welfare state. Franklin D. Roosevelt's use of the federal government in combating the depression and Lyndon Johnson's war on poverty gave progressive liberalism its most salient characteristic. It was surely this characteristic that Ronald Reagan had in mind when he referred to *liberalism* as the "L-word," too abhorrent to be pronounced in full.

Why do progressive liberals favor governmental efforts to promote welfare? Four answers are advanced, and the four are compatible with one another.

The first answer is oriented toward those in dire distress or threatened with it. According to progressive liberals, such people have a right to life and to the various liberties, just like everyone else. Further, to adopt the approach that Rawls takes, considerations of justice require that their liberties have worth. Measures must be taken "to insure that all citizens have sufficient material means to make effective use of [their] basic rights," and the basic rights and liberties of everyone are to be "guaranteed their fair value" (Rawls 1993, 5, 157). Inequalities are acceptable, but only as long as they are consistent with fair equality of opportunity (281).

Other liberals are inclined to emphasize not so much the worth of liberties as the sense of worth of the individual—the importance of self-respect. A problem develops immediately here, for people are sometimes their own worst enemies, making choices that later undermine their self-respect and that may even jeopardize their lives. Modified on the basis of this consideration, the liberal's view is that, if at all possible, conditions beyond the control of the individual but subject to social control should not be allowed to make life, self-respect, and a sense of worth unduly difficult or impossible. Except perhaps for cases of willful choice or willful irresponsibility, people are not to be allowed to die unnecessarily or to live in circumstances that fall below an acceptable level of human decency. Liberals remember that the fetus had no opportunity to take out insurance against being born into poverty, and the newborn child has moral claims, that is, human rights.

Further, to make self-respect and a sense of worth possible, people must have an opportunity to achieve a degree of self-actualization or self-fulfillment. They must have the opportunity to develop and use at least some of their talents. Recall T.H. Green's view, mentioned in chapter 2, that the growth of a society in freedom is to be measured "by the greater power on the part of the citizens as a body to make the most and best of themselves."

Thoughts like these apparently lie behind the stand taken by the National Conference of Catholic Bishops in a pastoral letter of 1986. Its summary declaration is that "government [has] a positive moral responsibility in safeguarding human rights and ensuring that the minimum conditions of human dignity are met for all.... Basic justice calls for the establishment of a floor of material well-being on which all can stand" (Catholic Church 1986, xi, 38).

A comparable view is that the normal operation of the market can be expected to leave some in poverty, that poverty involves a kind of moral exile from society, and that we must avert or terminate such exiling if we are to maintain the values of self-respect and equal moral worth.

Critics point out, as we see in subsequent chapters, that those expressing thoughts along this line generally do it without specifying reciprocal obligations that the recipients of aid must meet—for example, that those in early life must take advantage of whatever opportunities they have to improve their education and training, and that the able-bodied who are not in school must actively seek work and be willing to accept almost any job that will reduce or eliminate their dependency.

The second answer to the question why progressive liberals favor governmental efforts to promote welfare is oriented toward society as a whole rather than toward the individual in distress: it is important to maintain the social order, the culture. Moreover, the social order, the culture, should be maintained in a stable and assured way, with threats and challenges held at bay insofar as possible. If this goal is to be achieved, serious discontent must be kept at a minimum, lest disaffected and desperate persons turn to drugs, crime, riot, or rebellion.

David Miller and Thomas Horne elaborate on this answer. Miller cites the view that the welfare state is "an insurance scheme taken out by the rich (or the capitalist class) to buy off the discontented poor" (Moon 1988, 164). Horne cites the view that property rights and welfare rights go together as parts of a bargain: on the one hand, property rights are to be accepted and protected, with primary reliance on the market; on the other hand, those whom the market leaves in acute distress are to receive aid (Moon 1988, 130).

A different answer oriented to society is that it is shameful and costly to waste talent. All possible talent needs to be used to enrich the culture and civilization. Thus social efforts are justified to salvage those in distress and to develop and take advantage of whatever talents they have.

The third answer is oriented toward middle- and upper-class observers. Up to a point they can shield themselves from knowledge of the poor in various ways, but in the age of television they cannot shield themselves entirely; and knowledge of the distress of others makes them uncomfortable. Perhaps they have a faith, or at least an outlook, that requires them to be compassionate and helpful; in addition to assuming responsibilities for themselves and their immediate families, they accept social responsibilities. They are serious about being their brother's keeper. Perhaps they know that they have succeeded at least in part on the basis of factors other than merit, such as pure luck or, perhaps, success in manipulating the market in such a way as to obtain unjustifiable gain. If incomes and salaries should be proportionate to contributions to social well-being, many are clearly excessive. In such instances, the affluent may find balm for their spirits and develop a sense of virtue through good works, and this is important to them.

The fourth answer relates to only one small part of the total problem: health care. As things stand, some employers include health care among the fringe benefits they provide, and some do not. This means that some employers face burdens not faced by their competitors, that workers enjoying the fringe benefit become less mobile, and that irrational differences exist in the treatment of workers. This adds to the other reasons that progressive liberals have for endorsing some kind of governmentally provided or mandated health care.

I might elaborate on the first of the answers given above, oriented to concern for those in distress, by citing the argument of Robert Goodin, who tacitly accepts the answer described but dwells on a supplement. The supplement assumes that in a market economy (and perhaps in any situation) some will take unfair advantage of others—will exploit others—if they can. Destitution—abject dependency—creates one of the major circumstances in which this might happen: the destitute are vulnerable to exploitation by those on whom they depend, with little choice but to accept almost any terms a rescuer chooses to impose. "Those who depend upon particular others for satisfaction of their basic needs are rendered, by that dependency, susceptible to exploitation by those upon whom they depend. It is the risk of exploitation of such dependencies that justifies public provision—and public provision of a distinctively welfare state form—for those basic needs" (Goodin 1988, 121).

Goodin's argument rests on "the crucial moral premise ... that we individually and collectively have a strong moral responsibility to protect those whose interests are especially vulnerable to our actions and choices." In other words, the strong have a moral obligation to protect the weak. It is wrong to take unfair advantage of others and wrong to leave people helpless against those who would do so. Thus we should guarantee everyone's basic needs through the impersonal and nondiscretionary agency of the state so as to render them less dependent upon and vulnerable to others.

> The essential function of the welfare state is ... to prevent the exploitation of vulnerable members of society. Put more positively, it is to protect the interests of those who are not in a position to protect themselves.... When people's needs are unmet they are likely to be desperate, dependent, and hence exploitable. The welfare state is justified ... as a device to guard against that possibility. (Goodin 1988, xi, 25)

Critics of AFDC and food stamps might respond that Goodin is looking in the wrong direction, that the exploiters are to be found mainly among the recipients of welfare: irresponsible teenagers who fail to take advantage of their educational opportunities and who produce babies they cannot support, and able-bodied people who do not work but depend on gullible taxpayers for support. Goodin's response presumably would be that people in these categories constitute no more than a small fraction of those on welfare—that the vast majority are either people who are not expected to work (children, mothers with small children, the handicapped, the elderly), people suffering a temporary misfortune, or people who are simply not able to find jobs. Goodin is not impressed by the argument that the availability of public welfare undermines self-reliance.

In other words, large numbers of people are bound to be dependent; it is inevitable. And rather than leave them vulnerable to neglect or exploitation, Goodin would have government provide aid impersonally according to law.

Whatever the specific answer to the question why progressive liberalism calls for governmental action on behalf of welfare, the general spirit involved is reflected in the following statement by Senator Hubert Humphrey: "The moral test of a government is how it treats those who are in the dawn of life, the children; those who are in the twilight of life, the aged; and those who are in the shadows of life—the sick, the needy, and the handicapped." Tip O'Neill, longtime Speaker of the House of Representatives, quotes this "beautiful statement," saying that it "spells out my own philosophy and values ... clearly and succinctly" (O'Neill 1987, 203).

I speak above of government as a provider of welfare without differentiating between the three types of welfare programs previously identified: insurance programs that in effect transfer income from one period in people's lives to a later period; charitable aid that transfers money from the advantaged to the disadvantaged; and tax expenditures that reduce some kinds of tax burdens and necessitate increases in others. The differences between the three types are significant, and reasonable persons make different judgments concerning them. The first two types tend to get the most attention, but the third type is the most costly to the government and does the most to shift tax burdens. Progressive liberals are inclined to accept all three.

The above arguments concerning welfare generally carried the day up until about 1980, when Reagan was elected to the presidency. They even persuaded some nonliberals. Recall from chapter 3 that Herbert Hoover described himself as a "strong advocate of expansion of useful public works in hard times" and as determined to "ask the aid of every resource of the Federal Government," if need be, to prevent hunger and suffering. In subsequent chapters we see that some libertarians, some champions of public choice, and some conservatives give some support to governmental programs to relieve distress. Ronald Reagan himself took the view that the federal government should provide a "safety net" and give help to the "truly needy."

## Taxes

Although the fact is not especially apparent on the basis of the performance of progressive liberals in the last quarter-century, progressive liberalism holds in principle that taxes should be progressive—for any or all of several reasons. One concerns ability to pay, or equality of sacrifice. Equality of sacrifice is not achieved if a person with an income of $20,000 and a person with an income of $200,000 pay the same amount, or even at the same rate; proportionality is not enough. If the pain is to be equalized, the tax rate must be progressive, going up as incomes go up. How much higher the rate should be on the higher income is a matter of judgment, and agreement is difficult to reach.

Another consideration relates to equality, or to the gap between the rich and the poor. In principle, taxes can be allocated so as either to increase or decrease the gap. Experience suggests to progressive liberals that the normal operation of the market tends to make the gap too wide and that taxes should be made progressive so as to weaken the tendency. Not that progressive liberals are levelers. They do not aim at equal incomes for all. But they want a society in which people at every level recognize the common humanity of people at every other level, sharing a sense of solidarity with them, and they believe that this recognition is jeopardized by gaps that are too wide. The evil to be avoided is suggested by the Salvadoran landowner who spoke dismissively of those peasants who did not have souls.

The Rawlsian formula is also relevant here: inequalities—in taxation as well as in other spheres—are acceptable only if they are to the advantage of the least advantaged. It is to the advantage of the least advantaged that people be rewarded for their contributions to society, and taxes should be adjusted to respect rewards. But the further assumption is that the advantage to the disadvantaged tends to decline as the gap between incomes increases, and that therefore tax rates should rise along with incomes.

The odd fact is that in the past several decades progressive liberals have not put emphasis on these beliefs. They have not voluntarily paid much attention to taxes. Their focus has been on the question what government ought to do, and they have tended simply to assume that the money would somehow be found to pay for it. It is conservatives, and more particularly economic conservatives, who have led the way in making taxes an issue. The imbalance in the concern for taxes is indicated by the fact that at the beginning of the 1980s, according to Benjamin Page, conservative groups focusing on federal tax policy had budgets twenty-two times as large as rival liberal and labor groups (Page 1983, 47). This subject is discussed mainly in coming chapters, but progressive liberal failures need to be acknowledged here.

## Underlying Postulates

A brief discussion of the principles of liberalism and their rationale is bound to be incomplete. It is a little as if you were asked what is important to you, and you failed to include the next breath of air on your list. We tend to focus on what is in doubt or in jeopardy or in some way controversial and to say nothing about what is shared with most others or what can, with a reasonable degree of confidence, be assumed.

As is at least intimated in the discussion of Rawls's principles of justice at the beginning of the chapter, progressive liberalism calls for social responsibility—for acceptance of the view that we are members of a community with shared interests and with ties of reciprocity. When libertarians speak of responsibility, they are likely to be speaking of the responsibility of individuals for their own personal well-being or fate. Progressive liberals are also concerned about this, but they go on to recognize, as John Donne put it, that no man is an island. Society is not and should not be looked upon as a set of Robinson Crusoes morally isolated from each other and concerned only for their own private welfare. We all depend on others. Alongside our responsibility for our own fate goes a responsibility for the community—for the social structure within which we live. Public interests exist, and public purposes are to be identified and pursued on a collective basis.

Progressive liberalism, like most ideologies, is identified mainly by its prescriptions for domestic politics. I should acknowledge, however, that it also concerns itself with foreign policies—a subject to be discussed in chapter 14.

## *Epilogue*

How can it happen that people can have such different views of liberalism as the following statements reveal? The first is by Michael Kinsley, editor of the *New Republic:* "My own political views are more or less liberal. They were not genetically implanted, and I hold them under no form of compulsion except that of reason. It seems to me they're the sort of views a reasonable, intelligent person would hold. Since most journalists I meet are reasonable, intelligent people, the mystery to me is not why journalists tend to be liberals but why so many other reasonable intelligent people are not" (Kinsley 1992, 6).

The second is by Samuel T. Francis, columnist and contributing editor of a conservative journal, *Chronicles:* "Liberalism barely exists as an independent set of ideas and values. Virtually no significant thinker of this century has endorsed it. Internally, the doctrines of liberalism are so contrary to established fact, inconsistent with each other, and immersed in sentimentalism, resentment, egotism, and self-interest that they cannot be taken seriously as a body of ideas. Liberalism flourishes almost entirely because it reflects the material and psychological interests of a privileged, power-holding, and power-seeking sector of American society" (Francis 1993a, 64).

John Rawls is presumably not amused by the statement that no significant thinker of this century has endorsed liberalism.

I said at the beginning of this chapter that I do not have an entirely satisfactory succinct definition of progressive liberalism. The following, however, may be helpful: Progressive liberalism is an ideology calling for (1) public policies designed to enhance the worth of liberty and promote fair equality of opportunity for all, (2) reliance on reason and the market, (3) tolerance of diversity, and (4) concern for the common good; and it regards democratic government as a useful instrument in promoting its goals.

# Chapter 7

# Libertarianism

THE PRECEDING three chapters illustrate progressive liberalism concretely, citing especially the New Deal and Great Society programs. I cannot illustrate libertarianism in a similar fashion, for libertarians have never controlled either the White House or the Congress; and neither have they controlled any other government.

Nevertheless, libertarianism is important both politically and intellectually. In the political world, both Ronald Reagan and Margaret Thatcher were clearly influenced by libertarian thought. David Stockman, who served under Reagan as director of the Office of Management and Budget, describes himself as a disciple of one of the founding fathers of libertarianism, Friedrich Hayek, and pictures himself in office as wielding a sword forged in Hayek's free-market smithy (Stockman 1986, 30, 38). Alan Greenspan, chairman of the Federal Reserve Board under Bush and Clinton, is described as "a man who, when pressed on the matter, still ... professes the fiercely libertarian beliefs of Ayn Rand" (*Economist,* 327 [12 June 1993], 26). And Governor William Weld of Massachusetts speaks of at least a partial commitment to libertarian doctrine (Meyerson 1993, 12, 15–16).

Intellectually, libertarianism is supported by impressive argument. In addition to Hayek, two other economists, Milton Friedman and Murray Rothbard, advance the argument most prominently, joined by the philosopher Robert Nozick in his *Anarchy, State, and Utopia.* And others might be named. The Center for Libertarian Studies, the Cato Institute, and various journals (for example, *Critical Review, Liberty,* and *Reason*) concern themselves with libertarian thought. A Libertarian political party, scorned by many libertarians, nominates a candidate for the presidency every four years.

Not all of those whom I call "libertarian" accept the name. Hayek preferred the name "Old Whig," and Friedman calls himself a classical liberal. Declaring that the name "libertarian" has been "hopelessly tainted" by the "antics" of the party bearing the name, Justin Raimando suggests that people who might otherwise call themselves libertarians should instead call themselves "American nationalists," and officials of the Cato Institute suggest the name "market liberalism." Murray Rothbard seeks to distinguish between different sets of libertarians by calling himself and those aligned with him "paleolibertarians."

I use the term *libertarian* in the belief that it reasonably applies to all those named and to many others as well. They share a fundamental outlook, even if they also have their disagreements. I think of libertarianism, in its variations, as stemming from classical liberalism as conceived by Herbert Spencer.

Libertarianism is an individualistic ideology. Its central feature is the glorification of liberty or freedom for the individual and the condemnation of collectivism and coercion. Questions arise almost automatically. How do libertarians define liberty, and why so much emphasis on it? What kinds of policies and attitudes does it suggest? What about values in addition to liberty? How do libertarians propose to treat those unable to provide for themselves: children, the unemployed, and many of the elderly, the sick, and the handicapped? What about social justice? What about community? How does individualism fit with the need for national security? What do libertarians propose when one person exercises liberty in such a way as to harm others?

"Public choice" theorists have much in common with the libertarians, but discussion of them awaits the following chapter.

## Liberty and the Market

Libertarians uniformly adopt the negative conception of liberty. Hayek expresses a common libertarian view in defining liberty as "independence of the arbitrary will of another" or as what exists in the absence of coercion by other persons (1960, 11–12, 19). What counts as the "arbitrary" will of another and as "coercion" are questions without clear answers. Suffice it to say that most libertarians regard the enforcement of criminal law as reasonable and not arbitrary and so they do not treat it as coercion—or at least not the kind of coercion that they condemn. In contrast, they regard redistributive tax policies as unreasonable and arbitrary; so they condemn the collection of such taxes as coercive.

Libertarians give little or no attention to the possibility that conditions may be such as to make liberty worthless. Those who live in the slums and those who live in the suburbs are equally free, and so are the sheep and the wolf in the same field. In other words, individualism is rugged. Liberty is a formal conception, treated as a good in itself, regardless of the conditions that affect its worth for particular persons in particular circumstances. This means, although Hayek was not entirely clear on the point, that when libertarians demand freedom from coercion, it is coercion by the state that they have in mind. David Boaz and Edward Crane, officials of the Cato Institute, make this explicit in identifying liberty with "the liberation of the individual from the coercive power *of the state*" (Boaz and Crane 1993, 1; italics added).

The market is the primary arena in which people exercise liberty. The libertarian prescription is that people, left free to develop their talents, should also be left free to acquire property and engage in enterprise as they see fit. They should be free to make contracts as they please, free to produce, and free to exchange goods and services (including their own labor) on any terms that those involved accept. And they should be self-reliant, responsible for their own destiny, nothing being done to weaken their motivation to look out for themselves.

Of all the free individuals operating in the market, entrepreneurs are the heroes. Entrepreneurs are persons who take economic initiatives and risks, deciding what kinds of economic activities should be undertaken and providing organizational and managerial skills. They thus provide jobs for others and contribute in myriad ways to human progress. Without entrepreneurs, society would stagnate and everyone would suffer. With them, economic and cultural development occurs for the general benefit. As Milton and Rose Friedman put it: "In every country a tiny minority sets the pace, determines the course of events. In the countries that have developed most rapidly and successfully, a minority of enterprising and risk-taking individuals have forged ahead, created opportunities for imitators to follow, have enabled the majority to increase their productivity" (1980, 60–61).

The implication is that government should give entrepreneurs free rein and stay out of the way. Arthur Seldon spells out this idea in his analysis of capitalism: "Even bad men are led by the market process to do good, but good men are induced by the political process to do harm.... The object has to be not the 'limited' state, based on no clear principle of the functions of government, but the minimal state, based on the principle that government shall do only what it must." Government is so inefficient, so unaccountable, and so corrupt that it is best to avoid its use wherever possible. "The Gulliver of capitalism has long been tied up by Lilliputian politicians. Compared with the best deeds of little political people, capitalism [that is, the market] has the potential for good of the giant" (Seldon 1990, x–xi, 239, 242).

## Why Liberty and the Market?

For the most part, libertarians advance their doctrine on what they regard as a pragmatic basis: freedom works, producing good results and doing it better than any known alternative. But a few go beyond pragmatism to offer a supporting rationale. Hayek is among them.

Hayek bases his rationale on experience and tradition, but his theme has a distinctive twist. To him, human ignorance is the basic all-important fact—pervasive and inevitable ignorance. Even in simpler times the world was so complex that no one could fully know or understand what went on. Large numbers of persons had wants and desires of many kinds, and in their efforts to satisfy them they made contact with others. Each producer and each consumer came to be involved in a series of networks for purposes of exchange, and interconnections developed among the networks. No one planned or created the general system of production and exchange, and it is preposterous to assume that anyone could have done so. It emerged naturally, to our great benefit (Hayek 1984, 135; 1988, 6, 14).

The heart of the system is the free market, which offers a discovery procedure that enables people to act effectively on the basis of limited knowledge. Producers and consumers, buyers and sellers, including entrepreneurs—all motivated by a desire to advance their own self-interest and perhaps the interests of their families—know something of their own circumstances and goals. They know what kind of innovation or what kind of exchange will advance their interests, or at least they know enough to make an educated guess; and they do not need to know much more. The general good of society need not be their concern; in truth, they cannot really know what the general good is or what will promote it.

Focusing on their own interests, then, people make bargains and contracts with each other, buying and selling labor, goods, and services—producing and exchanging—gambling on the prospect that their interests will be served. Some deals turn out to be bad, but on the whole the interests of those involved are in fact served. The system works in such a way that productivity increases, higher standards of living are achieved, and progress of all sorts occurs.

Hayek makes much of the point that this system was not deliberately created but is the product of spontaneous evolution. "We stand in a great framework of institutions and traditions—economic, legal, and moral—into which we fit ourselves by obeying certain rules of conduct that we never made and which we have never understood" (1988, 14). Barry describes this doctrine ("that institutions develop as the unintended and unanticipated consequences of human action") as "one of the major foundation stones in the structure of Hayek's thought" (Barry 1979, 9).

For political purposes, one of the strengths of the doctrine is that it makes the system seem to be somehow foreordained—a gift of history for which the present generation should be grateful. Just as the system was not deliberately created, so it cannot be deliberately improved. Any deliberate tampering with it is automatically suspect, likely to be wrong-headed and dangerous.

Hayek's reading of history is obviously selective and judgmental. He does not say how it happens that the developments that he likes are all spontaneous and natural whereas other developments are perversions and mistakes.

## Collectivism? Coercion?

Extolling individualism, libertarians condemn collectivism and coercion. That is the other side of the coin.

Socialism (including communism) is the most abhorred form of collectivism, with nationalism a close second. Moreover, government itself is a collective endeavor, and so must be carefully and strictly limited. Whatever happens in the free market is likely to be good, for those involved in the exchanges are likely to have enough relevant knowledge to serve their respective interests. In contrast, whatever happens on a collective basis, including what happens in political life, is at best suspect, for those who make the decisions cannot possibly have the knowledge and understanding that they need.

Hayek has developed this thought most fully. In his eyes socialism is bad in that it calls for centralized planning and control, involving the abandonment of tradition and subordinating individuals to the will of the government, which by definition means that their liberty is reduced. Moreover, those who support socialism assume that our rational capacities and our knowledge are great enough that we can shape the future to our benefit, whereas in fact our ignorance is too great to make this possible. Governments can of course mobilize the knowledge of many individuals, but, even so, they cannot mobilize enough to justify the exercise of many powers, and it is presumptuous and dangerous for them to assume otherwise. The farther they go in the direction of centralized control, the more they will be acting out of inadequate knowledge; and thus the more danger that what they do will be harmful. Least of all should they attempt to guide or manage economic life.

Put in more esoteric terms, what Hayek warns against is "constructivist rationalism," the assumption that "social institutions are and ought to be the product of deliberate design." He speaks of the illusion that we can rationally control or direct social processes, that we can deliberately "create the future of mankind." In his eyes, rationalists—people (for example, progressive liberals) who believe in following the dictates of reason rather than the dictates of tradition—fail to understand how limited their knowledge is. And if rationalists attempt to redesign the world on the basis of their imperfect knowledge and understanding, they are heading toward totalitarianism and the terrible coercions it involves. Socialism is *The Road to Serfdom.* Hayek published a book with that title and theme in 1944 and thus became famous, endearing himself especially to people on the right politically.

Not only does Hayek warn against socialism but he also warns against any effort to find a "middle way" between capitalism and socialism, for such an effort will only lead to socialism and to the subordination of economic processes to politics. His horror of collectivism goes to the point that he objects to the use of the word *economy,* for he thinks that this word suggests an organized, purposeful collective enterprise. To avoid any such suggestion, he replaces the word *economy* with the word *catallaxy,* meaning an individualistic system with a free market—the cherished product of evolution.

## Social Justice? Social Responsibility? Uphold Virtue? Equality?

As a rule, libertarians do not concern themselves with social justice, nor do they call for social responsibility. They differ about upholding virtue, and they deplore what they see as liberal support for equality.

Hayek is scornful of the very idea of social justice, calling the search for it a "mirage." Justice, he holds, relates to the "deliberate treatment of men by other men," not to outcomes that no one plans or intends (1960, 99). And since neither society nor any other agency or person plans or intends the outcomes of economic activities in a free market, it is improper to speak of social or distributive justice. People simply play the game according to the rules, making gains and suffering losses, and it is no more proper to speak of the justice of the outcome than it is to speak of the justice of the outcome of a baseball game. Justice is not the object of the game. An effort to promote or assure it would mean interference in the operations of the market—interference in the game—with a social purpose superseding the purposes of the individual participants and with coercion (the denial of liberty) as a necessary feature. As I note later, Hayek explicitly objects to an effort to promote justice through redistributive taxing policies.

Friedman (1962, 133) decries the idea of social responsibility. The aim of competitors, in his eyes, should be to promote their own interests or the interests of those whom they represent. If they are thought of as exercising social responsibility, the logical implication is that they should be elected or appointed, just as government officials in a democracy are elected or appointed, and this would reduce economic life to the deplorable level of waste and inefficiency that characterizes political life.

As to virtue, libertarians generally deplore any governmental action designed to promote it but disagree about action in the private realm on its behalf. They object, for example, to laws against the sale and use of drugs and to any governmental effort to prohibit prostitution or pornography. But they differ on the role of institutions intermediate between the individual and the state (for example, the family, the church, and other private organizations) and on the importance of a sense of personal responsibility. The extreme view is expressed by Frank S. Meyer: "freedom means freedom: not necessity, but choice; not responsibility, but choice between responsibility and irresponsibility; not duty, but the choice between accepting and rejecting duty; not virtue, but the choice between virtue and vice" (quoted by Carey 1984, 5). The argument is that no action can be virtuous unless it is freely chosen, which apparently means chosen voluntarily, without any pressure (let alone coercion) from any source.

The less extreme libertarian view is that although coercion from any source is unacceptable, private agencies may act on behalf of virtue, and personal responsibility is desirable. Ostracism, boycott, rebuke, and like means are all available and acceptable. Here again arises the question of what counts as coercion.

Llewellyn Rockwell reflects the division among libertarians when he denounces the Libertarian Party and pleads that libertarianism must be cleansed of its "cultural image," which is that libertarians are libertines who endorse behaviors that they would legalize, rejecting "the standards of Western civilization."

> Arguments against the drug war, no matter how intellectually compelling, are undermined when they come from the party of the stoned. When the Libertarian Party nominates a prostitute for lieutenant governor of California and she becomes a much-admired Libertarian Party celebrity, how can regular Americans help but think that libertarianism is hostile to social norms, or that legalization of such acts as prostitution means moral approval?

Rockwell argues that freedom from the coercions of the state does not mean freedom from all social authority. "Authority will always be necessary in society." It should be lodged, however, in such voluntary social units as the family, the church, the private school—even in Rotary and the Boy Scouts (Rockwell 1990b, 5, 10–12). Similarly, Boaz and Crane consider it "essential for leaders in all fields ... to affirm our commitment to the moral and cultural values that underlie political freedom: honesty, self-reliance, reason, thrift, education, tolerance, property, contract, and family" (Boaz and Crane 1993, 11). They would simply reduce or eliminate reliance on government to uphold these values.

Stressing liberty, libertarians expect inequality. And they see good in it. Not only is inequality evidence of successful entrepreneurship, with an implicit social contribution; but one of the spillover effects is the presence of economically powerful individuals who can stand out against the ever-encroaching power of the state.

The counterpart of the welcome given to inequality is a tendency to attack progressive liberals for allegedly seeking equality of outcomes or results. Thus Friedman says that "a central element in the development of a collectivist sentiment in this century, at least in Western countries, has been a belief in equality of income as a social goal and a willingness to use the arm of the state to promote it" (1962, 161). Friedman no doubt believes this to be the case, but he cites no supporting evidence or testimony, and I know of none that relates to progressive liberalism. It is true that many people, including many progressive liberals, think that some business leaders are overpaid and want to reduce the gap between the rich and the poor. It is also true that some people want equality of results in the sense of proportional equality for large groups—for example, want blacks to graduate from college in the same proportion as whites. But it is not clear what basis Friedman thinks he has for the view that significant support exists for "equality of income as a social goal." John Rawls's prescription is not that incomes should be equal but that differences should be to the advantage of the least advantaged.

Libertarians have difficulty with the idea of equality of opportunity. For the most part, they ignore it. If they take note of it, the likely assumption is that equal liberty—equal freedom from coercion—automatically implies equal opportunity. Thus the Friedmans (1980, 132) say that the "real" meaning of equality of opportunity is expressed by the French revolutionary demand for careers open to talent—a statement that implicitly defines equality of opportunity as what exists in the absence of "arbitrary obstacles" such as racial discrimination. But, as I note later, they do not want any governmental intervention in the market for the purpose of eliminating arbitrary obstacles or for the purpose of providing redress to those whom the obstacles have handicapped. Self-reliance and responsibility for one's own destiny are the values that go with liberty, not equal treatment or equality of opportunity.

## Criticisms of Government

Being hostile to collectivism and coercion, libertarians are, at a minimum, suspicious of government, and their suspicions grow into outright hostility the more a government interferes in the market. Big government is bad government. A government that imposes a central economic plan, like the Soviet government, is anathema.

That a government is democratic does not save it from criticism. Hayek, for example, thinks that as history has unfolded, legislatures have acquired too much power. In fact he speaks of the "unlimited power of the majority" in legislatures, and he considers this "unlimited power" to be "the root of all evil ... in modern democracies" (1991, 385). Given the unlimited power of legislatures, political parties are irresistibly tempted to confer benefits in order to win votes, and government thus becomes in effect a coalition of interest groups seeking to get what they can at the expense of the rest, expanding without limit (1979, 9, 11–15, 31).

Further, to win votes democratic governments are inclined to promise social justice and then to interfere in the market coercively, reducing individual liberty. Hayek applies this thought directly to the United States: "It is difficult to know what to do when the enemies of liberty describe themselves as liberals, as is today common practice in the USA" (1979, 136). He names no names, but presumably he ranks Franklin Roosevelt and Lyndon Johnson among the enemies of liberty.

Friedman advances a variation on the same theme. He speaks of the possibility that a small group may get large benefits from government, with the costs spread thinly over the population at large. The small group is then highly motivated to go after the benefit and to keep it coming, whereas the large numbers who pay the costs are not burdened enough individually to make it worth while to put up a fight. Friedman speaks of an Iron Triangle; at one corner of the triangle are the direct beneficiaries of a program; at a second corner are bureaucrats whose jobs and livelihoods depend on governmental programs and their continuation; and at the third corner are elected officials. The pressures go from the first two corners toward the third, with little or no counterpressure from the many taxpayers among whom the costs are thinly divided. Effective power is thus in the hands of the small percentage of the population who benefit, and as more and more of these small groups get their benefits, government becomes bigger and bigger and taxes go higher and higher. Moreover, the same relationship of forces enables the small groups to keep their benefits coming. "Big government" develops, with corresponding reductions in liberty; and cutbacks in the functions of government are rare (Friedman in Theroux 1984, 30–31; Friedman 1976, 13; 1980, 293–94, 302–3).

Note that the beneficiaries of government include those whom it employs—the bureaucrats. They join others in seeking to avert developments that might reduce the role of government. The welfare bureaucracy, for example, does not really want to reduce poverty but to keep it going. In addition, the national press serves its interests by supporting not only big government but bigger government. "Just as government's basic incentive is always to accrue power, funding, and personnel—that is, to aggrandize itself, to expand its turf—collaterally its watchdog, the media, quickly discovers that the bigger and more powerful government becomes, the bigger and more powerful the media become. With more and more turf to watch, more and more watchdogs are needed" (Brookes 1993, 10). Big government, then, is the product of a great conspiracy, a conspiracy that must somehow be countered. The favored strategy, adopted by libertarians and others as well, is to demand reduced taxing and spending, on the one hand, and limits on the number of terms during which a given person may hold office, on the other (Boaz and Crane 1993, 53–64).

## Limited or Minimal Government

Libertarians range from those who seek limited or minimal government to those who would do away with government entirely. Hayek is among those seeking limited government. Government is needed, he thinks, to create "an adequate framework for a functioning competitive market and a law of corporations." It is also needed to promulgate "not only the principles of taxation but also all those regulations of safety and health ... that have to be enforced in the general interest" (1979, 115). Government can promote economic stability and prevent major depressions (1960, 264). It may require people to take out insurance to reduce the danger that they may otherwise become public charges (1960, 286). It should make education compulsory and should support it, but should not necessarily administer the schools itself; perhaps, in accordance with a proposal by Friedman, to be mentioned below, it should issue vouchers that parents can use in paying tuition to the school of their choice (1960, 377–81; 1979, 61). Government alone can conduct foreign relations and perhaps wage war. In fact, after making the "crucial point [that] individual freedom cannot be reconciled with the supremacy of one single purpose to which the whole society must be ... subordinated," Hayek goes on to grant that "war and other temporary disasters" create exceptions that require subordination as the price of preserving freedom in the long run (1944, 206). Hayek would concede government other functions too. Where no coercion is involved, he fixes no limits, even though the noncoercive activities, like all others, depend on taxes that are collected coercively.

At the same time, while seeing needs for government, Hayek's main emphasis is on limiting its role. He proposes fundamental constitutional reforms, designed to bring the "unlimited power of majorities" to an end. He would divide legislative powers among three bodies, the central one charged with fixing the general, abstract rules on the basis of which government should proceed and charged with determining how much government can take in taxes. Its members would be elected for fifteen-year terms and would be ineligible for reelection, the hope being that this arrangement would enable them to resist pressures from interest groups. Of the other two legislative bodies, one would meet only to consider questions of constitutional reform and the other would be the workhorse, determining how to apply the general, abstract rules to concrete circumstances and how to allocate the money that it is permitted to raise (Hayek 1979, 38, 126–27; 1984, 396).

Hayek is especially concerned about taxes. He holds that general rules of just conduct (the kind of rules that the central legislative body would lay down) preclude any governmental effort to redistribute income or wealth. The use of force to redistribute benefits, he says, is "the heart of socialism" (1979, 150). He is willing that taxes be proportionate to income, but not that they be progressive in their general effect. If an income tax is made progressive, it must be only for the purpose of counterbalancing the regressive nature of other taxes (1960, 307, 318–23). Roger Pilon is more blunt: "Majority decisions to redistribute property ... are simply illegitimate, however large the majority behind them.... They are morally illegitimate because in no way do they conform to the higher law ..., the theory of natural rights ... " (Pilon 1991, 12). David Bergland, Libertarian candidate for the presidency in 1984, is even more extreme, treating taxation as theft. "Taxation is simply some people using the force at their disposal to steal the earnings or property of other people" (Bergland 1990, 41).

Milton and Rose Friedman are like Hayek in seeing need for government, expecting it to provide "a stable monetary framework for a free economy" and a stable legal framework, which includes the enforcement of law and order. They are also like Hayek, however, in putting the emphasis on reducing the role of government. Too many of its actions are coercive and thus incompatible with liberty. Milton Friedman begins his book on *Capitalism and Freedom* by deploring the plea that John F. Kennedy made: "Ask not what your country can do for you—ask what you can do for your country." According to Friedman, these questions are not "worthy of the ideals of free men in a free society." The proper question is what to do through government, what to do without using government, and how to keep the government from "becoming a Frankenstein that will destroy the very freedom we establish it to protect.... Our minds tell us, and history confirms, that the great threat to freedom is the concentration of power" (1962, 1–2).

The Friedmans do not attempt an exhaustive list of functions to be taken from government any more than they list the functions that it should retain. But they mention all of the following as unjustified: various welfare programs, including social security; tariffs and import quotas; the licensing of persons for various professions, including the practice of medicine; minimum wage legislation and any regulation of prices or interest rates; public housing, and governmental subsidies for housing; rent control; the governmental monopoly on carrying mail; governmental ownership and administration of national parks; fair trade laws; support for higher education; support for agriculture; support for the National Science Foundation and the National Foundation for the Humanities; the "detailed" regulation of industries; and the FCC's control of radio and television. They think that toll roads should be privatized. They would repeal right-to-work laws and laws outlawing yellow-dog contracts (contracts making nonmembership in a union a condition of employment). And no doubt they could easily add to the list. In general, they are against governmental regulation of private enterprise. In their view, "what we urgently need, for both economic stability and growth, is a reduction of government intervention, not an increase" (1980, 68, 190–92). And of course what we urgently need is a reduction in taxes, including a shift from a progressive income tax to a flat tax rate on all incomes above a certain level (1980, 306; Theroux 1984, 6).

The Friedman prescription with respect to education bears elaboration. In an article published in 1991 Milton Friedman describes schooling as, "next to national defense, the largest socialist enterprise in the United States," and he considers it "as much of a failure as the socialist enterprises in Poland or Hungary or Czechoslovakia or East Germany." He recommends that, as the ultimate goal, people should be made responsible for their own education and for that of their children, with governmentally administered schools eliminated. Milton Friedman is especially hostile to governmental support for higher education, holding that it is mainly a means by which students prepare themselves for lucrative careers; and since the potential benefit is mainly theirs, they should be the ones to pay for it (1962, 100–103; Theroux 1984, 34). He would have the government ease the transition from socialist to private education by having government provide vouchers that people could use in paying a portion of the costs (Friedman 1991, 20).

I noted earlier that libertarians tend to ignore the question of equality of opportunity. Along with this neglect goes the problem of what to do about arbitrary discrimination based on such grounds as race, sex or sexual orientation, language, religion, or handicap. The most recent major libertarian attack on the problem is that of Richard A. Epstein, who denounces governmental intervention on behalf of equal employment opportunity and urges a regime of strong property rights, freedom of association, and freedom of contract. He would "allow all persons to do business with whomever they please" (Epstein 1992, 3).

Epstein argues that competition in a free market is the best kind of attack on discrimination, for competitors aim at efficiency and tend to lose out if they allow irrelevant considerations to influence their policies. Employers who recruit and promote on the basis of merit rather than on the basis of such characteristics as race or sex will be rewarded, and those who engage in arbitrary discrimination will be penalized. Not that this will necessarily bring all discrimination to an end. The efficiency of some kinds of enterprise will be enhanced rather than reduced if considerations such as race and sex are taken into account. But free competition will drastically reduce discrimination and will do it without coercion (Epstein 1992, 91).

In Epstein's view, the fact that the Jim Crow system developed and prevailed for so long does not undermine his thesis. That system, which he denounces as a "national disgrace," stemmed from the workings of democracy and "the abnegation of the principles of limited government." Democracy permitted racists and bigots to outvote the more moderate, and the racists and bigots adopted legislation requiring discrimination. The market would not have permitted such an outcome, for it does not operate on the principle of majority rule.

For example, the railways in Louisiana segregated people by race a century ago only because the law required it, not because the owners and managers were prejudiced or saw profit in segregation. Then in *Plessy* the Supreme Court failed to do its duty, adopting the "separate but equal" principle that left legislatures free to intervene in the private market and that, in effect, permitted continued discrimination. Virulent majorities in the electorate and in the legislatures choked off measures that blacks could otherwise have taken to improve their circumstances and adopted legislation tending to deter outsiders from coming in and undermining the discriminatory system. Moreover, racists and bigots in control of government did not let it perform its minimal function of protecting people from private violence, such as the violence of the Ku Klux Klan. In short, Jim Crow is to be explained by the fact that "government fell into the hands of the wrong people" (Epstein 1992, 94–96). And the solution, according to Epstein, is to cut back the government's role and trust to damage suits brought by aggrieved parties.

The analysis leaves problems unresolved. Jim Crow practices developed not only in situations where competition might theoretically have provided a cure but also in numerous situations that competition did not reach: in the employment policies of government itself (for example, in municipal fire and police departments, in state police systems), in the public schools, and in public utility companies. To expect that damage suits might have taken care of the problem is like expecting that the Jews of Germany could have averted the Holocaust by filing suits in Hitler's courts. And it is scarcely plausible that a reduction in the role of government would have included the elimination of all governmental agencies that engaged in discrimination. Further, to the extent that the discriminations of Jim Crow resulted from acts of omission or commission by state and local governments, a reduction in the role of government is by no means the obvious solution. An enhancement of the role of the federal courts and of Congress looks more promising, and this is the path that history has in fact taken.

Other libertarians offer prescriptions for the problem of discrimination that are no more satisfactory. They generally resist any line of thought that might suggest governmental action. Friedman's discussion of the subject shows no awareness of the extent to which government itself has in the past denied equal treatment, or of the extent to which it still does. And as for discrimination in the private realm, Friedman is like Epstein in supporting "freedom of contract," including the freedom of employers to refuse to hire blacks if this will enhance their profits.

Friedman treats racial discrimination not as a moral issue but as a matter of taste, and he holds that it is not appropriate for those who oppose discrimination to use the coercive powers of government to force their taste on others. Moreover, Friedman argues, the principle that government can prohibit discrimination might also lead government to require it. He sees no moral difference between prohibiting and requiring, and he explicitly rejects the view that those who have suffered arbitrary discrimination in the past should get preferential treatment as a matter of redress (1962, 110–15). Since discrimination is a matter of taste and an aspect of profit seeking, and since all who are not coerced are free, he sees nothing that calls for redress.

Like many others, libertarians have tended to become more sensitive to racial issues since the time Friedman wrote (recall Epstein's characterization of Jim Crow as a "national disgrace"), and a few are disposed to favor some kind of action on behalf of equal treatment. But according to Llewellyn Rockwell, paleolibertarians (libertarians of the Old Right) reject any such attitude. Paleolibertarians "reject not only affirmative action, set-asides, and quotas but the 1964 Civil Rights Act and all subsequent laws that force property owners to act against their will" (Rockwell 1990b, 14).

Samuel Francis goes further, denouncing the subordination of public policy to what he regards as the "illusion of equality." He holds that "the natural differentiation of the races in intellectual capacities implies that of the two major races in the United States today, only one possesses the inherent capacity to create and sustain a level of civilization that has historically characterized its homelands in Europe and America." The war against discrimination, he further holds, is "actually a war against those institutions of civil society such as property, patterns of association, education, and employment that naturally reflect inequality and differentiation." He thus denounces not only affirmative action, quotas, and set-asides but also enterprise zones and all sorts of "egalitarian experimentation." To him, these are all aspects of a crusade against "social manifestations of the reality of human inequality" (Francis 1993b, 23). How widely this view is shared among libertarians, I do not know.

Charles Murray, who identifies himself as a libertarian and who glorifies Ayn Rand, directs his attack mainly against the welfare system. But he generalizes: "We [libertarians] think government is a waste of money." He would like to restore what he thinks of as a "Jeffersonian republic" (Murray 1993a, 41).

## Welfare and the Welfare State

I noted earlier that Hayek is scornful of the idea of social justice. Nevertheless, he mentions the problem of those unable to provide for themselves, and he sees no reason why government should not provide for them, assuring them a minimum income, as long as it does not act in the name of social justice. Moreover, any provision for such people must occur "outside the market," whatever that means. Hayek does not elaborate on his view, nor does he explain how assistance to the poor, even if "outside the market," squares with the injunction against redistributive taxation.

The Friedmans take a similar line. They think that "most of the present welfare programs should never have been enacted" (1980, 119). Milton Friedman explains his position at least in part when he says that the "fundamental fallacy of the welfare state ... is the attempt to do good at somebody else's expense.... Nobody spends somebody else's money as carefully as he spends his own." Further, taxing so as to make welfare payments possible reduces the freedom of the taxpayer (1976, 11). Friedman does not mention the logical counterpart: that welfare payments increase the freedom of those who receive them.

Although opposing welfare, the Friedmans are like Hayek in that they accept the view that government must provide somehow for those who otherwise might starve. Their solution is a negative income tax. They would eliminate all or nearly all of the existing welfare programs and put a negative income tax in their place. The general principle is that government should levy a tax on incomes above the poverty level and should itself make payments to those whose incomes fall below that level.

Two major differences between "welfare" and the negative income tax are immediately obvious. The first is that the benefits of the negative income tax would go only to the poor, whereas some of the welfare programs (most notably Medicare and social security) serve all those in a given age bracket even if they are rich. The second is that the negative income tax would be administered by the Internal Revenue Service and the bureaucratic structure that now administers the various welfare programs would be dismantled.

How great other differences might be is uncertain. Much would depend on the fixing of the poverty level—the dividing line between those who pay taxes and those to whom negative income taxes are paid. And much would depend on the amounts involved. The Friedmans want to make negative income tax payments high enough to alleviate destitution but not high enough to undermine the principle that people should provide for themselves.

Since 1984 the principal libertarian voice concerning the poor has been that of Charles Murray. In *Losing Ground* he argues that the various welfare programs do more harm than good. Despite them, we are "losing ground" in the struggle against poverty, for the aid given has the perverse effect of undermining the work ethic. Murray speaks of "scrapping the entire federal welfare and income-support structure" for working-age persons, expecting that a high proportion of those cut loose would shape up, or at least find a way to survive, and that private charities and local governments would take care of the rest.

Murray repeats the prescription in a more recent article focusing on the problem of single mothers and their babies. "My proposition," he says, "is that illegitimacy is the single most important social problem of our time—more important than crime, drugs, poverty, illiteracy, welfare or homelessness because it drives everything else." To solve the problem, he would send the signal that government will no longer subsidize women who have babies they cannot support. For them, AFDC would go to zero, and they would be ineligible for subsidized housing or food stamps. They should give up for adoption any babies they are unable to support, and those not adopted should go into orphanages. Murray does here concede a role for government, for it should provide "lavishly" for the orphanages, treating them as "24-hour-a-day pre-schools" (Murray 1993b, A14). He does not say what to do about mothers who are unwilling to give up their babies. If they are denied welfare, pushing drugs and resorting to prostitution are among their obvious alternatives.

Libertarians vary in their prescriptions relating to social security. Niskanen and Moore take the view that it involves a tacit contract that must be honored. They would, however, make various changes, including a shift to sixty-eight as the retirement age, designed to bring down the costs (Boaz and Crane 1993, 71). Bergland too would honor the contract, but he would do it by giving everyone in the social security system a lump-sum payment equal to their equity in the fictitious trust fund and then bring the government's role to an end (Bergland 1990, 62–63). Others satisfy themselves with emphasizing the view that it is morally wrong to tax some in order to benefit others (Waldron 1986, 466).

Assuming that the social security program is terminated, Milton Friedman, unlike Hayek, opposes any governmental requirement that people buy annuities so as to provide for their own old age. This infringement on freedom, he argues, is justifiable only to make sure that people do not become public charges, and his guess is that so few would become public charges that the precaution is unnecessary (Friedman 1962, 188).

## Private Coercion

The question of private coercion came up earlier in connection with the discussion of upholding virtue. Now the question concerns private coercion in the economic realm.

Discussions of coercion in the economic realm usually rest on the assumption that it is governmental. Many of Hayek's statements, however, refer to coercion in general, as if he opposes coercion whatever its source, including the coercion that one person might bring to bear against another. To some degree he does in fact oppose coercion in the private realm. The brief definition of liberty cited earlier suggests this: that liberty exists in the absence of coercion by other persons. Likewise, his definition of coercion suggests it: that coercion occurs when people abandon their own purposes and pursue the purposes of another in order to avoid a greater evil that the other is able to inflict. And the reason for objecting to coercion suggests a generalized concern for it: that coercion is bad because it "eliminates an individual as a thinking and valuing person and makes him a bare tool in the achievement of the ends of another" (1960, 20–21, 133–37).

Further, Hayek acknowledges that "life in society necessarily means that we are dependent for the satisfaction of most of our needs on the services of some of our fellows," and that "our fellows" may make their services available only if we meet conditions that they fix—a statement that suggests sensitivity to the possibility of coercion in the private realm (1960, 135–36). Moreover, as Barry summarizes

Hayek's position, "the main justification for the use of coercion by centralized authority is to prevent coercion by others" (Barry 1979, 72).

But, given all this, Hayek seems arbitrary in deciding what constitutes coercion. On the one hand, he seems to assume that as long as people act on their own as individuals and in conformity with law, they are equal bargaining agents accepting the imperatives of the market, and nothing that they do should count as coercion. Every bargain made "voluntarily" is compatible with liberty. Thus no coercion is involved even if the only choice that an applicant for a job sees is between starving and accepting onerous terms of employment. The lack of education does not mean a lack of liberty, for the greater knowledge of some does not enable them to coerce others.

On the other hand, Hayek seems to think that when people enter the market in an organized way to get what they want, coercion is likely. Not that monopolies are a threat. Few exist, and those few are more likely to be creatures of governmental protection (through tariffs or patents, for example) than creatures of the market. Neither are owners or managers a threat, regardless of how great their profits or their power; if they refuse to hire or threaten to fire, they are simply operating within the rules of the market. Corporations are not threats either, even if they are the collective enterprise of many stockholders who combine their resources in pursuit of a common goal. It is trade unions that are the threat. They diminish freedom by adopting bullying tactics designed to compel the workers to join and give support. And they diminish the liberty of employers through strikes or the threat of strikes, compelling the payment of higher wages or the granting of better fringe benefits than the market justifies.

I quote Barry earlier to the effect that the main justification Hayek sees for the use of coercion by government is to prevent coercion by others. In the light of the above, it is clear that the statement should be narrowly construed. It does not apply to everything you might think of as coercion. Barry illustrates his point by referring to the protection that government can offer against "violence, fraud, blackmail, and so on," that is, against crime. Hayek does not call on government to protect one person from the economic coercions that another can bring to bear, for he would think of this as an unjustified governmental intervention in the market. The term *coercive* thus seems to be flexible, permitting a definition that reflects a predisposition to favor property owners and entrepreneurs.

Friedman seems more sensitive to the problem of private coercion, granting that liberty exists only when choice is possible. But his view is that the market provides choice—to whom to sell, from whom to buy, for whom to work, and so on. And those dissatisfied with the choices available in one locality can move to another.

The Libertarian Party once adopted a "Statement of Principles" that accepts private coercion as long as it is not "forcible." The statement insists on the right of all to live as they please as long as they do not "forcibly interfere" with the right of others to do the same (Bergland 1990, 18).

Hayek's general approach calls for comment. It is rationalist and intuitive, not empirical. On the basis of reason, he prescribes both rules of conduct and organizational arrangements, thus himself exhibiting a "fatal conceit" that he denounces in others—the "fatal conceit that man is able to shape the world around him according to his wishes" (1988, 27). Having taken the stand that "constructivist rationalism" is the road to disaster, he takes that road himself (1984, 364). He condemns others for thinking that they can improve on what has developed "spontaneously," but then he himself rationally prescribes a return to what "spontaneity" would presumably have created in the absence of ill-considered deliberate intervention. Moreover, he does not say why the various developments favoring a free market count as "spontaneous" while developments going in the other direction do not. Nor does he take up the question why "spontaneity" produced one kind of system in western Europe, say, and a different kind in China, and still a different kind in India. Why should we assume that these developments are all a reflection of the workings of nature? And if deliberate decisions gave the West a system that Westerners prefer to the systems of China and India, is it not possible that additional deliberate decisions might also have beneficial results?

Hayek's impressionistic and intuitive approach—his failure to be empirical—leads to questions about his evaluation of democracy and his recommendations for reform. Empiricism would presumably have led him to ask about the relative responsiveness of different systems, democratic and other, to the pressures of special interest groups, but intuition does not lead him to do this. Instead, he focuses on democracy alone and condemns it because it is so responsive. My own supposition is that all kinds of governments are responsive to the demands of one or more kinds of interest groups and that no government is entirely fair. The question is whether it is not one of the virtues of democracy, rather than one of its failings, that it puts few limits on the opportunity of interest groups to get their desires considered. Are not undemocratic regimes more likely to be biased toward a relatively narrow range of interests?

Finally, I should recall that Hayek does not supplement his conception of liberty with a concern about conditions affecting its worth. He even speaks out against governmental action on behalf of equality of opportunity on the ground that coercion would be involved.

Experience with communism redounds to Hayek's credit. Communism proved to be a "road to serfdom" and to additional evils. But empiricism might have led Hayek to ask whether social democracy is also a road to serfdom, as he claims on the basis of reason and intuition. Are the people of Sweden on the road to serfdom? How about the people of other countries where social democratic parties are strong? Did the New Deal and the Great Society put the American people on the road to serfdom? Hayek and his disciples must say yes, but others can hold that, at the least, the evidence is not in.

## Robert Nozick

In *Anarchy, State, and Utopia* (1974), Robert Nozick concludes "that a minimal state, limited to the narrow functions of protection against force, theft, fraud, enforcement of contracts, and so on, is justified; that any more extensive state will violate persons' rights not to be forced to do certain things, and is unjustified" (ix). Since every state in the world, including the United States, is more than minimal, Nozick's position is that they are all unjustified. From his point of view, the welfare state is far beyond the limits of legitimacy.

How does Nozick arrive at his conclusions? The answer is that, without acknowledging the fact, he starts with certain assumptions. He is a state-of-nature theorist, and he assumes that individuals get rights in the state of nature—the right to liberty (the right "not to be forced to do certain things") and the right to property. The rights of each person are qualified by the need to respect the comparable rights of others, but they are not qualified in any other way. They are absolute (32–33). For example, the right of people to property includes the right to property in their own bodies and lives, and it is so absolute and unqualified that they may sell themselves into slavery if they so choose (331). Absolute rights are not inalienable.

At one point Nozick speaks of the idea that people may have other kinds of rights—"a right to various things such as equality of opportunity, life, and so on"—but he cannot imagine that these other "things" are really rights. In referring to them, he puts the word "rights" in quotation marks, not accepting it as appropriate. The objection to recognizing "equality of opportunity, life, and so on" as rights is that they depend on a "substructure of things and materials and actions" to which "other people ... have rights and entitlements" (238). In other words, the right of individuals to property, being absolute and unqualified, precludes other rights that might impinge.

In Nozick's scheme, owners of property in the state of nature voluntarily create protective associations—ultraminimal states. In time, by "an invisible hand process and by morally permissible means, without anyone's rights being violated" (114–15), one of the ultraminimal states becomes a minimal state, the difference being that it achieves a monopoly in its territory and serves everyone under its jurisdiction. The claim that the minimal state develops by "an invisible hand process" presumably means that it develops with at least the tacit consent of all involved. The minimal state has only such rights and powers as individuals concede to it, having no aboriginal rights of its own (92, 118). Since no extension of the functions of the state beyond the minimal can possibly occur without violating rights of liberty and property, any extension that occurs is necessarily illegitimate and immoral (149).

The few functions that the minimal state performs involve costs, so taxes must be imposed; and they are sure to be in some degree redistributive. But, like the functions of the state, taxation must be kept at a minimum, for it is in about the same category as forced labor (168–70, 172).

If you grant the assumptions with which Nozick begins, you may be carried along to his conclusions. But you do not need to accept the assumptions. No one knows that a state of nature ever existed corresponding to the one that Nozick imagines. It is inherently implausible. The more likely situation is one in which family groups and perhaps small clans, not isolated individuals, struggle to survive. Survival depends on mutual cooperation and sharing, people accepting obligations toward one another as well as being accorded rights. Children are especially dependent on parents, who accept obligations toward them and inculcate in them attitudes supportive of the family and the group. Property rights, including the right of people to their own bodies and lives, are qualified and contingent, subordinate in some degree to the needs of the group—subordinate, for example, to the need to collect taxes or the equivalent and to the need to have individuals perform services (such as fighting) on behalf of the group. By agreement or conquest, small groups join together, and eventually organizations emerge recognizable as states, with no natural limits on their functions.

In this alternative scheme, nature does not confer rights. In truth, if you take this alternative view, you can well say that those claiming that rights are natural are akin to con artists in that they are attempting to give undeserved authority to their own thoughts and preferences. The alternative view is that people create rights and are always revising their conceptions. They create rights by putting interests in an order of importance and saying that the most important interests should be classified separately and given a special name: rights. Of course, an interest does not become a right simply because someone thinks it should, but in many cases a widely shared consensus develops. Thus, a widely shared consensus now exists on the human rights listed in various international treaties.

Rights that come into existence in this way are not absolute, if for no other reason than that conflicts of rights are always developing; the longer the list of rights, the more numerous the conflicts. For example, one group may claim the right to parade down the street as a matter of freedom of expression, while another group claims the right, as a matter of freedom of communication and travel, to use the same street at the same time for their automobiles. Further, various public interests are important enough that they override private rights. Thus your right to property must give way in part to the public need for tax money, and your right to liberty must give way at times to the public need for soldiers.

Nozick does not discuss these possibilities. Ignoring them, and assuming that individuals have absolute rights to liberty and property derived from the state of nature, he makes a powerful case for a minimal state. He might still favor a minimal state if he accepted the alternative conception of the origin and nature of rights, but he would have to do so for other reasons.

## Anarchocapitalism

In *For a New Liberty, The Libertarian Manifesto* (1978), Murray N. Rothbard presents the case for anarchocapitalism. Rothbard does not want even minimal government. Instead, his ideal is to do away with government all over the world. The assumption is that government is the enemy of liberty and that, with government eliminated, liberty will flourish.

In Rothbard's eyes, the "central core of the libertarian creed is the absolute right to private property" (39). He is in accord with Nozick on this point. This absolute right, belonging to individual persons, is a natural right that no one, not even the government, is entitled to abridge or take away. Along with the natural right to property goes a "nonaggression axiom"—that no one may initiate the use or threat of physical violence against the person or property of anyone else (23). And government is a major source of aggression. "What is the State anyway but organized banditry? What is taxation but theft on a gigantic, unchecked scale? ... If you wish to know how libertarians regard the State and any of its acts, simply think of the State as a criminal band, and all of the libertarian attitudes will logically fall into place" (46, 236).

Since the state is to disappear, so must governmental title to any property. All property is to be privately owned, including roads and highways, lakes, streams, and rivers. Rothbard would even put airlanes, microwave channels, and the oceans under private ownership, although he is unclear about how this could be arranged.

The assumption of course is that private property owners, motivated by self-interest, would see to it that their property is properly maintained, utilized, and protected. For some purposes they would act individually and for others they would cooperate voluntarily. Thus the owner of a highway would want to keep it in good repair so that people would pay the toll for using it, and merchants wanting to prevent crime in the business district would voluntarily join in hiring the necessary police. Homeowners wanting protection against fires would subscribe to the protective service offered by a private company, and parents wanting to educate their children would choose among privately owned schools. And so on. Whatever function government performs—if it is a necessary function—will be performed more satisfactorily and more economically through private enterprise. One can imagine how underworld figures would relish the possibilities.

Rothbard acknowledges that people get into disputes, but he rejects this as a justification for government. Disputants can simply resort to a judge of their own choice or to an arbitral tribunal that they select, paying the costs of the judicial process themselves; and economic and social pressures will be sufficient to induce the defeated party to accept the outcome. Law will develop not through the action of legislatures but on the basis of successive precedents, as the common law developed in England.

Implicitly acknowledging that government is not going to be eliminated overnight, Rothbard wants meantime to cut its functions to a minimum. Asking what government can do to help the poor, he answers that it can "get out of the way." It can get out of the way by abolishing taxes or reducing their level, and reducing governmental expenditures accordingly. In particular, it can reduce the taxation of the poor for the benefit of the rich, as in connection with the subsidies given to higher education and to farmers. It can remove legal roadblocks to productive energies; for example, it can repeal minimum wage laws, laws that prohibit peddling, and laws that give privileges to trade unions (163–67). Most important, government can stop paying people to be unproductive. That is, it should completely abolish all public welfare programs, relying instead on private charity to provide whatever help the deserving poor may need (147–48). Rothbard explicitly rejects Friedman's proposed negative income tax, which he says would only lead to a "massive flocking to the guaranteed dole," and he disassociates himself more generally from Friedman's willingness to use government for so many purposes. Among other things, Friedman wants government to regulate the supply of money, whereas Rothbard wants "a money that emerges from and whose supply is determined by the free market." He thinks that governmental control of money is inherently inflationary.

The foregoing reflects the position described in the book cited. In 1992, in a presidential address to the Randolph Club, Rothbard says that his minimum demand (and the minimum demand of paleo-libertarians) is the total abolition of the "whole kit and kaboodle of the welfare state," including the Wagner Act and the Social Security Act. He deplores the abandonment of the gold standard, holding that governmental control of the currency is bad. He speaks of abolishing the Federal Reserve system and repealing the income tax. In fact, he is quoted as saying that "we shall repeal the twentieth century." Even that may not be enough, for he also speaks of repealing the Federal Judiciary Act of 1789 and perhaps even restoring "the good old Articles of Confederation" (Rothbard 1992, 2; Gottfried 1993, 161).

For the most part, I am reserving the discussion of foreign policy issues for chapter 14, but should note here that foreign policy and, most particularly, provision for national security, present a special problem for libertarians. Hayek and Friedman both grant the need for government to provide for national defense, which means that they are in an uncomfortable position. Distrusting government in every other way and wanting to limit it, they nevertheless open the way to the almost unlimited government that war may involve.

Nozick ignores the problem. Rothbard solves it by holding that foreign policy and war will disappear along with the state. And if libertarianism triumphs in the United States before it sweeps the world, we would nevertheless be safe. A libertarian America would not be a threat, for libertarianism rules out aggression against anyone or any country. "Being no longer a nation-state, which is inherently threatening, there would be little chance of any country attacking us" (1978, 238). In saying that, Rothbard was obviously not thinking of the fate of the American Indians after the arrival of Columbus, or of the more recent fate of Afghanistan and Kuwait. But he does say that if, against all expectations, an invader were to come in, he would find no governmental structure through which to work and would be bogged down in guerrilla warfare, waged voluntarily by individuals insistent on their freedom (240).

Rothbard's short-term solution to the problem of national security is twofold: to play down foreign threats and to urge isolationism. Libertarians, he says, must call on the United States to disarm itself and "to abandon its policy of global interventionism: to withdraw immediately and completely, militarily and politically, from Asia, Europe, Latin America, the Middle East, from *everywhere*." It should maintain a policy of strict political isolation and neutrality (291–94). This will presumably give it safety.

## Social Rigidities

Mancur Olson advances a theory that is relevant to libertarianism. As in the case of the libertarians, his concern is with economic growth, and he starts with the assumption that "in these days, it takes an enormous amount of stupid policies or bad or unstable institutions to *prevent* economic development.... An economy with free markets and no government or cartel intervention is like a teenage youth; it makes a lot of mistakes but nonetheless grows rapidly without special effort or encouragement" (Olson 1982, 175, 177). Olson goes well along in the direction of the view that, given a completely free and untrammeled market, prices and wages go up or down as need arises so that everything offered for sale is bought and everyone who wants work is employed. In the absence of "stickiness," the market clears, and growth goes on apace (213, 229).

But in practice the market is never completely free and untrammeled. Olson endorses the analysis ascribed earlier to Milton Friedman, who speaks of small groups gaining benefit by inducing government to favor their interests, the costs being spread over large numbers. But Olson does not go along with what he calls "monodiabolism," that is, with treating the government as the only devil. As he sees it, devils also beset the market. Their evil influence shows up in collusion among those who otherwise might compete—collusion in the form of "distributional coalitions" (Olson 1982, 177; Olson 1984, 244).

For example, those who grow oranges may find it to their advantage to get together to fix prices or share out the market or regulate the flow of oranges to the market. Firms selling insecticides used on the orange trees may collude so as to get higher prices. Workers who pick oranges, grocers and others who sell them, and truckers who take them to the market may find it to their advantage to organize so as to be in a stronger position to protect and advance their interests. Soon, instead of a number of persons pursuing their individual interests competitively, you have a much smaller number of distributional coalitions (cartels, trade unions, merchandising associations, etc.) trying to rig the market in their favor. The tendency pervades the professional world as well as the business world, with physicians and lawyers, for example, employing various devices to limit the competition they face. Instead of wanting to keep competition free, everyone in the market wants to limit it. Pursuing their own self-interest, they have no reason to be concerned about the costs they are imposing on others.

This does not necessarily mean that those pursuing their interests forget about government. They may seek and get help from it too. For example, orange growers may seek tariff protection from foreign imports, workers may seek legislation fixing a minimum wage or requiring employers to engage in collective bargaining, consumer organizations may get government to ban the use of a dangerous insecticide, and so on. And those in various professions, from medicine and law to cosmetology, may seek laws restricting the profession to those who are licensed, ostensibly to protect the public from unqualified practitioners but with the incidental result of reducing the competition they face.

The damage done by "encompassing" groups may be limited to the extent that their interests approximate the general public interest. ("What is good for General Motors is good for the country.") But many of the interests of less encompassing groups can be satisfied only at the expense of others. Moreover, the smaller groups, including small groups of large firms, find it easier than the encompassing groups to get organized so as to pursue their special interests. In any event, as time goes on, given social and political stability, both private collusion and governmental interventions lead to "social rigidities," to "institutional sclerosis." Prices and wages become "stickier," and the market does not clear. Economic growth slows down and perhaps stops. This is sometimes called the "aging democracy" theory, distributional coalitions restricting competition more and more as time goes on.

Olson does not offer a clear solution to the problem. It obviously follows from his analysis that government should not intervene in the market so much for the benefit of special interests. But it also follows that government might well play more of a role in "trustbusting," in preventing the kinds of collusion that interfere with the free operation of the market. And implicit in Olson's analysis is the idea that periodic restructuring of some sort may have desirable effects (whatever undesirable effects it may also have). West Germany and Japan may have gained from the restructuring that followed their defeat in war, and the countries of Europe may gain through the common market that they are forming. The United States may make a comparable gain through NAFTA. The longer a country goes along in a peaceful and stable way, according to Olson, the more social rigidities are likely to take hold.

Olson's theory is provocative but is not uniformly endorsed. Lester Thurow, for example, points to a number of factors that influence growth in addition to those that Olson emphasizes, mainly technological change and good and bad luck. The economy of Massachusetts grew in the nineteenth century when water power gave it an advantage. Then it declined, only to be revived by the revolution centering on electronics. The economies of countries on the Persian Gulf have all grown because of oil. Moreover, stability does not necessarily lead to rigidity; otherwise, Switzerland and Sweden could not have done so well (Thurow 1983, 9). The boom in postwar Germany and Japan may be due less to restructuring brought on by defeat in war than to the special impetus obtained by importing technologies developed elsewhere. Further, even if we could somehow put a stop to the collusions and lobbying of special-interest groups, it does not automatically follow that we should do so. To do it would scarcely be compatible with the ideals of liberty and democracy, and it would be to reinforce a status quo reflecting the successes of interest groups in the past. Moreover, it is not necessarily to be assumed that economic growth is so important that it should override concern for all other values.

## Externalities

Externalities confront all advocates of limited or minimal government with a problem. As indicated in the preceding chapter, externalities are side effects, "neighborhood effects": the consequences of an action or a choice for persons not party to it—consequences for bystanders and for values of concern to bystanders. Being hostile to government, libertarians can scarcely urge its use to prohibit or regulate choices that produce externalities. What they tend to do is to make any of several claims designed to undermine the case for governmental action. They may claim that the danger (or the harm done) is exaggerated and that little or no need for governmental action exists. Or they may claim that governmental action itself involves dangers and costs that ought not be accepted. These sorts of reactions are especially prominent in relation to the environmental movement, which libertarians (and conservatives influenced by libertarians) are likely to regard as a threat to free enterprise. These responses to the problem of externalities have some merit, but a major problem for libertarians remains.

## Reprise

Speaking not of all kinds of libertarians but only of paleolibertarians, Llewellyn H. Rockwell says that they see

I. The leviathan State as the institutional source of evil throughout history.

II. The unhampered free market as a moral and practical imperative.

III. Private property as an economic and moral necessity for a free society.

IV. The garrison State as a preeminent threat to liberty and social well-being.

V. The welfare State as organized theft that victimizes producers and eventually even its clients.

VI. Civil liberties based on property rights as essential to a just society.

VII. The egalitarian ethic as morally reprehensible and destructive of private property and social morality.

VIII. Social authority—as embodied in the family, church, community, and other intermediating institutions—as helping protect the individual from the State and as necessary for a free and virtuous society.

IX. Western culture as eminently worthy of preservation and defense.

X. Objective standards of morality, especially as found in the Judeo-Christian tradition, as essential to the free and civilized social order. (Rockwell 1990a, 35)

Libertarians other than paleos might not have the concern for a "just" society included in point VI, and they might have hesitations or doubts about the last three points, but otherwise libertarians of all sorts are likely to find Rockwell's points acceptable.

Another statement by way of reprise: "Society is produced by our wants and government by our wickedness.... Society is in every state a blessing, but government, even in its best state, but a necessary evil" (Tom Paine, quoted by Sullivan 1982, 199).

# Chapter 8

# Public Choice

**B**ROADLY CONCEIVED, *public choice* refers to group or collective decision making, as opposed to decision making in the private realm. So conceived, it does not necessarily identify an ideology. But the term also refers to a special school of thought about group or collective decision making—the Virginia School—with James Buchanan and Gordon Tullock as its founders and principal exponents. And as the Virginia School expounds *public choice,* it is ideological in the sense that it is intended to guide and explain behavior and provide a basis for judgment.

The object in this chapter is to describe and appraise the theory. With what assumptions do Buchanan and Tullock begin? What arguments do they advance, and how convincingly? To what sorts of policy prescriptions does their theory lead? What criticisms are appropriate?

## Assumptions

To Buchanan, "the ideal society is anarchy, in which no one man or group of men coerces another" (1975, 92). The statement indicates that, like libertarianism, *public choice* theory is highly individualistic. It focuses on adult individuals, not on any group, be it a family, community, or society. The individuals in the ideal society have complete liberty, Buchanan specifying that he means liberty "in its negative sense: an individual is at liberty or free to carry on an activity if he or she is not coerced from doing so by someone else, be this an individual or a group" (1986, 169). Individual liberty, according to Buchanan, should be "the overriding objective for social policy."

The further assumption is that, ideally, individuals enjoy their liberty in a free-market situation, where they make bargains and conclude contracts. They are "well informed and fully rational in their choices," and are "motivated by utility-maximizing considerations" (Buchanan and Tullock 1962, 297). "Utility-maximizing" persons are persons who serve their own interests. The terms *utility* and *interest* are both broad, referring to anything of value or anything that gives pleasure or satisfaction, but it is clear that (as a rule, with qualifications to be noted later) Buchanan and Tullock do not intend to make the words include altruistic or disinterested motives or actions. If utility-maximizing persons do good for others, it must be in order to gain advantage for themselves. They are completely selfish.

Although regarding anarchy as ideal, Buchanan does not endorse it as practical; nor does Tullock. Given anarchy and complete liberty, everyone could act in such a way as to impose costs on others—"external costs," costs associated with externalities—and both Buchanan and Tullock accept the view that this is a major problem, making government necessary: government (the state) is necessary to regulate and control conduct for the purpose of eliminating or minimizing external costs. Moreover, government is also necessary to enforce contracts, to maintain order, and perhaps to serve other purposes such as national defense.

But government itself involves costs, costs associated with the process of achieving agreement, costs in the form of infringements on liberty, and costs in the form of taxation. In constitution making, as perhaps in other activities, tradeoffs have to occur, but in working out the tradeoffs the presumption is always in favor of individual liberty. The burden of proof is on those who want government and want to give it functions and powers.

## The Argument

The major joint work of Buchanan and Tullock is *The Calculus of Consent. Logical Foundations of Constitutional Democracy* (1962). In this work they are not descriptive or historical. They do not ask, for example, how the Constitution of the United States came to be adopted or what considerations influenced the members of the convention of 1787. Instead, they ask in effect what thoughts concerning government would influence rational and logical utility-maximizers in working out a constitution. The thoughts that they project onto the constitution makers are clearly their own.

According to Buchanan and Tullock, the logical formulators of a constitution, assuming universal selfishness, are more fearful than hopeful. For good reason, they are reluctant and suspicious about government, concerned mainly with the dangers. They are and should be more concerned with protecting themselves than with planning for a government that will help them solve problems and achieve progress. They are tempted to make unanimity a constitutional requirement: only by giving everyone a veto can everyone be sure that government will not become too costly. It would be a nightmare if, at the other extreme, anyone could order an action and impose the costs mainly on others. But unanimity itself would be costly in that it might make government totally ineffective or require the bribing of holdouts. So the constitution makers agree on majority rule.

How does majority rule work out? Forget the constitution makers now, and think of 100 persons authorized to govern themselves by majority rule. Any 51 of them can order an action, knowing that the other 49 will have to pay part of the costs. Moreover, the majority need not always consist of the same 51. People can regroup themselves in connection with every issue that comes up, with any group of 51 able to order action and impose part of the costs on the other 49. The result is similar to the one that Hayek and Friedman both bewailed—a great expansion of government, surely an overexpansion.

The problem is accentuated by *rent seeking*. Rent seeking has nothing to do with the kind of rent that landlords collect. It refers instead to "transfers of wealth through the aegis of the state." It "includes activities aimed at profit through inducing the government to intervene or to terminate its intervention."

> We behave as rent seekers when we support expanded spending programs or tax breaks to benefit our own industry, occupation, region, local authority, or, quite simply, our own pet version of some 'public interest.' ... If I seek a special tax exemption for my industry, my profession, my region, I am rent seeking. If I seek a special spending program that will benefit my pet project, whether this will provide me with personal pecuniary gain or not, I am rent seeking. I am seeking to secure differential gains that are not shared by the full constituency. (J. Buchanan 1989, 2, 10)

The lobbyist for General Motors who wants government to restrict the importation of Japanese cars is a rent seeker. So is the bureaucrat who seeks a raise. So are those who oppose restricting imports and oppose giving the bureaucrats a raise. In short, any effort to gain advantage through the action or inaction of government is rent seeking, and so is any effort to thwart the rent seeking of others.

Rent seeking is thus suggestive of profit seeking, but it has a pejorative connotation that profit seeking lacks. Profit seeking is ordinarily associated with productive effort and thus with some kind of contribution to social well-being, but rent seeking involves the use of resources (if only the time and talents of the lobbyist, for example) in an essentially unproductive way. It consists of "resource-wasting activities." By diverting resources from productive activities it may even diminish aggregate wealth. This characteristic is prominent enough to lead to the suggestion that the references ought to be not to "rent seeking" but to "Directly Unproductive Activities" (Rowley 1987, 143). And it is prominent enough that Tullock speaks of "Rent Seeking as a Negative Sum Game," expressing the view that the extraordinary amount of rent seeking in Third World countries is, to a large extent, the explanation of their backwardness (Buchanan et al. 1980, 35).

Bureaucrats are among the utility-maximizing (i.e., selfish) rent seekers. Their immediate concern is for their own jobs and the accompanying salary and perquisites, and their larger concern is for the agency within which they work. Their own career prospects are ordinarily better if their agency is growing, with new people being hired and with the budget expanding. Thus, on the one hand, they look for additional functions that they can perform and for needs that they can meet, justifying expansion; on the other hand, they try to ward off or to interpret away any development that might lead to a reduction in the number of people employed or in the size of their budget.

The illustration of their outlook most commonly cited concerns their behavior as the end of a fiscal year approaches: they spend every last dollar, fearing that if they acknowledge a surplus, their budget for subsequent years will be cut. Better to create evidence that they were not allotted enough. Further, the complaint is that bureaucratic agencies never die or even fade away; rent seekers manage to keep them alive and perhaps even manage to have them grow after the reason for their existence is gone.

Like bureaucrats, military personnel are among the selfish rent seekers. Among other things, they must view with special alarm any developments that suggest even a remote threat to national security so that the need for their services remains unquestioned.

You can elaborate on the above. The more complex point is that voters are assumed to vote to advance their own interests, electing legislators who respond to their desires. Legislators in turn are motivated by self-interest, which usually means a desire to be reelected, and so they vote to serve the interests of their special constituencies and to impose the costs on others insofar as possible. The pressures on legislators to expand government and thus add to its costs are far greater than any pressure to cut back, especially since expansion can continue on the basis of borrowed money rather than on the basis of taxes if need be.

John A. Ferejohn puts the Buchanan/Tullock thesis to an empirical test by examining the record of Congress and gives it some credence. The processes of Congress are, of course, more complicated than the description above suggests. Above all, assignments to committees and subcommittees are important, with chairpersons having special powers. The record indicates that members of Congress are likely to be able to use the power provided by their votes and their committee assignments to get special favors for their districts or their states (Ferejohn 1974, 233–52). At the same time, it should be recognized that majorities and committees can block expenditures as well as provide for them. More generally, check-and-balance arrangements put limits on what the self-interested can do.

To some it is a witticism that the state is a "fictitious entity by which everybody tries to live at the expense of everybody else," but *public choice* theorists are deadly serious about this thought. To them, that is precisely what goes on. The witticism, incidentally, is found in the work of Bastiat, a French author who died in 1850.

## Qualifications

If the above were the sum total of the argument, the conclusions would be fairly easy to draw: those being rational about formulating a constitution for a democracy had better restrict government to the minimum essential powers. And Buchanan and Tullock usually give the impression that this is in fact their conclusion.

But selfishness (including rent seeking) is not the whole story. Even when emphasizing selfishness, Tullock grants that "in private life people are willing to give away perhaps five percent of their incomes to help the poor or other worthy causes." And he assumes that a comparable willingness—even if a bit more restricted—operates in public life. Whether you think in terms of 5 percent of the GNP or 5 percent of the federal budget, that makes possible a great deal of altruism.

Further, Tullock identifies issues on which people take stands even though they have little or no personal interest at stake, or at least little or no immediate interest. In fact, he says that "the bulk of the people voting on any given issue have no particular selfish motive.... They will vote in terms of the public interest." They want to provide for national defense and thus to maintain an armed establishment. They want to maintain a system of unbiased courts. They support or oppose certain policies relating to the treatment of homosexual persons and relating to abortion, even if they have nothing at stake personally. They may share an interest with so many people that action to promote it is indistinguishable from action to promote a public good, as when they support a governmental weather service or a social security program or the development of a highway system. Moreover, people are divided on many issues, or lack relevant knowledge or interest, leaving their representatives in Congress to vote what they regard as the national interest.

Tullock wrote a whole book on *Private Wants, Public Means.* The subtitle of the book is what is most significant here: *An Economic Analysis of the Desirable Scope of Government* (1970). The book concerns mainly the problem of externalities.

A high proportion of our activities involve some kind of an externality: doing anything that affects public health or safety, getting an education or failing to do so, improving a property or letting it run down or using it in such a way as to affect the value of surrounding properties, creating noise or polluting the environment, establishing a business, building a road, going nude in public, extracting oil from a pool that extends under the property of a neighbor, doing anything that causes large numbers of people to assemble or to flee, and so on and on.

Harmful externalities raise the question of governmental action. Should government regulate, prohibit, or tax the activity, or should it let private parties work the problem out by themselves? What are the prospects that the benefits of governmental action will justify the costs? Tullock does not offer a clearcut prescription, but he accepts the principle that government is needed to handle some of the problems that externalities create. Government is not all bad.

Buchanan also qualifies his jaundiced view of government and his assumptions concerning the virtues of the market. The fact shows up in his treatment of equality of opportunity, meager as that treatment is. He takes the view that rational utility-maximizers who work out a constitution would want to "establish institutional structures within which some equalization of starting positions may be encouraged.... Constitutional design might allow for institutions that take some of the more apparent rough edges off gross inequalities in starting positions." It might, for example, tax inheritances and gifts and provide for governmentally financed education. The enjoyment of "fair chances," he says, "is vitally important in the generation of personal attitudes toward the 'justice' of any social order." He thinks that "libertarians go too far ... when they reject ... constitutional ... arrangements that act to promote some rough equality in pre-market positions and act so as to knock off the edges of post-market extremes."

## The Prescription

In 1986, in connection with the receipt of a Nobel prize in "economic science," Buchanan gave a lecture (1988) in which he focused on the idea of the "transfer state"—the state that transfers wealth from one group to another. He divides the transfers into two categories, although granting that the categories overlap, and on this basis he speaks of the "welfare state" and the "churning state." The welfare state, of course, transfers wealth from the better off to the worse off. The churning state transfers it from the politically weak to the politically strong, benefiting those rent seekers who manage to organize into interest groups strong enough to use government for their private advantage.

Buchanan holds that "no justification can be mounted for the transfers of the churning state." And the implication is that the utility-maximizing persons who are rational and logical in formulating a constitution would constrain government—limit its powers—so as to prevent "churning," or at least so as to keep it at a minimum.

In the lecture, Buchanan devotes much more space to the welfare state. He speaks of its "quasi-legitimacy," granting that rational people drafting a constitution might think it morally desirable to authorize government to help those in need. Nevertheless, he has doubts about the wisdom of the concession. And he forgets his earlier view that a constitution might well authorize government to "act to promote some rough equality in pre-market positions and act so as to knock off the edges of post-market extremes." In the Nobel lecture he holds that once political leaders are authorized to make transfer payments of any sort they are irresistibly tempted into undue generosity to more and more people. At the same time, they are loath to impose taxes, so fiscal difficulties develop. Further, the benefits, given out widely and generously, undermine the work ethic, and the associated rules may actively discourage work; at the same time, such taxes as are imposed discourage work on the part of those required to pay. On top of the other evils, welfare programs tend to accentuate rent seeking and churning as people who are not in need come more and more to look to government for their well-being.

I might note parenthetically that Buchanan speaks elsewhere of "the confiscation through taxation of goods that [the citizen] treats as 'his own,'" implying that the right to property is absolute. Some of his statements are suggestive of President Reagan: "Lower tax rates encourage saving, investing, working, and risk-taking.... As people respond to the higher after-tax income and wealth, or greater profitability, incomes rise and the tax base grows, thus feeding back some of the lost revenues to the Treasury." Buchanan also objects to governmental regulatory activities—at least to some of them; he speaks of the regulation of the trucking industry by the Interstate Commerce Commission as "an invasion of the natural liberty" of those who might want to participate in it. Like Friedman, he objects to the licensing of businesses and professions, tariffs and subsidies relating to foreign trade, union-shop restrictions in labor contracts, and other interventions in the market.

In the Nobel lecture, Buchanan does not offer a solution to the problems that he describes. He emphasizes that those receiving benefits, or expecting to receive them, are likely to be adamant in opposing adverse change; social security, for example, has become politically sacrosanct. And he grants that perhaps we should not entirely dismantle the welfare state even if we could. "But we can trim its edges, we can stop the bleeding, and, above all, we can work at restoring that sense of basic values that deems productive effort in the marketplace as 'good' and that scorns the receipt of governmental handouts as unworthy."

Buchanan makes no comparable suggestion with respect to the churning state even though the transfers that characterize it are greater than the transfers associated with the welfare state and even though he does not grant the churning state even quasilegitimacy. In a later publication, however, he extols what he calls *constitutionalism*. The constitutionalists, prizing liberty and regarding everyone as a rational utility-maximizer, want severely to limit the role of government. Buchanan contrasts rent seeking and constitutionalism, saying that Reagan flubbed a chance to shift from the one to the other. He hopes for a "return to some semblance of the eighteenth-century wisdom about the potential for abuse of political authority," and he dreams of the "strictly protective state." He wants to "promulgate and instill and transmit the 'civic religion' of traditional classical liberalism, in which the self-reliant individual remains jealous of his own liberty and confident of his own ability to secure his own welfare under the legal umbrella of a constitutionally constrained state."

## Critique

Public choice theory has critics as well as supporters. No one denies that self-interest, including rent seeking, plays a significant role in politics, but most observers believe that public choice theorists accentuate the negatives. Most observers dwell on what I called "qualifications" earlier, made mainly by Tullock. Fears based on what the majority of the voters will do are clearly unfounded. Voters rarely vote on projects that directly concern their well-being. They vote for members of town councils, state legislatures, Congress, and so on. And studies of electoral behavior do not support the view that they vote their pocketbooks. Checking on this question, Sears and several colleagues find that "symbolic attitudes [are] consistently much more important than self interest in determining policy preferences." "Symbolic attitudes" relate, for example, to "party identification, liberal or conservative ideology, nationalism, or racial prejudice." Such factors are "the main predictors of respondents' policy attitudes; self-interest contributes only trivially" (Sears et al. 1980, 673). Kinder and Kiewiet arrive at a similar finding (1979). Buchanan and Tullock would have done better to emphasize the role of interest groups rather than the selfishness of individual voters.

But even the role of interest groups can be exaggerated. Kelman takes up the role of self-interest theories generally and argues that they "have a difficult time explaining most of what has been important in American politics over the past twenty years." He holds that "as a general rule, self-interest becomes a less powerful influence as the importance of a policy choice increases" (Reich 1988, 390). "The story of government growth in the 1960s and of its limitation in the 1980s," he says, " ... are both stories of the power of ideas." He calls persuasiveness "the most underrated political resource," and he points out that a desire to contribute to the public good is an important motive of many civil servants and political leaders. Even those who are in fact out to serve their own interests through government normally have to justify themselves by claiming that what they want is for the public good (Kelman 1987, 239–40, 251–61).

Mueller points out that if self-interest theories are correct, and if redistribution is from the rich to the poor, then all those with incomes above the median should vote against the redistribution policies and all those with incomes below the median should vote in favor. But this is clearly not what happens (1989, 456–57). Schultze grants that people and legislators vote their self-interest, particularly on matters that affect them starkly and directly, but they also have views about the public good. People who favor gun control, a large defense budget, capital punishment, and balanced budgets are not trying to maximize their own utilities (1977, 67).

Orren stresses not rent seeking but the importance of widely shared values as the engine behind such successful social movements as the environmental movement and such major pieces of legislation as the civil rights acts (Reich 1988, 26–28). Reich cites public policies in a number of areas, including some of those mentioned earlier, and contends that they "were not motivated principally or even substantially by individuals seeking to satisfy selfish interests. To the contrary, they were broadly understood as matters of public rather than private interest." He thinks that in politics people "put aside personal interests to a surprising degree" (1989, 261, 269).

James Q. Wilson has looked at the question by examining the *Federalist Papers,* particularly the contributions of James Madison.

> Though Madison's view of human nature was certainly sober, it was not bleak. In various places (Nos. 40, 55, 57) Madison suggests that interests alone do not drive citizens. "As there is a degree of depravity in mankind which requires a certain circumspection and distrust: So there are other qualities in human nature which justify a certain portion of esteem and confidence" [No. 55]. In particular, there seems to be "sufficient virtue" to make republican government possible. (Wilson 1990, 559)

Wilson goes on to say that public choice theories "tend to understate the power of motives, such as duty or fairness, which seem at odds with any conception of immediate self-interest. . . . " He thinks that "many contemporary political scientists systematically understate the role of deliberation, the influence of norms, and the power of passion in human affairs. . . . " For example, many people vote even though the chance that their vote will make a difference is so remote that it would be in their interest to use their time and energy in another way. People take stands on many issues, and may be intensely aroused over them, even when they have no personal interest at stake—on the issue of abortion, for example. Candidates differ in the stands they take even when rational calculation would lead them all to "move to the center of every discernible preference distribution."

Further, Wilson points out that legislators appeal to motives in addition to self-interest and argues that this is significant.

> Legislators defend their votes or criticize those of others by making arguments about justice, fairness, and the public good. These arguments may be dismissed as rationalizations, as they often are, but they are not mere rationalizations; the fact that they are employed

means that people are affected by them, and if they are affected by them, then their behavior can be altered by them. If none of us took seriously an argument about fairness or the common good, we would ignore—or laugh at—all such arguments, and soon they would no longer be employed. (561)

And although interest groups of a utility-maximizing sort are formed, so are *pro bono* groups, some of them large. Moreover, people support certain kinds of interest groups—for example, those representing ethnic, national, or racial communities—even though the payoff for them as individuals is at best highly uncertain.

Wilson concludes by quoting Madison's statement that "the aim of every political constitution is or ought to be first to obtain for rulers, men who possess most wisdom to discern, and most virtue to pursue, the common good of the society; and in the next place, to take the most effectual precautions for keeping them virtuous, whilst they continue to hold their public trust." Wilson's summary of Madison's view is that "man is sufficiently self-interested and calculating as to make checks and balances necessary but sufficiently virtuous and deliberative as to make it possible to design and operate a constitution that supplies and maintains that system of restraints."

# Chapter 9

# Conservative Conservatism

I F YOU SEE a statement that conservatives believe this or that, beware. Conservatives, or at least people who call themselves conservatives, differ so much among themselves that generalizations covering all of them are suspect; conservatives do not even classify into neat categories, for many are eclectic, selecting and combining conservative ideas in different ways.

But a classification scheme is possible if we think of kinds of conservatism rather than kinds of conservatives—that is, if we think of classifying ideas rather than persons. At the same time, for illustrative purposes we can cite some individuals who identify themselves prominently with the ideas in question. Given this perspective, five kinds of conservatism suggest themselves: conservative, economic, social, progressive, and neo-. This chapter is devoted to conservative conservatism; succeeding chapters are devoted to the other four kinds.

I hesitate about the term *conservative conservatism* for obvious reasons, but consider it appropriate. If some conservatives call themselves progressive (Canada has a Progressive Conservative Party), is it not logical to think that others can properly be called conservative? *Traditionalist conservatism* is the most likely alternative name. *Standpat conservatism* would not do, for few conservatives insist on standing pat. Conservative conservatives are sometimes referred to as adherents of the Old Right.

My objective in this chapter is to characterize and appraise conservative conservatism.

## Distrust of Rationalism

Note that the reference is to the distrust of *rationalism,* not to the distrust of rationality or of reason. Conservative conservatives join almost everyone else in prizing rationality and making use of reason. What they deplore, they call *rationalism.*

In the chapter on libertarianism I mentioned Hayek's scorn for "constructivist rationalism"—his scorn for the belief that we can rationally "create the future of mankind." His main point was that we are so ignorant of so much that it is unwise to fix on general social goals and attempt to pursue them in a coordinated way. Better to let individuals look after their own interests, producing unplanned social results as a kind of incidental by-product.

Conservative conservatives hold a similar view, illustrated by Michael Oakeshott (1962). Oakeshott divides knowledge into two categories, giving the categories labels that are not very helpful—technical knowledge and practical knowledge. Technical knowledge is the kind that can be articulated in a clear and explicit way, and practical knowledge is knowledge of tradition, akin to understanding and wisdom, reflecting what the generations have found to be acceptable. Those who command technical knowledge, according to Oakeshott, are tempted to believe that they can get unerring guidance from it in the pursuit of chosen ends. In contrast, practical knowledge is vaguer, even if more profound, not lending itself to concise expression. It corresponds to the artistry of pianists, as opposed to their technique.

According to Oakeshott, rationalists may command technical knowledge, but they neglect practical knowledge. Wrongly believing that technical knowledge is enough to justify their leadership, they adopt general social goals and prescribe courses of action for achieving them. But, like as not, their decisions turn out to be bad, and they do harm rather than good.

The position is easily illustrated. Oakeshott names Marx and Engels as "the authors of the most stupendous of our political rationalisms" (1962, 26). They developed a grand theory presuming to explain an array of social ills, and their work led to the communist movement and all the harm that it has done to so many countries and people. Robert Owen did not do as much harm, but he was guilty of rationalism in writing about Utopia, and so were the French revolutionaries when they called for the deliberate reconstruction of society. In truth, all those who want to reconstruct society on the basis of a theory or principle or rule (for example, that human rights should be observed or that national self-determination should be granted) are rationalists and therefore dangerous. They are acting on the basis of technical knowledge that is necessarily limited.

Rationalism is all the more dangerous when it gives rise to ideologies and to fanaticism in supporting them, as with Marxism-Leninism.

Ideologies save people from thinking and tend to inspire support as a matter of blind faith. They lead to intolerance, for rationalists find it "difficult to believe that anyone who can think honestly and clearly will think differently from [themselves]." They are likely to regard the past as an encumbrance, somehow to be overcome, for they want to start anew—to see unrolled before them a "blank sheet of infinite possibility. And if by chance this tabula rasa has been defaced by the irrational scribblings of tradition-ridden ancestors, then the first task of the rationalist must be to scrub it clear; as Voltaire remarked, the only way to have good laws is to burn all existing laws and to start afresh" (Oakeshott 1962, 2, 5). Conservative conservatives find this appalling.

An ideology is especially dangerous when it calls for the concentration of power, whether in the state or in any other organization. Russell Kirk expresses the view in saying, with respect to the United States, that "in politics, conservatives should labor energetically to resist centralization of power and to restore to state governments and to local agencies, so far as possible, the functions constitutionally assigned to them.... In economic policies, the conservative approach is to encourage small-scale and competitive enterprise, and to cease to favor economic concentration and oligopoly" (Kirk 1990, 24). Freedom is to be prized, and the most general condition of freedom is the diffusion of power, maintaining diversity and competition. Kirk bewails "the decay of community, particularly at the level of the 'little platoon'" prized by Burke. Subsidiarity should be the rule, with everything done at the lowest feasible level. In the United States, the trend toward centralizing powers and functions in the federal government ought to be reversed. Central planning ("the ideal of all rationalistic politics") is anathema. The ultimate evil toward which rationalism tends is totalitarianism.

## Preference for the Known

Russell Kirk quotes a statement contrasting conservatives and liberals: conservatives are enamored of existing evils, whereas liberals want to replace them with others. Kirk himself speaks of conservatives as "a loose league of people who prefer the devil they know to the devil they don't," and Honderich caricatures conservatives by saying that, according to them, "nothing should be done for the first time." George Will quotes the statement of a Frenchman that if a conservative had been present at the Creation, he would have exclaimed, "Mon Dieu, conserve le chaos!"

These statements suggest a central feature of conservative conservatism: a preference for the known, for the traditional—a preference tempered by prudence. The preference appears in the works of Edmund Burke, described by Kirk as the "founder of modern conservatism." Burke's "central premise" was that it is "inexpedient to tamper with existing institutions without good cause. . . . 'I feel an insuperable reluctance,' he told the Commons, 'in giving my hand to destroy any established institution of government, upon a theory, however plausible it may be.'" He wanted to "distinguish between a profound, slow, natural alteration and some infatuation of the hour. . . . Even the wisest and shrewdest of men are ridiculously conceited if they presume to set the products of their reason against the judgment of the centuries" (Burke 1966, 150, 152). From his point of view, revolutionaries are "at war with nature," seeking to "change and pervert the natural order of things" (Lock 1985, 15). He identified what exists with the natural. By this standard, slavery in the United States was natural, and so was the system of apartheid in South Africa.

Oakeshott recommends a similar attitude in saying that the characteristics of what he calls the conservative disposition "center upon a propensity to use and enjoy what is available rather than to wish for or look for something else; to delight in what is present rather than what was or what may be."

> To be conservative . . . is to prefer the familiar to the unknown, to prefer the tried to the untried, fact to mystery, the actual to the possible, the limited to the unbounded, the convenient to the perfect, present laughter to utopian bliss. Familiar relationships and loyalties will be preferred to the allure of more profitable attachments. . . . (1962, 168–69)

Implied in the preference for the known is a reluctance about change. "Hasty innovation," warns Kirk, "may be a devouring conflagration, rather than a torch of progress." "Heaven," according to Oakeshott, "is the dream of a changeless no less than a perfect world." The attitude translates into a respect for tradition and custom, for they reflect what people have in practice found to be tolerable. Burke expressed the attitude in saying that society is to be regarded as "a partnership not only between those who are living but between those who are living, those who are dead, and those who are to be born." And Kirk reflected it in saying that "we have no right to imperil the happiness of posterity by impudently tinkering with the heritage of humanity." G.K. Chesterton put a different spin on the same idea in saying that the emphasis on tradition amounts to an extension of the franchise to ancestors and thus to an acceptance of the democracy of the dead.

Kirk and some others follow Burke in commending not only tradition but also prejudice and prescription. They do not think of prejudice in the usual sense of bias founded on ignorance. Prejudice is to them an intuition reflecting the wisdom of the past—what the generations that preceded us learned. Prescription is a method by which rights or titles are gained or lost: a usage followed long enough creates a custom, and a custom followed long enough creates a prescriptive right. A prescriptive right is a "customary right which grows out of the conventions and compacts of many successive generations." Prejudice and prescription are good.

## Change

Although conservative conservatives are reluctant about change, they recognize that it is inevitable and, in a sense, desirable. The present is itself "the latest point reached by the past in a continuous, seamless growth," and growth should continue. "Change," according to Kirk, "is the means of society's conservation, just as the human body exhausts its old tissue and puts on new. But the conservative statesman goes about this delicate task of guiding society from old forms into new only with caution and prudence" (Burke 1966, xviii). The problem is how to distinguish "healthy change from the processes of dissolution." Kirk is scornful of those who think that conservatives have difficulty coming to terms with modernity.

Oakeshott suggests an approach to the problem of judging which changes are desirable. First he defines politics as "the activity of attending to the general arrangements of a set of people," emphasizing the idea of "attending to" rather than "making" arrangements (1962, 112). His view is that these arrangements are not made in a deliberate and self-conscious way but that they evolve incrementally. If they appear to be introduced suddenly in one country, as in France at the time of the French Revolution, the appearance is at least in part deceptive, for many of the old arrangements continue and what is new is a small proportion of the whole. Moreover, many of the seemingly new arrangements evolved in a kindred society where they were put to the test of time.

In Oakeshott's view, we should not accept ideology as a guide. Instead, we should look for intimations in existing arrangements—intimations that something about these arrangements is out of tune with the rest, that an incoherence exists, that a "sympathy" needs to be more fully expressed. In such circumstances, change is to be sought —change that reduces incoherence, change that brings one aspect of life into fuller harmony with the rest, change that responds to an already existing "sympathy."

The illustration that Oakeshott offers concerns the extension of the suffrage to women. He denies that this was a question of giving effect to a natural or human right or a question of justice; instead, the need for change relating to the suffrage was intimated by other changes that had already been accepted concerning human equality and the role of women. It was a question of moving toward consistency or coherence (1962, 123–24).

Not that we always know which of the intimated changes is desirable. Conservatives see no way to escape the need for judgment in these matters, but caution is the rule—caution in lawmaking, for example. Joseph Sobran makes the point in recalling Aristotle's recommendation that there should be few laws, seldom changed: "This is so for several reasons. One is that those laws are best that require least enforcement—laws that are rooted in the moral habits of the citizens.... Another is that it is a general function of rules, tacit or explicit, to make social life predictable. If the law itself is unpredictable, it loses its appropriate character.... Moreover ... positive law should have the quality of seeming to be discovered or elicited from tacit moral understandings commonly shared, rather than imposed by an effort of will" (Sobran 1985, 28).

An implication of the above is that social engineering is to be avoided, although what should count as "social engineering" is uncertain. Presumably incremental change should not. Even when the cumulative effect of many incremental changes over a period of years is profound, it should not count as social engineering. But deliberate and self-conscious innovation on an extensive scale, occurring in a limited period of time, should. On this basis the development and spread of Christianity, and the development of the Catholic Church, was not social engineering, but the adoption of the Constitution of the United States was.

## Ideology, Tradition, and God's Will

Oakeshott and Kirk both deny that their kind of conservatism is an ideology. Oakeshott speaks of a conservative disposition and Kirk of a conservative approach and conservative principles.

It is no wonder that Kirk abhors ideology, for he defines and characterizes it in a way that makes it automatically bad. An ideology, he says, is a "sham religion and sham philosophy." It is "hostile to enduring order and justice and freedom." Ideological politics is "the politics of passionate unreason," leading to "fanaticism and utopian schemes." Ideology is dogmatic, promising paradise but actually creating hell (Kirk 1993, 1, 5–6, 9).

Kirk ignores the possibility, described above in chapter 1, that *ideology* may be defined as a coherent set of ideas and principles designed to guide action, that is, as action-oriented theory. So defined, an ideology may have the bad characteristics of which Kirk speaks, but need not. To use a term that Kirk likes, it may even be prudent.

Kirk's rejection of ideology has a possible basis apart from any special definition. In a sense, the rejection goes with the preference for the known and thus with a preference for what is traditional or customary. Acceptance of this preference makes for what Samuel P. Huntington calls a situational definition of conservatism—conservatism being supportive of different principles and practices depending on the situation confronted (1957, 455). After all, what is known or what is traditional or customary is bound to vary in different times and places. What is traditional in Britain today differs from what was traditional when George III ruled, and what is traditional in the United States differs from what is traditional in India. Thus, conservative conservatism calls for the denial of women's suffrage at one time and the grant of it at another. It calls for acceptance of a form of egalitarianism in one country and the acceptance of a caste system in another. "Paradoxical as it may seem," Huntington says, "conservatism, the defender of tradition, is itself without tradition" (1957, 469). Depending on time and place, conservative conservatism calls for the acceptance of differing sets of arrangements.

Edmund Burke illustrated this feature of conservatism. In preferring the known, he was thinking of what is known in each community or society. He did not contend that what was known in Britain should be extended over the world. The idea that prejudice is virtuous and the idea that prescription is to be respected applies not to just one set of prejudices or one set of prescriptive rights but to the different prejudices and prescriptions of different countries and different traditions. Every social order is the product of long evolution and is to be respected.

With respect to the people of India, for example, Burke's contention was "that we, if we must govern such a country, must govern them upon their own principles and maxims, not upon ours; that we must not think to force them to our narrow ideas" (Newman 1927,

189). They must be governed by "some mode of justice ... correspondent with their religion, correspondent with their manners." Britain should keep the disturbance of their way of life at a minimum (Marshall 1965, 181). Thus conservative conservatives can be expected to uphold different customs, rules, and principles depending on the time and place in question. They cannot be guided by any one ideology other than respect for tradition and custom.

The above view of conservatism leads to the view that conserving is its central feature. Daniel Patrick Moynihan takes this view, and goes on to comment that sometimes conservatives conserve liberalism (1986, 66). In recent years, too, frequent references occur to "conservative communists" in what was the Soviet Union. And according to Gottfried and Fleming, "it is possible to regard conservatism as a series of trenches dug in defense of last year's revolution" (1988, xv).

But in stressing tradition and custom, conservative conservatism gets itself into a contradiction, for some traditions and customs turn out to be unacceptable. Whatever Burke may have thought, Kirk and Oakeshott make it clear that they are not willing to be indiscriminate in what they accept. They want to be selective. Kirk provides a basis for this position in going beyond the features of conservatism so far described—the distrust of rationalism, the preference for the known, the reluctance about change—and adding others.

A major additional feature is a concern for religion, or at least for the idea of a transcendent, enduring moral order. Kirk calls for deference to the divine intent that, he believes, "rules society as well as conscience, forging an eternal chain of right and duty which links great and obscure, living and dead." Man and the state are both "creations of God's beneficence," and "God's purpose among men is revealed through the unrolling of history" (1974, 140). With obvious sympathy, Kirk cites Burke's view that the foundation of social tranquility is reverence.

At bottom, Kirk thinks, political problems are moral problems, and the great division in modern politics is between those who accept and those who reject this view. Virtue is a prime concern. Writing at mid-century, Kirk thought that during the remainder of the century one of the principal problems for conservatives to address was "the problem of spiritual and moral regeneration; the restoration of the ethical system and the religious sanction upon which any life worth living is founded" (1953, 414). He considers churches important, along with other institutions intermediate between the individual and the state. This is not the outlook of a person who wants to uphold custom and tradition regardless of their nature.

Note the statement quoted earlier that God's will is revealed "through the unrolling of history." This contrasts with the claim of some evangelical Christians that God's will is revealed to them personally as a response to their prayer—a claim that is a potential basis for an authoritarian theocracy. It also contrasts with the claim advanced by some that they have reliable knowledge of natural law and can therefore tell you what it requires. Further, it contrasts with the position that liberals are most likely to take: that people do and should decide for themselves what is moral and immoral—what is right and what is wrong—and that public standards (to which individuals may demur) are those on which a substantial consensus is achieved. Kirk rejects all of these positions. "How are we to know God's mind and will? Through the prejudices and traditions which millennia of human experience with divine means and judgments have implanted in the mind of the species" (Kirk 1986, 29). This suggests that Kirk is an empiricist, looking simply to history to determine the kind of social order to support.

But given the emphasis on a transcendent, enduring moral order, Kirk cannot be strictly empirical. Customs and traditions are not necessarily of equal merit. Although asking what history teaches, Kirk also emphasizes the role of "intuitive reason" in providing a standard for determining what is good and what is bad (Kirk 1986, 137). The implications become clear when Kirk refers scornfully to references to conservative communists. Communists who want to conserve communism are not conservative.

According to conservative conservatives, once the principles of good and bad are identified, they are absolute. Relativism is the enemy. The truths that American conservatism advances are allegedly immutable and the values immemorial—sustained through four thousand years of Judeo-Christian civilization (Cribb 1990, 24).

Kirk describes conservatives as chastened by the thought that human beings are imperfect and doomed to remain imperfect. The idea is akin to the idea of original sin. And, given the principle that people are imperfect, no perfect social order can ever be created. "To aim for utopia is to end in disaster." Kirk contrasts his own position with that of "radicals" who, he thinks, are not sufficiently deterred by the human tendency toward depravity, sin, and violence and believe that education, positive legislation, and the alteration of the environment can make men like gods.

In various ways Kirk stresses the importance of property and rejects most kinds of egalitarianism. Property and freedom, he holds, are closely linked, so a socioeconomic hierarchy is to be expected and accepted (1986, 9). Variety is desirable, and "for the preservation of a healthy diversity in any civilization, there must survive orders and classes, differences in material condition, and many sorts of inequality" (1993, 20). Any attempt at leveling invites social stagnation. Kirk cites Burke's view that "nature has furnished society with the materials for an aristocracy which the wisely-conducted state will recognize and honor, always reserving, however, a counterpoise to aristocratic ambition" (1986, 61–62). Among other things, the natural aristocracy can be expected to uphold a moral order of obligation and personal responsibility, which is "essential to the survival of a democracy."

Although concerned about democracy in the United States, Kirk notes shortcomings, and he refrains from championing democracy for the world. "The vaunted 'democratic freedom' of liberal society," he says, "in reality is servitude to appetites and illusions which attack religious belief; which destroy community through excessive centralization and urbanization; which efface life-giving tradition and custom." He is caustic about what he calls the Welfare Lobby: "Democracy amounts to the opportunity to plunder other people—that is, the general public; for hasn't the American democracy a limitless supply of money and goods, the products of exploitation, the rightful spoil of enterprising egalitarians? Doesn't everybody deserve more of everything, and isn't the apparatus of taxation well designed to secure that more for tolerably-organized factions?" (1993, 281).

The attitudes of both Kirk and Oakeshott raise the question whether the traditional comes up to date or includes only the principles and practices of an age gone by. Huntington holds that Kirk is so unhappy with so many aspects of the current situation that he is reactionary rather than conservative. "Instead of a vigorous defense of American constitutional democracy, Kirk's books are filled with a strained, sentimental, nostalgic, antiquarian longing for a society which is past." He seeks "to conserve an intellectual tradition which does not exist rather than institutions which do exist" (Huntington 1957, 471–72).

The same kind of problem arises concerning Oakeshott. On the one hand, he seems to be what Huntington calls a situational conservative. He says that the wellspring of the conservative disposition "is to be found in the acceptance of the current condition of human circumstances." Now the "current condition" includes an expectation that government will engage in various substantive activities designed to promote full employment and the general welfare.

But, on the other hand, in 1948 Oakeshott censured another conservative who approved governmental action to rearrange incentives

in industry, and he used language suggesting that the other conservative—and conservatives generally—had sold out to the enemy: "The
bug of rationalistic politics," he said, "has bitten the Conservative."
True conservatism, in Oakeshott's view, called for a "policy of diffus-
ing all those morbid concentrations of power which have grown up in
our society during the last fifty years" (Oakeshott 1948, 488). In other
words, far from accepting the "current condition of human circumstances," he wanted to go back to the conditions that prevailed at the
turn of the century.

Further, Oakeshott spoke of governing as "a specific and limited
activity, namely the provision and custody of general rules of conduct." The statement is suggestive of Hayek. Government is to be
"limited." It is to lay down rules of conduct, but the rules are to be
"general." Oakeshott went on to say that the general rules of conduct
"are to be understood, not as plans for imposing substantive activities,
but as instruments enabling people to pursue the activities of their
own choice with a minimum of frustration" (Oakeshott 1962, 184).
The fact is, of course, that the British government has been "imposing
substantive activities" for a century, and the U.S. government has been
doing so at least since the time of the New Deal.

Moreover, Oakeshott made a number of other statements suggesting that he wanted to restore the conditions not simply of the turn
of the century but of the century before that. For example, he held
that "the office of government is merely to rule." And "the image of
the ruler is the umpire whose business is to administer the rules of the
game, or the chairman who governs the debate according to known
rules but does not himself participate in it." In the economic realm,
"the main (perhaps the only) ... activity appropriate to government is
the maintenance of a stable currency" (1962, 186–87, 190–91).

These views are reactionary. They do not reflect an acceptance of
the circumstances prevailing when Oakeshott wrote. In truth, it is
questionable whether the circumstances that he idealized ever existed,
for government has rarely if ever confined itself to the role of an umpire. The strong presumption has always been that the persons or
groups controlling government will use it in a way that, as a minimum, is compatible with their interests and, more probably, in a way
that advances those interests. The question is not whether government
can be an umpire but whose interests it upholds and promotes.

### "Fusionism"

Some conservative conservatives and some libertarians have raised the question whether "fusion" of the two outlooks is desirable and possible. Discussion of the question has sharpened the differences between them; and the usual answer is no.

Nisbet speaks of the two as "uneasy cousins" (Carey 1984, 13–24). They perceive people differently. Libertarians pulverize society into a sandheap of individual particles, thus endangering the social order and setting the stage for collectivist nationalism. Conservatives, in contrast, are more concerned with "the natural groups within which individuals invariably live—family, locality, church, region, social class, nation, etc." Conservatives attach importance to such groups and want to maintain them. Libertarians make liberty the highest of all social values, whereas conservatives make it one among a number of values, subject to restriction when it undermines national security, the moral order, or the social fabric. Implicitly the conservatives, though wanting to limit the power of the state, nevertheless attach importance to authority in society and want it maintained.

Kirk is likewise critical of the idea of fusion (1993, 156–71). He regards libertarians as "radical doctrinaires, contemptuous of our inheritance from our ancestors." They are "philosophical anarchists in bourgeois dress." They reject the idea of a "transcendent moral order, ... admitting no transcendent sanctions for conduct." Stressing individualism, they say that the nexus of society is self-interest, whereas conservatives declare that "society is a community of souls" cohering through what Aristotle called friendship and Christians call love of neighbor. Libertarians generally believe that human nature is good, whereas conservatives hold that "in Adam's fall we sinned all" and that, although human nature includes good features, it cannot be perfected. Libertarians treat the state as the great oppressor, whereas conservatives regard the state as a necessary instrument for conducting the common defense, restraining the unjust and the passionate, and carrying on a variety of undertakings important to the general welfare. Libertarians give reign to "the ego, with its appetites and self-assertive passions," whereas conservatives stress duty, discipline, and sacrifice. The cosmos of the libertarian is "an arid, loveless realm," whereas conservatives join Marcus Aurelius in believing that "we are made for cooperation, like the hands, like the feet." "What the doctrinaire libertarian offers us is an ideology of universal selfishness—at a time when the country needs more than ever before men and women who stand ready to subordinate their private interests, if need be, to the defense of the Permanent Things."

# Chapter 10

# Economic Conservatism

E CONOMIC CONSERVATIVES concern themselves primarily with material well-being, naming growth and development as their goal—a flourishing economy, prosperity. They obviously share this goal with many others. They set themselves apart in decrying turns made in the past that in their view militate against economic growth—turns toward "big government," higher taxes, increased regulation of business and commercial life, and the redistribution of wealth in the name of equality and welfare. They want to restore emphasis on individual liberty, private property, the free market, personal responsibility, and political decentralization. From their point of view, it is bad enough to increase the functions of government at the local level, worse to do it at the state level, and intolerable to do it at the federal level. If at all possible, government should be cut down in size, taxes and the regulatory activities of government should be reduced, and laws leading to "excessive" litigation should be changed. Granting that government must provide a "safety net" and give aid to the "truly needy," economic conservatives are nevertheless hostile to "the welfare state," wanting (vaguely) to curtail or eliminate it. They approve governmental activism only against foreign dangers and domestic crime.

Despite the emphasis on the wrong turns of the past, economic conservatism is predominantly forward-looking. For example, President Reagan, treated by economic conservatives as their paragon, spoke of "morning in America" and repeatedly proclaimed that the best is yet to come.

The economic conservatism of President Reagan had a libertarian streak in it; he also embraced some features of social conservatism, to be described in the next chapter.

I should note that the claim that economic growth is the goal of economic conservatism does not stand unquestioned. For example, granting that growth was "the stated ultimate goal" during Reagan's period in the White House, Robert Solow denies that it was "the real goal." In his eyes, the real goal was "the redistribution of wealth in favor of the wealthy and of power in favor of the powerful." Solow goes on to cite areas in which the Reagan administration pursued the " real" goal—areas that I deal with below (Solow 1987, 182).

## Hostility to Government

The central features of economic conservatism are hostility to government and praise for individual liberty and the market. Hostility to government manifests itself mainly in hostility to taxes, regulatory activities, and certain welfare programs.

Reagan in his first inaugural declared, with respect to the economic ills of the country, that government is the problem, not the solution, and he said that he wanted to curb the size and influence of the federal establishment. A year later he said: "This can be an era of losing freedom or one of reclaiming it. I think we've made our choice and turned an historic corner. We're not going back to the glory days of big government.... The best view of big government is in a rearview mirror as we leave it behind." The function of government, he said, is "not to confer happiness on us but to give us the opportunity to work out happiness for ourselves." "The overwhelming goal of my administration is to put limits on the power of government.... " He aimed "to get the Federal Government out of your pockets and off your backs" (*Public Papers* 1982, 1:17; 1982, 2:1121; 1986, 1:38). The more extreme libertarians go farther, speaking of the state as the enemy.

Reagan's disparagement of government carries on a theme that Barry Goldwater espoused when running as the Republican candidate for president in 1964. Seeking "freedom at any cost," Goldwater wanted to "restore the restraints on the federal government which the framers of the Constitution intended to impose, [restricting it to its] proper role.... Our great reverence for freedom requires us to resist the use of power to coerce or control the individual beyond restraining him from inflicting injury on others" (Goldwater 1979, 14, 48, 99, 304).

Current members of the Senate play on the same theme. According to Senator Malcolm Wallop,

> Government touches almost everything in America and harms almost everything it touches.... Over one generation government has

doubled the amount of money it takes from us.... [It] has turned our public spaces over to criminals and our public schools into factories of ignorance. It has driven us apart on the basis of race and even of sex and, in the name of tolerance, has made us intolerant. ... Disdain for government is wise, patriotic—even lovely.... The dominant issue of our time is whether the state will grow or be cut back." (1994, 36, 41)

And Senator Phil Gramm wants to scale government back "not because it doesn't do anything right, but because it *can't* do anything right." It is irredeemably incompetent, so the more we dismantle it the better (Segal 1994, 40). The outlook is widespread enough that George Will speaks of "a kind of scorched-earth, pillage-and-burn conservatism that loathes government" (Will 1992, 180).

Michael Ledeen offers the view in colorful extreme: "Government must be slashed down to size, its gluttonous tentacles torn out of the body of society, its insidious poisons purged from the lifeblood of enterprise and education, its mindless bureaucrats blown away from their telephones and fax machines, its presses stopped, its linen washed, its babies and bathwater thrown out together in a great tidal wave of purifying destruction" (Ledeen 1992, 24). This view is indistinguishable from that of some libertarians, even though printed in a journal that can reasonably be classified as conservative.

Economic conservatives rarely say how much government they think we should have. Grover Norquist responds to the question by recalling the answer that Samuel Gompers, the labor leader, gave when asked what working Americans want: "More."

But Norquist turns the answer on its head: "What do we want? ... Less. And a year from now, what do we want? Less. And when we cut it [government] down by a third, what do we want? Less. And when we've cut it down by a half, what do we want? Less." Norquist calls for an end to the situation in which "22 percent of our GNP is going to be stolen from us by the federal government" (Barnes and Norquist 1991, 68). The 22 percent refers to the amount the federal government takes in taxes.

Note that the disparagement of government is ordinarily indiscriminate. It is not that government is ill suited to perform some particular functions or that it could do well given this or that reform; the usual claim is that government is all bad. Reagan himself, however, accepted some qualifications. Government is needed, he said, "to ensure that liberty does not become license to prey on each other." He accepted government as an instrument for combating fraud and crime and for dealing with the problem of externalities. And of course he accepted the need for government in providing for national security, a point on which I touch below.

One aspect of the disparagement of government is an antipathy toward "bureaucrats." The charge is the same as the one advanced by public choice theorists—that bureaucrats are self-serving careerists interested primarily not in the public good but in preserving their own jobs and the importance of their own agency. Any reduction in their budget is a threat to them, whereas an ever increasing budget is a source of security and a basis for personal pride and power.

Bureaucrats are also looked on as potentially corrupt. If their duties permit them to do favors, or include the letting of contracts, they act in their own self-interest. Perhaps they are angling for jobs with private firms; perhaps they are making payoffs to business concerns whose lobbyists invite them to nice vacation spots or even give them kickbacks or bribes. Theoretically, of course, political leaders and bureaucrats are all accountable to someone, so theoretically this kind of thing should be preventable. But some political leaders and some bureaucrats get into positions of such power as to make a mockery of the idea of accountability.

The counterpart of the disparagement of government and the bureaucracy is a glorification of individual liberty and the market. Thus Reagan spoke of "the need to develop a new state of mind, to look first not to what government can do to help, but to what we can do as individuals or private organizations." The key to progress is "individual initiative, leadership, and personal responsibility." Providing a basis for George Bush's later metaphor of "a thousand points of light," Reagan praised the work of "natural, voluntary associations." "Our economic system—based on individual freedom, private initiative, and free trade—has produced more human progress than any other in history."

Wanting to liberate the powers of the individual, above all of the entrepreneur, Reagan quoted George Gilder's statement that entrepreneurs are "the heroes of economic life," and he added that too often they are "forgotten heroes." He wanted to look to them instead of the federal planner, to the free-enterprise system instead of the bureaucracy. The best thing a government can do for a free people is to get out of their way.

It is curious that, despite hostility toward government and disdain for it, so many conservatives are nevertheless willing to serve in it, Reagan among them. Further, at the end of Reagan's second term, his political appointees were asked whether they wanted to return to private life or stay on with Bush; almost all of them wanted to stay on (Barnes and Norquist 1991, 69). It is impossible to know, of course, how many are deterred from entering public service in the first place because of antigovernment attitudes.

Surely, however, the disparagement of government must have consequences. Surely it undermines public trust in government and public willingness to support government through taxes and otherwise. Why support a bunch of selfish and bungling bureaucrats? And scorn must surely demoralize the "bureaucrats" themselves, leading many of the best of them to seek more satisfying employment. Whether hostility to government undermines respect for law is less certain. Although Reagan was referred to as the Teflon president, on whom scandal did not stick, his administration was nevertheless marked by scandal, suggesting the possibility that the lack of respect for government translated itself into a lack of respect for law.

Most notorious during Reagan's administration was the Iran-*contra* affair, marked by circumventions and violations of the law on the part of persons in and near the White House itself—circumventions and violations arising out of efforts to extend help to those in Nicaragua whom Reagan called "freedom fighters." More sordid was sleaze and outright corruption—the questionable or illegal use of government for personal gain, as in the Department of Housing and Urban Development and the Environmental Protection Agency.

The reasons that lead economic conservatives to favor reducing the functions of government are about the same as those influencing the libertarians. First, the coercions of government reduce liberty, and economic conservatives, like libertarians, are inclined to focus on the coercions rather than on the liberty-enhancing activities that are often their counterpart. Liberty is a major value—defined negatively as the absence of governmental restraint. Second, governmental decisions are too likely to be made on the basis of inadequate knowledge. The higher the level at which decisions are made, the greater the danger. The federal government is a special threat to the liberties and the interests of individuals and local communities. Third, as the other side of the coin, private persons, including entrepreneurs, are likely to use or invest their money more wisely and constructively than government will if it takes that money in taxes. Fourth, by implication, the farther you go toward an individualistic, *laissez-faire,* competitive system, the more efficient the system will be and the more likely to stimulate innovation and make for economic growth. And fifth, resistance is necessary to two related tendencies: the tendency of government to give favors to special interests while imposing the costs on others and the tendency to let every governmental program continue even after the need for it is gone.

I note above that Reagan faced a problem in that he wanted both to leave "big government" behind and to make government strong in the name of national security. The dilemma has plagued most conservatives. Did the danger posed by the Soviet Union, and the danger that communism might spread, justify a high level of military preparedness? The reluctant but determined answer of the economic conservatives, along with most other conservatives, was yes. And so in the decades following World War II conservatives found themselves in the uncomfortable position of both condemning "big government" and wanting it to be big enough to wage the Cold War effectively. And they were in the uncomfortable position of relying on government to promote military purposes while denying that it could be useful in promoting social and economic purposes.

One of the reactions to the end of the Cold War is that conservatives can once again be "unequivocal champions of small government." "No longer having to support a massive military establishment, conservatives can redeploy their most formidable artillery —strong philosophical principles rooted deeply in the lessons of history—to besiege the state grown fat during the Cold War.... [They] can insist, in scores of ways, on power devolving from the distant federal center back to localities" (Pines 1992, 23). They can resist the alleged tendency of liberals to "view life as a series of problems to be solved by government."

## Taxes

When Reagan said that he wanted to get government "out of your pockets," he of course meant that he wanted to reduce taxes. He was no doubt emboldened in his hope by the "tax revolt" that led California to adopt its Proposition 13 in 1978, limiting property taxes. Subsequently, more than a dozen other states adopted comparable measures. Bush dramatized the issue in the 1988 campaign, using the slogan, "Read my lips: No new taxes!" And sensitivity about taxes has become so acute that political leaders of both parties, and candidates for public office, have been exercising extreme caution with respect to it.

I discuss the subject under five headings: (1) taxation as theft; (2) tax rates and revenue; (3) taxation and prosperity; (4) Reagan's tax policies; and (5) tax expenditures.

## TAXATION AS THEFT

Reagan's statement about getting government "out of your pockets" implied a desire to lower taxes, but even more significantly it intimated that government has it hands where they do not belong, taking what is rightfully yours: taxation amounts to theft. Reagan seemed to believe this. He spoke literally of "theft" when inflation put people into higher income tax brackets, and he proposed "indexing," saying that this would prevent government "from stealing a greater percentage of your earnings" (*Public Papers* 1983, 1:415). It would keep people from being "robbed." Like Goldwater, he spoke of taxation as "confiscation" (Goldwater 1979, 54; *Public Papers* 1988–89, 2:1307). He said that government had "plundered" the earnings of small businessmen and workers.

Such language implies that taxation is morally unjustified and that government itself is illegitimate. Recall the rhetorical questions of Murray Rothbard, quoted in chapter 7: "What is the State anyway but organized banditry? What is taxation but theft on a gigantic, unchecked scale?" The implication is that those with income and property have an absolute right to it—a right not qualified by any obligation to society or to the government that provides for order and law.

## TAX RATES AND REVENUE

Hating taxes, but granting implicitly that they are going to be collected, economic conservatives insist that they be low. They disagree, however, about relationships between the tax rate and the amount of revenue produced. Sometimes the assumption is that revenue will go up or down along with tax rates, but sometimes it is that an inverse relationship is to be expected: revenue will go up when tax rates go down.

The assumption that tax rates and revenue vary directly with each other is rarely stated explicitly. It is implicit, however, in the view that taxes should not be raised even to reduce the deficit, the argument being that Congress will end up spending the extra money for other purposes. It is also implicit in the argument—advanced by Milton Friedman, among others—that tax rates should be reduced as a means of starving government of funds (Friedman 1991a, 54).

The more common question (this one often dealt with explicitly) is whether an inverse relationship exists between tax rates and the revenue produced—whether lower rates will produce greater revenue. Niskanen, whose economic conservatism includes a heavy dose of libertarianism, calls any claim of this sort "irresponsible" and says that "no administration economist or revenue projection" ever advanced it (1988, 313).

But supply-side theory, which economic conservatives generally endorse, encourages the belief, irresponsible as it may be. Supply-side theory contrasts with demand-side theory, that is, with Keynesianism. Keynes's theory is that the key to economic growth is in continued demand for goods and services. Given demand, production is maintained, investment is encouraged, and employment is high. Further, Keynes's prescription is that if popular demand slacks off, government should step in with expenditures of its own, perhaps expenditures on public works. Or perhaps government should reduce taxes, leaving more money in the hands of the consuming public and thus maintain or increase demand.

Supply-siders, as described by James Buchanan, put the focus not on demand but on incentives. "High income tax rates and regulation are seen as disincentives to work and production regardless of the level of demand." Buchanan illustrates the theory by pointing out that if a tariff rate is high enough, it eliminates any incentive to import the item to which it applies, which means that no economic activity occurs and no revenue is produced. In such circumstance a reduction in the tariff leads to both expanded economic activity and increased revenue, encouraging further investment (J. Buchanan 1989, 26).

The implication is that, just as high tariffs reduce or eliminate the incentive to import goods, so do high taxes reduce or eliminate the incentive to work or produce. Instead of investing in productive activity rendered unattractive by high taxes, people may invest in art or seek pleasure in travel or other consumption; or they may invest abroad. Conversely, lower taxes open up the potential for higher profits and thus provide an incentive to invest in domestic job-creating enterprises and to work harder. The result is that more people will be paying taxes, and more will be paying on higher incomes, so governmental revenue will not be reduced and may even be enhanced.

Despite Niskanen, it is common for economic conservatives to make claims based on this line of reasoning. George Gilder is among them. Speaking of the tax rate reductions he urged in *Wealth and Poverty*, he says that after they took effect in 1983 and 1984 "total revenues at all levels of government rose some 9 percent a year in real terms, far faster than during the high-tax 1970s" (Gilder 1993, 35).

More significantly, Reagan made statements along the same line. With respect to the capital gains tax, he laid it down as a virtual economic law that a higher tax rate produces less revenue, and that a lower tax rate increases the revenue (*Public Papers* 1981, 1190). And he generalized more broadly, saying in 1988 that "every time we have reduced the rates, we have increased the total revenue.... And so, no, the deficit has not been caused by the cut in taxes. The deficit would increase if we yielded to those who want us to increase taxes" (*Public Papers* 1988, 1:18). Reagan gave no rule for deciding when taxes had been cut enough, nor was he explicit about the rule for deciding whose taxes should be cut. Whereas Keynesians may seek tax cuts for the general public so as to maintain or increase demand, supply-siders are more likely to want tax cuts for entrepreneurs so as to give them an incentive to produce.

The correct answer to the question whether lower taxes mean higher revenue surely depends on circumstances. Buchanan made the answer easy by assuming a prohibitive tariff—so high as to preclude any importation of the goods to which it applies and thus to preclude the collection of any revenue. It is automatic, then, that if the tariff is lowered enough that imports begin to come in, governmental revenue is increased. The same reasoning applies to the income tax. If the income tax is at the 100 percent level, people have little incentive to work—or strong incentive to fail to report some or all of their income. In either event the government gets little or no revenue. But if the tax is lowered enough that income-producing activity comes to seem worthwhile, and if the reporting of income does not lead to too great a penalty, governmental revenue is increased.

In other words, if you start with excessively high tax rates, you can increase revenue by reducing them. By the same token, if you start with absurdly low rates, you can increase revenue by raising them. No one has yet advanced a reliable rule for determining where the dividing line is—that is, how high the tax rate can go without reducing the revenue produced. The signs are that within a broad middle range taxes can be fixed to respond to governmental needs and that (other things remaining the same) revenue will go up or down along with the rate selected.

A special hazard besets efforts to predict the effects of a tax increase, for people do not always look on income-producing activity in a purely economic way. Many people work for the joy of working. Work is challenging, and success at work is self-fulfilling. The income produced by work may be necessary as a livelihood, but is nevertheless an incidental result of an activity in which people would want to engage anyway. Achievements through work are a source of pride, and (once a certain level of income is exceeded) money becomes mainly a source of more pride. A higher income is like a higher score in a game, and many like to run up the score. For people with an outlook of this sort, the level of taxes has little effect on what they do.

What this means is that sweeping generalizations about the relationship between tax levels and revenue are automatically suspect. It is obviously true, however, that something about the taxing and spending policies of the federal government since 1980 has left it with huge deficits and a monstrous debt.

## TAXATION AND PROSPERITY

Economists do not agree on the factors that promote or impede economic growth. They come up with different explanations of the fact that some countries grow economically at a much faster rate than others. One theory is that government plays an indispensable role, stimulating, assisting, and guiding entrepreneurs so as to produce growth that would not otherwise occur. I mention this theory in chapter 6. A second theory also focuses on the role of government but advances the opposite argument: that efforts by the government to promote economic growth are likely to do more harm than good. According to the second theory, government should keep hands off and depend on the entrepreneur and a free market.

A third theory, advanced by Mancur Olson and described in chapter 7, also stresses the entrepreneur and a free market, but warns that during periods of stability social rigidities develop that tend to throttle growth. The rigidities may stem from governmental policies but are at least as likely to stem from collusion among entrepreneurs who want to restrict competition. So the problem is to keep the market open. Olson does not say how this should be done, but the use of government for the purpose is an obvious possibility.

A fourth theory is the "catch-up" theory—the theory that economic growth is likely to be especially rapid in countries that are taking advantage of technological and other advances already made elsewhere.

Each of these theories gets some support, which means that none of them is universally accepted. Those who explain the rate of growth by citing governmental policies may include tax policies among those that are relevant, but other policies get attention too (Weede 1986).

The World Bank analyzes the problem in *The East Asian Miracle* (1993), focusing on the economies of eight countries in East Asia: the "Four Tigers" (South Korea, Taiwan, Hong Kong, and Singapore), plus Japan, Indonesia, Thailand, and Malaysia. The study speaks of the "immense variety of policies" followed and says that "the sheer diversity of these policies precludes drawing any simple lessons or making any simple policy recommendations, except perhaps that pragmatic adherence to the fundamentals is central to success."

For economic conservatives in the United States, the most striking feature of the World Bank's study is that taxes are treated as simply one of many conditions affecting growth and get no emphasis at all. The next most striking feature is that, with the partial exception of Hong Kong, all of the governments played active roles in promoting economic development. The study divides the activities into "fundamentals" and "selective interventions," but both categories refer to activities of governments. Hong Kong limited itself largely to the fundamentals, except that it engaged in "selective intervention" with respect to housing. If any one activity gets more emphasis than the others, it is probably the development of human capital through education and measures relating to health, listed among the fundamentals. And the study emphasizes the fact that, to win general public support as well as the support of the elites, the governments "introduced mechanisms that drastically increased opportunities to share the benefits of growth.... Growth with equity was the leaders' primary concern." Income gaps were not to become too wide.

The World Bank study contrasts sharply with the explanation offered by the editor of the *Wall Street Journal* of what he calls "the seven fat years" during Reagan's presidency. The fat years, according to him, were due to low taxes, small government, and relative freedom for the entrepreneur, but he offers no supporting evidence or argument. He dwells on the correlation between Reagan's tax cut and "the seven fat years," assuming that a correlation must be a causal relation. What comes first must be the cause of what comes next (Bartley 1992). But what has already been said makes this position inherently implausible, and additional considerations are in point.

In the first place, it is not to be assumed that lower taxes mean greater investment in the private realm. "Lower tax rates on wealthy people in the early and mid-1980s had no discernible net effect at all on American rates of investment, productivity, incomes, or growth" (Shapiro 1993, 23). If people or corporations are left with extra funds because of lower taxes, they have a number of possibilities open to them in addition to investing in some new entrepreneurial activity. Among other things, they may lend the money to the government.

Further, investment occurs in the public realm too, which means that the lowering of taxes may possibly have a perverse effect, failing to produce greater private investment and leaving government without the means (other than borrowing) for making public investments.

In the second place, government does not put tax money under a mattress, but spends it with reasonable promptness, mainly for goods and services. And what it transfers to those on social security and those on welfare also tends to get spent, keeping up the demand. In the net, therefore, taxing does not necessarily reduce either demand or incentives.

In the third place, a question is raised by the possibility mentioned just above that government may simply borrow the funds left in private hands by the tax reduction. Insofar as that happens, it is difficult to see how a reduction in taxes would produce gain for the economy—unless some of the borrowed money comes from foreign sources, which is of course what happened during the Reagan years. Rather than say that lower *taxes* brought "seven fat years," it is more plausible to say that massive *borrowing* brought what prosperity there was—massive borrowing by the government (a significant portion of it from foreign sources) and a credit-card spending spree by the public (Harrison and Bluestone 1988, 147–51). If so, Reagan stimulated the economy by applying Keynesian demand-side policies unintentionally while claiming to be a supply-sider.

Whether taxes in the United States are too high is of course a matter for judgment. People in other industrial countries pay more. In 1990 twenty-two of the twenty-four countries in the Organization for Economic Cooperation and Development (OECD) took a higher proportion of the GDP in taxes than the United States. If social security taxes are excluded from consideration, twenty-three did. In 1989 total tax revenue was almost 50 percent of the GDP in Denmark, 38 percent in Germany, and only 30 percent in the United States. Yet from 1972 to 1988 the other six major industrial countries in the OECD achieved greater increases in their standard of living than did the United States. The American standard of living index went up about a fourth as much as theirs (OECD 1992, table 3, p. 73; Phillips 1990, xix).

## TAX POLICIES

Income tax rates were in fact reduced during Reagan's years in office. In 1981 he signed a measure cutting them by 25 percent, with 50 percent as the rate for the topmost incomes, and in 1986 he signed another reducing the highest rate from 50 to 33 percent. The incomes of those in the top quintile increased during the Reagan years more than enough to offset the reduction in their tax rate, so they ended up paying more into the treasury than they had before. But they paid less—about $24 billion less—than if the tax rate of 1977 had remained unchanged. In contrast, Reagan's changes required those in the bottom 80 percent of the households to pay more—about $24 billion more—than the 1977 rates would have required (U.S. Congress 1990a, 3). Moreover, apart from changes in the income tax, changes relating to inheritance and gift taxes favored the rich. On the other side, Reagan signed a measure substantially increasing the regressive social security tax.

The combined effect was to shift the tax burden. Economic conservatives complain that the American tax system and the system of transfer payments are between them redistributive—transferring money from the rich to the poor. Some redistribution obviously occurs, but it would be easy to exaggerate its extent. In a book published in 1983, Page's conclusion is that "taxes in the United States have done little or nothing to redistribute income" (Page 1983, 211). Although the income tax was progressive, many other taxes, especially at the state and local levels, were regressive, and the two kinds of taxes tended to balance each other. Then Reagan reduced the progressivity of the income tax and raised the payroll tax, with the result that the tax burden shifted away from the rich and toward the poor. Comparing the 1980s with the 1970s, the revenue of the federal government from the personal income tax went down from 40 percent of total revenue to 38 percent, and revenue from the corporate income tax went down from 13.3 to 7.7 percent. For the same periods, revenue from payroll taxes went up from 27.7 to 29.2 percent; and revenue from borrowing went up from 11 to almost 18 percent (Shapiro 1991, table 2).

After Bush became president, Senator Moynihan created a problem for economic conservatives. He held that the government was financing its programs to an undue extent from the surplus produced by the payroll tax (the social security tax), and he therefore proposed that this tax be reduced. It was an embarrassing proposal, and the conservatives split. Some remained consistent in their antitax stand, but others seemed to say that although tax cuts for upper-income groups were to be desired, cuts for lower- and middle-income groups were not. Moynihan's proposal was not adopted.

## TAX EXPENDITURES

I mentioned tax expenditures in chapter 4. They take the form of a reduction in a normal tax liability. The clearest example is the exemption of mortgage interest from the income tax. A homeowner who pays $10,000 a year in interest on a mortgage, for example, may deduct that $10,000 from his or her income before figuring income tax. The result is the same as if the government collected the normal tax on the $10,000 and then returned it. Similarly, a tax expenditure occurs when those who carry health insurance, or employers who provide health insurance for their employees, are permitted to deduct the premiums in determining how much of their income is taxable. Tax expenditures also take several other forms—for example, an investment tax credit or an accelerated depreciation schedule. Some of them are called loopholes.

Whatever the specific form, tax expenditures are, in a sense, hidden. No appropriation is voted. No check is written. No money changes hands. But tax expenditures nevertheless leave the beneficiaries richer than they otherwise would be, and the government has to make up in some other way for the tax that it forgoes. In other words, tax expenditures shift the burden just as open and explicit transfer payments do.

Tax expenditures are not identified exclusively with economic conservatism. Many progressive liberals vote for them too. The situation leads Mancur Olson to comment that ideology does not always predict action—that whatever those on the right and left say, they in fact devote themselves mainly to serving organized interests ("paying clients"). "Most redistributions are from the unorganized to the organized, and these redistributions are not closely related to the ideology of the government" (Barfield and Schambra 1986, 261–62).

Reliance on tax expenditures burgeoned in the 1970s and 1980s. The federal government had fewer than fifty tax expenditure programs in 1967 and more than 100 in 1985. The amount of money involved went up from less than $37 billion in 1967 to ten times that much in 1985 (Surrey and McDaniel 1985, 33–34).

Apart from the expansion of the programs, the most striking feature of tax expenditures is that those with the highest incomes gain the most. For example, only those with enough money (and credit) to buy a home can take advantage of the mortgage-interest deduction, and the bigger the mortgage, the bigger the benefit. In 1985 the top 4 percent of taxpayers received 36 percent of the tax expenditures of this sort, and the bottom 30 percent of the taxpayers received 0.1 percent. In this realm, what amount to transfer payments go disproportionately to the rich.

## The Seven Fat Years

The claims of economic conservatives with respect to the performance of the economy under Reagan are suggested by a book entitled *The Seven Fat Years*. Under Reagan, the stagflation that had marked the Carter administration came to an end. Inflation went down, and the economy picked up. Unemployment went down, from 7.6 million in 1980 to 6.5 million in 1989. Continuous growth occurred for ninety-six consecutive months, an extraordinary record. The stock market soared, nearly tripling in value. From 1977 to 1990 the average income of all families increased by 14.3 percent (U.S. Congress 1990a, 2).

Even so, the economic achievements were modest. Real GNP grew by an annual rate of 2.67 percent in the 1980s, as compared to 4.05 percent in the 1960s and 2.83 percent in the 1970s. The percentage of individuals in poverty went up from 11.5 in 1979 to 13.5 in 1990 (Green Book 1992, 1273). Although the average family income went up, as noted, the gain was by far the greatest for upper-income groups. The gain was 1 percent for those in the lowest quintile, 24.3 percent for those in the middle quintile, and 35 percent for those in the highest quintile, which means that inequality increased (Green Book 1992, 1350, 1451; cf. Krugman 1992).

Reagan and others kept boasting of the number of new jobs created during the decade, and many were in fact created. But they were created at a lower rate than during the preceding years: from 1965 to 1980 "the work force grew by 40 percent, swelling by almost 30 million workers" (Schwarz 1988, 115). Schwarz's conclusion is that "far from being stronger, economic growth during the recovery years in the 1980s has generally been weaker than in the 1970s" (1988, 166). Reagan's main contribution was not so much economic as psychological, for he uplifted people by his air of confidence and optimism.

I do not mean to attribute the limited successes of economic conservatism entirely to the policies associated with it, or to "trickle down" economics. Other factors, beyond anyone's control, were surely at work, and it is difficult to know what relative weight they should have. Economic "globalization" is occurring, meaning that competition is more and more with foreign as well as with domestic enterprises and suggesting that cheap labor abroad may outcompete low-skilled labor in the United States. The substantial increase in the number of single-parent families has economic implications, as does the aging of the population. If it were not for changes such as these, the achievements of economic conservatism might be more pronounced.

## Hostility to Regulatory Activities

When Reagan spoke of getting government "off your backs," the principal reference was to what he thought of as the burdens of overregulation. He spoke in 1982 of "the growing thicket of Federal regulations that was stifling business and industrial growth," and he went on to say: "The intrusive hand of government can only hinder creativity, stultify growth, and suffocate enterprise, initiative and diversity. Our goal is to take government out of areas where it does not belong" (*Public Papers* 1982, 2:1011).

The principle that Reagan endorsed applied potentially to a wide range of governmental activity. David Vogel spoke in 1989 of the federal government's forty-two regulatory agencies (1989, 248), among them the Environmental Protection Agency (EPA), the Federal Trade Commission (FTC), the Food and Drug Administration (FDA), the Occupational Safety and Health Administration (OSHA), and the National Labor Relations Board (NLRB). Many other executive offices and agencies also issue and enforce regulations in the normal course of their administration of the law, for example, offices concerned with the enforcement of antitrust laws and prohibitions of discrimination based on race, sex, or disability.

Among the regulatory activities to which economic conservatives especially object are those concerning trusts, the environment, and employment practices. And policies with respect to endangered species, the collection of statistical and other information, and litigation have come in for attention.

Jonathan Cohn picks out antitrust law as "the quintessential victim" of Reagan's determination to curtail regulatory activities. The principal methods were to put people in charge of the Department of Justice and the Federal Trade Commission who shared his views and to cut the budget and the staff of the offices directly involved. The result was that "antitrust enforcement virtually vanished" (Cohn 1993, 64–66). This raises a question that is reinforced by the line of argument advanced by Mancur Olson, described in chapter 7. Although Olson clearly goes along with Reagan in viewing some kinds of regulation as bad, he would regard others as good. Olson's question is whether a regulation promotes or diminishes free and open competition. Olson would approve regulatory activities of a trust-busting sort, and, more broadly, activities directed against all kinds of collusion that tend to make prices and wages sticky (Olson 1982, 141; Olson 1984, 240).

Economic conservatives tend also to be hostile to environmentalism. The environmental movement, according to writers in the *National Review*, is "the biggest impetus for the growth of government in our time.... The very same people who so recently marched under the banner of socialism now pursue precisely the same ends under the green banner" (Codevilla 1993, 60). "The whole anti-capitalist agenda has found a new home in the environmentalist cause.... [Environmentalism] challenges the whole technological basis of Western civilization" (Rusher 1993, 40–41). The 1992 Earth Summit at Rio de Janeiro was a "Carnival of Dunces." "Belief in progress has been replaced by the notion of a planet in peril caused by too many people consuming too much." The conference was "disheartening," perhaps marking "the demise of the Western idea of progress" (Smith 1992, 31). According to economic conservatism, the claims of environmentalists are unsubstantiated or exaggerated or both.

Implied in the above criticisms is the view that environmentalism costs too much. Thus Weidenbaum comments that "every time a government agency attempts to safeguard the environment, it imposes on business a more expensive method of production.... Environmental regulations alone cost each family more than $1,000 a year" (Weidenbaum 1992, 40). Henderson stresses the same point: "the economic costs of environmental regulations are staggering." He cites a claim that the Clean Air Act alone will cost $40 billion a year while providing benefits valued at no more than $15 billion (Henderson 1992, 5).

Partial exceptions can be cited. DeMuth, for example, declares that improving the environment "is an important and appropriate function of government in the modern world, and one that political conservatives should embrace with enthusiasm." But he complains that "the policies we are pursuing to protect the environment are ... enormously wasteful—we could be achieving the same degree of environmental quality for much less cost or far more quality for the same cost" (DeMuth 1992, 17).

Economic conservatives are also generally hostile to governmental efforts to regulate employment practices. After all, it is not surprising that those who extol entrepreneurs would want to leave them as free as possible to work their economic magic. Among other things, this means that economic conservatives oppose minimum wage legislation, the public argument usually being that the absence of such legislation makes for fuller employment, and most particularly the employment of the young and the unskilled. It also means opposition to policies and laws that strengthen the position of trade unions. Reagan made his attitude on this subject clear early in his first administration when he broke the strike of air traffic controllers and barred the rehiring of strikers. He appointed a management attorney as chairman of the National Labor Relations Board, with the result that, as compared with earlier decades, the percentage of decisions favoring management doubled (Judis 1992, 250). Such policies help explain the fact that American trade unions are weaker than at any time since the New Deal.

Opposition to regulatory activities extends to much of what the federal government does on behalf of minorities. Economic conservatives tend to ignore the long record of discrimination against blacks and women (governmental as well as private discrimination), and to ignore the fact that this discrimination had as its counterpart the preferential treatment of whites and men. They ignore the question whether, during the Jim Crow period, people were treated according to merit and afforded equality of opportunity. They take it for granted that we start now with a clean slate, with no one advantaged or disadvantaged by the illegal governmental and private discrimination and preferential treatment in the past. Or they take it for granted that they have no responsibility for the behavior of their fathers and grandfathers.

Goldwater reflected this outlook when he voted against the Civil Rights Act of 1964, declaring that the proper aim of government is to preserve a *free* society, not to establish either a segregated or an integrated society. He failed to note the fact that government itself had played a major role in creating a segregated society. And he obviously assumed a negative definition of freedom.

Having taken no notice of preferential treatment as long as the beneficiaries were whites and men, economic conservatives experienced a conversion once court decisions and congressional legislation began calling for the preferential treatment of blacks and women. They quickly saw virtue in the rule of merit and the principle of equality of opportunity, and thus they began denouncing quotas and set-asides. They ignored the question whether remedial action was called for, except where the rule of "victim specificity" applied. I discussed this issue in chapter 5.

Not only do conservatives ignore the case for redress, but some of them deny that white racism is responsible for black problems and failings, arguing instead that the responsibility lies with the blacks themselves. The argument is that blacks who behave in the same way as successful whites achieve approximately equal success. That is, blacks who take full advantage of their educational opportunities, who marry and stay married, and who live by a work ethic do about as well as comparable whites; perhaps better. In contrast, blacks who drop out of school, who get involved somehow in drugs or crime, who father or give birth to babies out of wedlock, and who lack a work ethic do badly. The implication is that their fate is in their own hands and that whites are not responsible for those who fail to shape up. Whites may even accentuate the problems of the blacks if, like those who turn out to be "enablers" when dealing with alcoholics, they provide welfare that shields blacks from the full consequences of their irresponsibility (Taylor 1992).

Discrimination against those with disabilities also occurs, and the fact led Congress to adopt the Americans with Disabilities Act designed to assure them equal opportunity to benefit from a wide range of services and activities. Economic conservatives are appalled by the regulatory implications of the act, an editor of *Human Events* describing it as a "horrendous piece of regulatory nonsense." Coupling this act with the Clean Air Act, the editor of *Reason* describes them as "the most intrusive, expensive, onerous pieces of legislation to come out of Congress in years. They will be dragging down the economy long after this recession is past."

Mark Ahlseen provides a summary statement about "so-called 'civil rights' legislation": "Besides being a restriction on human rights of freedom of association and employment, [such legislation] places an unbearable drag on the American economy in competition with the economies of the newly industrialized nations which now undersell legislation-burdened American manufacturers, obliged to employ inefficient workers and deprived of the freedom to fire those who fail to do their job efficiently" (Ahlseen 1992, 18).

Protecting an endangered species is not as big an issue as those described above, but economic conservatives respond in about the same way to the regulatory measures taken. And others join in. The objections do not come from economic conservatives alone. Some years ago, many questioned the wisdom of holding up the construction of a dam in order to protect snail darters, and more recently many have questioned whether the desire to save the spotted owl justifies restrictions on logging when the restrictions cost so many jobs. Evolution has included the extinction of many species.

Similarly, litigation is not a big issue, but it is nevertheless getting attention. Examples include litigation over the liability of an employer for injury to a worker, the liability of a manufacturer for harm done by his product, and the liability of a physician for alleged malpractice. Vice-President Quayle spoke of the problem, pointing out that insurance and other costs associated with litigation affect the competitiveness of American enterprises. The conservative *Policy Review* ran an article on the subject in 1992, focusing on the problem in Texas, where litigation is said to be "the largest growth industry." After all, litigation consumes human energy and talent, often with no corresponding contribution to public well-being.

I noted earlier that one of the methods of curtailing regulatory activities during the Reagan years was to put persons in charge of reg-

ulatory agencies who were out of sympathy with the regulatory purpose. This policy naturally extended to the bureaucracy. Eager regulators who got no support tended to resign, and their replacements were
likely to be economic conservatives.

Although Reagan also cut budgets and staffs, conservatives do
not credit him, or Bush, with much overall success in this respect. For
example, James C. Miller, head of OMB under Reagan, says that "in
1991 the federal government spent 22 percent more in real dollars on
regulatory agencies than in President Carter's last year" and that,
although Reagan cut down the number of regulators by about 16 percent from 1980 to 1985, the number in 1992 was back up above the
1980 level (Miller and Mink 1992, 4; cf. Niskanen 1988, 115).

The reasons are not far to seek. Once a regulation is issued, those
adversely affected can be expected to look for loopholes and methods
of evasion, which is likely to lead to a further elaboration of the regulation. Growth in the population and in the economy is likely to be
accompanied by a growth in troublesome externalities (consequences
of actions for persons not party to them), giving rise to needs for regulation. And public expectations that government will protect them
from harm and provide for the good seem to be growing stronger,
even if the will to pay for governmental services is not.

In describing the objections of economic conservatives to environmental regulations, I cited claims about their costs. Laffer offers
what is apparently a claim about the comprehensive costs of all kinds
of regulations. He says that "the total regulatory burden is costing the
American people between $810 billion and $1.7 trillion per year—or
between $8,400 and $17,000 per household" (Laffer 1993, 319).
How he arrives at those figures I do not know.

Economic conservatives do not try to estimate the costs, either
human or material, if most or all governmental regulatory activities
were terminated.

## Equality of Opportunity

As noted earlier, economic conservatives appeal to the idea of equality
of opportunity, but only in restricted circumstances; and they give the
idea a narrow meaning. Their emphasis is not on governmental action
to enhance equality of opportunity but on the responsibility of individuals for their own fate.

Affirmative action gives economic conservatives their principal
reason for appealing to the idea of equality of opportunity. The paradox here is that both conservatives and liberals appeal to the idea in

this connection. Liberals want to promote equality of opportunity for those who have traditionally been denied it through discrimination, and conservatives want to promote it on behalf of those whom they see as victims of reverse discrimination. In each case, the attitudes fit with the more general attitudes concerning the proper role of government. Liberals favor governmental activism to give worth to liberty by redressing past wrongs, whereas conservatives want to leave property owners and entrepreneurs with untrammeled liberty, defined as the absence of restraint or coercion. The conservative desire to restrict the role of government, to leave property owners and entrepreneurs as free as possible from governmental regulations, and to uphold individual responsibility and self-reliance as values lead them to oppose most governmental action on behalf of equality of opportunity. Most economic conservatives, like most libertarians, do not even want government to administer the schools, which are a major means of promoting equality of opportunity for the poor.

## Welfare

As noted in chapter 4, the terms "welfare state" and "welfare" have potentially misleading meanings. The welfare state offers a variety of aid programs serving both able-bodied people and persons not expected to be self-supporting. Most prominent among the aid programs are the following: social security, supplemental security income, Medicare, Medicaid, AFDC, food stamps, and aid to those with disabilities. The listing of programs is based more on convention than on logic. The price-support program for farmers and the interest exemption for those with mortgages on their homes—and a number of other programs—might be listed as welfare programs, but usually are not.

Economic conservatism views the different programs differently, whether out of concern for votes or out of concern for principle. Reflecting a degree of libertarianism, some conservatives want to get the government out of the business of providing social security, but they are the exceptions. Most economic conservatives endorse the programs providing support for the elderly. For example, early in Reagan's first administration he pledged to "protect the benefits of Social Security recipients now and in the future," and he never made an issue of Medicare. Like many others, the various kinds of conservatives are appalled at the costs (the rising costs) of such programs (something like two-thirds of the welfare dollars are spent for them), but older people have achieved so much clout that political leaders handle the problem of containing the costs in a gingerly and circumspect way.

For that matter, the welfare state, broadly conceived, benefits the middle and upper classes especially. According to Peter G. Peterson, the typical household with an income over $100,000 receives more total federal benefits than the typical household with an income under $10,000.

When people speak not of "the welfare state" but simply of "welfare" the probability is that they have in mind not the whole gamut of welfare programs but only those directed toward the poor—mainly AFDC, food stamps, and Medicaid. Those who get AFDC payments are "on welfare."

Economic conservatives are unhappy about welfare, reluctant to give support, especially long-term support, to able-bodied persons. They deplore the development of what they view as a culture of dependency. As noted before, their stress is on personal responsibility and self-reliance. Adam Meyerson describes the view:

> Not too long ago, it was a social embarrassment to take charity, public or private, on anything but an emergency basis. It is fundamental to a conservative vision of America that this cultural attitude be restored.... Government should provide temporary help for people caught in an emergency, but should not permanently subsidize the able-bodied. Examples of justifiable temporary help might include disaster relief, unemployment insurance, AFDC payments of three or four years to single mothers, temporary import protection for industries suddenly clobbered by foreign competition, and temporary aid to farmers during an unforeseen crisis in the agricultural economy. (Meyerson 1990, 4)

Meyerson is relatively generous in suggesting AFDC payments for three or four years. Clinton suggests limiting them to two years.

Reagan's views were similar to Meyerson's. "Government," he said, "has a responsibility to help those who can't help themselves." "Those who, through no fault of their own, must depend on the rest of us—the poverty stricken, the disabled, the elderly, all those with true need—can rest assured that the social safety net of programs they depend on are exempt from any cuts." At the same time, according to Reagan, welfare programs, at least some of them, were eroding the sense of responsibility in individuals, families, and local communities, encouraging dependency, and entrenching the poverty they were intended to alleviate. He held that "misguided welfare programs" were turning "a shrinking problem [poverty] into a national tragedy." They degraded the moral worth of work. "Federal welfare programs have created a massive social problem. With the best of intentions, government created a poverty trap...." And in addition its welfare programs gave rise to fraud and abuse—"a lot of it." Reagan spoke of "welfare queens."

Lawrence Mead, who describes himself as a conservative, takes a comparable view of aid. In *The New Politics of Poverty* (1992), he focuses on long-term adult beneficiaries of AFDC—mainly black women —who dropped out of school and thus failed to qualify themselves for any but the most menial and low-paying jobs. That is, he focuses on the 6 to 7 percent of Americans who count as long-term poor, "and especially the 4 to 5 percent who are employable, that is, not elderly or disabled." He describes them as "nonworking" and says that the poor are largely in this category. That is, they do not work even though (according to Mead) jobs are available and nothing prevents them from working. They do not have a work ethic. The women become pregnant (teenagers among them), not expecting the father to provide support but accepting dependency on government as a way of life.

In other words, the assumption is the same as the one described earlier in connection with the question whether government should follow policies of redress toward blacks: that the nonworking poor are not like everyone else but are failures in managing their own lives —irresponsible, incompetent, and undeserving. They are an "underclass" belonging to a "welfare culture"—without the various qualities that make for self-reliance. Apart from asking whether the need to care for children explains the failure of mothers to work, Mead scarcely mentions the fact that about two-thirds of those aided by programs for the poor are children. (For views that contrast with Mead's, see Patterson 1986, 115; Lockhart 1989, 20.)

In chapter 7 I spoke of Murray's *Losing Ground,* which takes an approach and makes an appraisal similar to Mead's. And the same point of view appears in Myron Magnet's *The Dream and the Nightmare* (1993), although Magnet places the ultimate blame on "elite, mainstream culture," not on the poor themselves. According to Magnet, the "haves" of mainstream culture communicated to the poor "exactly the wrong message and the most self-destructive values. [The message] told blacks in particular, and the poor in general, that they were victims, and that society, not they themselves, was responsible not only for their present but their future condition." From the 1960s on, the haves of mainstream culture, seeking personal liberation, "withdrew respect from the behavior and attitudes that have traditionally boosted people up the economic ladder—deferral of gratification, sobriety, thrift, dogged industry, and so on." "The new culture that the Haves invented—their remade system of beliefs, norms, and institutions—permitted, even celebrated, behavior that, when poor people practice it, will imprison them inextricably in poverty. It's hard to persuade ghetto fifteen-year olds not to get pregnant, for instance, when the entire culture ... is intoxicated with the joy of ... 'recreational sex.'" The haves "refused to assert to the poor and the black the most fundamental of ... values: the worth of the respectable working life, however humble." The upshot is "the panhandler begging outside McDonald's, right under the *Help Wanted* sign." That is, the upshot is a dependent underclass, lacking in initiative and industry. Jobs are available for them, but they do not want to work. Trying to do good, we have only made things worse.

Magnet's prescription is similar to Murray's. He wants to leave the poor and others with no choice but to shape up. We must "*stop* the current welfare system, *stop* quota-based affirmative action, *stop* treating criminals as justified rebels, *stop* letting bums expropriate public spaces or wrongdoers living in public housing at public expense, *stop* Afrocentric education in the schools."

Economic conservatives join social conservatives (to be described in the next chapter) in showing concern for the effect of aid programs on the family. The complaint is that the promise of aid to poverty-stricken mothers and their children undermines the family, deterring mothers from marrying, encouraging them to divorce, and encouraging husbands to desert.

Nevertheless, only the more extreme of the economic conservatives call for the elimination of these programs. Instead, the emphasis is on restricting aid to the "truly needy" and on requiring those without very young children (three years old or less?) to assume a reciprocal obligation, such as getting more education or getting training that may lead to a job. Many who do not count themselves as economic conservatives have come to take approximately the same view.

The shift toward mandatory "workfare" and "learnfare" began before Reagan entered the White House and culminated in the Family Support Act of 1988, which he signed and which imposes obligations on those receiving aid and thus attempts to put discipline and a sense of responsibility into their lives. The act involves the paradox that an administration hostile to big government and dedicated to liberty called for the use of government in a paternalistic and authoritarian effort to enforce social mores on the poor. Where the program is implemented, it requires recipients either to participate in some kind of training program or to work at some kind of job; preferably the job is to be in the private sector, but publicly funded jobs are theoretically to be available as an alternative.

The problem is that the program, especially the jobs part of the program, is expensive, and Congress as well as a number of the states have failed to appropriate anything like the amount theoretically required. In 1992 the states took up less than two-thirds of the federal funds available. Less that 1 percent of those on welfare now work in community-service jobs. More are enrolled for schooling or some kind of training. Welfare persists because it is cheap.

Speaking of the Great Society's war on poverty, Reagan once declared that poverty had won. He was correct in the sense that a higher proportion of the population was in poverty at the end of his second administration than in 1979. It is a good question to what extent this should be regarded as a failure of the war on poverty or a failure of the market and the economic policies that the government pursued. Reagan was incorrect insofar as the elderly and the disabled are concerned, for the war on poverty greatly reduced—virtually eliminated —poverty among them.

The views described above are by no means universally acclaimed. Murray's *Losing Ground* (libertarian, but endorsed by many economic conservatives) created a storm of controversy. Reactions in the academic and journalistic communities are predominantly negative. One of the statements characterizes Murray's arguments as "composed largely of misunderstanding and misdiagnosis. Almost nothing Murray says about the effects of welfare or welfare state policies on the poor is believed by serious students of the subject" (Marmor et al. 1990, 105; cf. Jencks 1992, 79–81; Harpham and Scotch 1988, 1989; Greenstein 1985, 12–17). Magnet's views will presumably evoke a similar appraisal. In fact, he does very little to support his interpretation with evidence. He provides no basis for deciding what proportion of those on welfare are "undeserving" and what proportion are simply down on their luck.

I note later that Jack Kemp, who styles himself as a progressive conservative, takes a different view of the problem of welfare. Like most progressive liberals, he rejects the view that the adults on welfare belong to a cultural underclass mired in poverty because of personal failings; instead, he views the adults on welfare as people who are pretty much like everyone else except that they have had bad luck and need to be tided over until they can get on their feet again (Reich 1988, 89–90). In fact, as indicated in chapter 4, about 30 percent of those on the AFDC roll are on it for less than two years and about 50 percent are on it for less than four. Those who take Kemp's kind of view are also likely to think of the aid as going not only to mothers but also to children, and to believe that aid to children is not only desirable on humanitarian grounds but a good investment. In truth, many liberals argue that even more should be invested in children in the hope of enhancing the prospect that they will avoid delinquency and crime and become self-supporting, constructive members of the community.

Some go further than Kemp in rejecting the libertarian/economic conservative diagnosis of the problem of poverty. For example, David Riemer, in *The Prisoners of Welfare* (1988), argues that poverty does not stem mainly from the personal failings of the poor, and this leads him to conclude that programs designed to solve the problem of poverty by providing schooling or training or work experience are bound to fail. According to his diagnosis, the problem of poverty stems mainly from the shortage of jobs and from low pay. In other words, it stems from inadequacies of the free market. He asserts that, as a rule, those on welfare and those unemployed want work but cannot find it. He cites data indicating that during the 1960s and 1970s there were 2.5 to 5 unemployed persons for every vacant job, which means that large numbers would have remained unemployed even if every job had been filled. And additional millions worked full-time the year around but were paid so little that they ended up below the poverty line.

Riemer joins many others in wanting to terminate "welfare," but he would do it by providing community-service jobs to those of working age who are able-bodied; and he would expand the earned income tax program for those who work but are still left below the poverty line. More on this in chapter 15.

For the most part, economic conservatives disowned the Bush administration and oppose the Clinton administration. Ambivalence prevails, however, in discussions of a national system of health care. On the one hand, the principles of economic conservatism call for leaving the problem in private hands. It should be a matter for the market. On the other hand, most economic conservatives who seek election and reelection apparently believe that they must seem to support the creation of some kind of national health-care system. The dilemma lacks a clear solution. It fits with economic conservatism to rely as much as possible on tax expenditures and vouchers. Premiums paid by employers or by individuals for health insurance would be a deductible expense. It also fits with economic conservatism to do whatever is necessary to appear to support a national health-care plan while criticizing and seeking to defeat the one that Clinton proposed.

Aid to agriculture needs to be mentioned in connection with the subject of welfare. One of the anomalies of the Reagan administration is the vast expansion of that aid. Whereas federal farm price supports cost about $3 billion in 1980, by 1986 they were costing $26 billion, "making farm programs the fastest growing part of the federal budget during the Reagan years" (Armey 1990, 24). The support went disproportionately to farmers who were better off, the 18 percent with annual sales exceeding $100,000 in 1989 getting 71 percent of all direct federal price-support payments.

## Crime

Economic conservatives claim that liberals are not sufficiently tough on crime. They spell out the thought by claiming that liberals are too inclined to assume (1) that everyone is potentially good and that if someone goes bad it must be the fault of society; (2) that the way to combat crime is through education and social reform; and (3) that the object in treating criminals is their rehabilitation. On the basis of such attitudes, liberals allegedly make it difficult to combat crime effectively, imposing too many restrictions on the police and the courts, meting out sentences that are too light, and releasing prisoners too soon.

The criticisms suggest that economic conservatives take opposite positions. To them, crime is not a failure of society but a manifestation of human nature; and the way to combat it is to rely on the police—perhaps on more police—and to strengthen the hands of the police and the courts by relaxing some of the safeguards designed to protect the innocent. If crime increases, the answer is to build more prisons. "Crime is not a hard problem," says Congressman Newt Gingrich. "We simply lock up violent criminals until they're too old to be violent. That means fewer welfare workers and more police officers and prosecutors and prisons." If more young black men are in prison than in college, that is where they belong, for society must be protected against disorder and crime. Like many others, economic conservatives tend to support the "three-strikes-and-you're-out" principle, which is that those convicted of their third violent crime should be locked up for life.

Attitudes toward gun control and the death penalty have come to play a symbolic role in connection with the problem of crime. To favor gun control, conservatives are inclined to argue, is to favor making law-abiding citizens more vulnerable to crime, and to oppose the death penalty is to support the coddling of criminals. In contrast, to uphold the right to bear arms and to favor the death penalty, and perhaps to ask for its extension to additional crimes, is to prove how tough you are.

One irony of the situation is that many of those who want to be tough on crime also want to keep taxes low, and toughness on crime costs money. Mainly because of the drug problem, the prison population in the United States more than quadrupled from 1970 to 1990, and in 1991 the country spent ten times as much on prisoners as on the women and children on AFDC. And the more widely the three-strikes-and-you're-out principle is adopted, the more rapidly the prison population will increase, presumably meaning that more taxes will need to be raised to house and feed them. In several states convicted criminals, including many convicted of violent crime, are already being released early not because of liberalism but because government will not impose the taxes necessary to keep them.

Economic conservatives are correct in saying that the solution most generally favored by progressive liberals is to spend more money trying to change the conditions that breed crime.

## Reprise

"Being opposed to government is what defines true conservatism. We know that government doesn't work even when the most brilliant people in the world—us—run it. We know government is an ineffective and morally unacceptable means of delivering life's benefits" (O'Rourke 1993, 20).

> After twelve years, the GOP must not only claim its successes—longest peacetime expansion in history, winning the Cold War—but concede its failures: the bureaucracy is larger, the deficit greater, the quota mind set more embedded, and the national debt four times what it was in 1981.
>
> The clean air act, the tax hike, the civil rights bill—all came down with crushing weight on an economy in which the GOP fortune was wholly invested. We imposed on small business the taxes and regulations that ate up their profit margins, and shut down the great American Jobs Machine of the 1980s. (P. Buchanan 1993, 87)

# Chapter 11

# Social Conservatism

N O ONE NAME for the subject of this chapter is widely accepted. People speak not only of social conservatism but also of cultural conservatism, moralistic conservatism, the Religious Right or evangelical right, the New Right, and the New Christian Right. The names differ a bit in their connotations, but "social" is broad enough to cover the rest.

Reagan champions some of the relevant ideas and attitudes, and so do Pat Buchanan and Pat Robertson, both of whom have sought the Republican nomination for the presidency. Jerry Falwell, Tim LaHaye, and Paul Weyrich are others identified with the kind of conservatism in question. Economic and social conservatism overlap, so on some issues economic and social conservatives are comfortable allies. But economic conservatism stresses liberty for the individual and hostility to government, whereas social conservatism stresses virtue as well as liberty and is ambivalent about government, wanting to limit it in some connections and use it in others.

The chapter is divided into two main parts. The first concerns the source of moral rules, and the second concerns the policies to pursue and their rationale.

## The Source of Moral Rules

Most of those who write on behalf of social conservatism hold that moral rules have a transcendental source—a source having nothing to do with human thought or reason, perhaps a divine source. They thus denounce secularism. In recent years, however, some cultural conservatives have drawn away from this position, welcoming into the fold those who come to the right judgments even by a secular route.

Thomas Jefferson appeals to the transcendental in the Declaration of Independence when he speaks of the laws of Nature and of

Nature's God and says that all men are endowed by their Creator with certain rights. It isn't that people deliberate on the matter and choose among the rules and principles that they might accept. It isn't that people learn from experience, use their own reason, and thus improve on the rules and principles developed by their forebears. What they do instead is to discover laws dictated by Nature and Nature's God—discover the rights with which the Creator has endowed them.

It is possible, of course, to treat such language as essentially figurative or rhetorical, designed to give a compelling quality to the ideas expressed. If Jefferson had said, "In our opinion all men should get equal treatment and be accorded certain rights," he would have admitted that he was expressing a human preference, potentially fickle. He could avoid this, and add to the credibility of what he said, by claiming (and perhaps believing) that the principles come from a transcendental source. How he knew what Nature or Nature's God or the Creator had done, he did not say. The weakness of his position is that others might read Nature or the mind of God differently, or might worship a different deity or none at all.

Most exponents of social conservatism make comparable claims and face the same problem. The claim is that "objective standards of right and wrong exist independently of human preference" (Bozell 1961, 341); in other words, the claim is that "moral absolutes [exist] that human beings do not create but discover" (Neuhaus and Cromartie 1987, 333). The less religious conservatives can say that these standards, or these moral absolutes, derive from natural law, and the more religious can say that they derive from God. Those who name natural law as the source can go on to make either of two claims: that natural law derives from a state of nature and is revealed by right reason or that it derives from the nature of man and is revealed in truths emerging from human experience. Alternatively, they can eliminate the distinction I am making by equating the law of nature to the will of God. Those who name God as the source can go on to make any of several claims: that God reveals His will to them through direct messages, perhaps in response to prayer, or that He reveals His will through the Bible or through nature. It goes without saying, of course, that the "objective standards of right and wrong" or the "moral absolutes" are to guide and limit all behavior and action, including behavior and action in the political realm.

Fundamentalists are preponderant among those who champion social conservatism and are most likely to name God rather than nature as the source of guidance. Thus in his autobiography Jerry Falwell, who led the Moral Majority, speaks of sending out a letter declaring that "God has told me what I must do," and in numerous other passages he reports direct personal help and guidance from God on specific matters. At the same time, Falwell acknowledges a problem in that, as he says, hundreds of other people had come to him with messages from God, making it necessary for him to decide whether to take them seriously. For the most part, he refused to do so, but he speaks of two exceptions—two messages that God sent him through others—that changed his life. How he knew that these messages were authentic whereas the others were not, he does not say (Falwell 1987, 385–87).

Aside from, or in addition to, getting messages from God, Fundamentalists claim to learn God's will through the Bible. Thus after declaring himself "a Fundamentalist—big F!" Falwell goes on to say that "a Fundamentalist believes the Bible to be verbally inspired by the Holy Spirit and therefore inerrant and absolutely infallible" (Neuhaus and Cromartie 1987, 119). Others testify similarly. Among those who might be cited is Pat Buchanan, who appeals to both natural law and the Bible: "I think there is a natural law which is consistent with Biblical Christianity, which tells you about man's moral obligations and moral rights." And at another point he says, "The Old and New Testaments are not only infallible guides to personal salvation; they contain the prescriptions for just laws and the good society—for building a city set upon a hill."

Pat Robertson has similar views, plus some that are more extreme. He regards the Bible as "a workable guidebook for politics, government, business, families, and all the affairs of mankind." Like Falwell, he believes that he gets guidance from God, and he thinks of God as performing miracles through him. He is pentecostal, speaking in tongues and engaging in faith healing; and he denounces the devil for daring to "come against the servant of God" (Harrell 1987, 117–18; Wilcox 1988, 671).

The counterpart of the emphasis on the transcendental in social conservatism is a rejection of secularism or, more fully, "secular humanism." The extreme nature of the Fundamentalist view is suggested by the fact that LaHaye describes Thomas Aquinas as "one of the most important thinkers helping to lay the foundation for modern humanism." Aquinas's mistake was that he took an incomplete view of the Fall of man. According to the incomplete view, the Fall left man with his intellect intact, permitting him to mix his own human wisdom with the teachings of the Bible in deciding what to do and how to live. With human wisdom thus given respectability, secular humanism developed—"a man-centered philosophy that attempts to solve the problems of man and the world independently of God," that is, independently of the supernatural (LaHaye 1980, 27–29).

The term *secular humanism* covers a range of attitudes. The secular humanism of John Rawls is of a limited sort, as evidenced by his warning that liberalism should not sponsor a comprehensive doctrine. It should be tolerant of all comprehensive doctrines, provided only that they are reasonable. Tim LaHaye, in contrast, holds that secular humanism rests on atheism and is amoral, rejecting absolutes and espousing relativism. It is thus totally unacceptable. To attempt to solve the problems of the world independently of God is preposterous. "Moral conditions have already become worse and worse in direct proportion to humanism's influence." Humanism "will ultimately lead to anarchy, and our culture will be destroyed" (LaHaye 1980, 26).

Others join LaHaye in his view, appalled by the tendency "to question moral truths that the Bible and great men of all ages have never dreamed of doubting" and by "the modern unbelief in the possibility of being sure about anything"; appalled, in other words, by "the absolute insistence that there is no absolute." Relativism is "the heart of our time's central error, ... the most deadly enemy of traditional Western values." As Pat Buchanan puts it: "The secularists who have captured our culture have substituted a New Age Gospel with its governing axioms: There are no absolute values in the universe; there are no fixed and objective standards of right and wrong. There is no God.... Every man lives by his own moral code. Do your own thing." Others say that secular humanism "rots the soul," deprives society of a basis for maintaining and imposing discipline, provides no basis for character building, and threatens Christian civilization. According to Falwell, "The rising tide of secularism threatens to obliterate the Judeo-Christian influence on American society.... We need to call America back to God, back to the Bible, back to moral sanity."

Fundamentalists—and evangelicals too—are torn on the question whether they should restrict themselves to saving souls or whether their mission extends to saving the country and its culture. In founding the Moral Majority, Falwell chose the broader mission. "We who are committed to the invisible world of God," he said, "cannot simply stand aside while the other world destroys itself." Pat Robertson made a similar decision (running for the presidency and founding the Christian Coalition, among other things) and Paul Weyrich says that the objective of his Free Congress Foundation has always been to "train the conservative movement so that it would be equipped to govern." LaHaye is so fully political that he can scarcely bear the thought of having a humanist in office. "No humanist is qualified to hold any governmental office in America." None is qualified to hold any position that "requires him to think in the best interest of America" (LaHaye 1980, 36, 93). LaHaye and others like him endorse "the triumphalist idea" that authority should be exercised by "the righteous." Christians should "take over" (Atwood 1990, 48–49).

Pat Buchanan operates mainly in the political realm, not having a ministry in the usual sense, but, as is already clear, he explicitly associates his religion and his politics: "There is a religious war going on in this country for the soul of America. It is a cultural war as critical to the kind of nation we shall be as the Cold War itself, for this war is for the soul of America." In this war the Fundamentalists and many evangelicals are confident that they fight on the side of the Lord, possessing direct knowledge of His will.

Buchanan's reference to war is obviously figurative; he is not thinking of a shooting war in which blood flows. Nothing on the Religious Right in the United States is in the same category with the view of a "mainstream Muslim cleric" in Egypt that "the secularist represents a danger to society and the nation that must be eliminated. It is the duty of the Government to kill him." Nor is it clear that Buchanan rejects the democratic process. After all, he participates in it. Even LaHaye, although believing that secular humanists are not qualified to hold public office, indicates that he wants them defeated in elections; he does not suggest that they be barred by law. Nevertheless, references to cultural war raise questions. Are those who disagree to be regarded not as honorable opponents but as enemies pursuing illegitimate and inadmissible purposes? Are these enemies to be subdued, and are social conservatives then to dictate the terms of peace?

Some of the language of social conservatism goes in this direction. A bumper sticker is epigrammatic on the point: "God said it, I believe it, that settles it!" And a question reflects a similar thought: "Why bother to pay attention to anyone else's ideas if we've already heard from God?" Falwell's statement is that when others hesitate and equivocate, "we [Fundamentalists] thunder, 'Thus saith the Lord'" (Neuhaus and Cromartie 1987, 119, 120).

This outlook is heady. It is not compatible with the principle of resolving social issues by a democratic process. What mere mortal should be permitted to voice doubts about the wisdom of God or to oppose the will of God? It is no wonder that a Republican leader in Georgia described the Christian Rightists who took over the party in that state as having the kinds of attitudes that led to the burning of Joan of Arc, the Salem witch trials, and Ayatollah Khomeini.

Addressing the problem of potential intolerance, Atwood, who was associated with Pat Robertson's presidential campaign, suggests that "some Evangelical activists ... have been too quick to put words into the mouth of the Almighty in the political context." They are "notorious for displaying an overconfidence in their ability to discern the Divine Will at any time, in any situation" (Atwood 1990, 47).

Another problem plagues the Fundamentalist perspective. It is illustrated by the point already made about the messages from God that others conveyed to Falwell. Christians agree on some broad principles, of course, but even those who assume that they (or someone they trust) can get direct guidance from God have to face the fact that through the centuries and around the Christian world the guidance has not always been the same. People who are confident that they know the will of God get conflicting messages from Him. And the same is true of those who seek instruction from the Bible: the instruction is likely to differ depending on which passage is selected for guidance and on the interpretation given to it. The problem is put in a special and odd light by references to "Hyper-Fundamentalists" who accept only the King James version of the Bible as divinely inspired. If a Falwell or a Robertson or a Buchanan claims that his message or his interpretation is the authentic one, skepticism on the part of others is understandable. To skeptics, including most secular humanists, those who claim to speak in the name of the Lord are either naive or brazen, claiming divine authority for what are in fact their own personal judgments and preferences.

The Free Congress Foundation, headed by Paul Weyrich, champions what it calls "cultural conservatism." Elaborating on it, Weyrich lists "major failures of the conservative movement." One of them is "the failure of the Religious Right to reach out beyond its natural base." The Religious Right has been "self-isolating," permitting the fear to develop that it wants to establish a theocracy. Weyrich dismisses this fear as "ridiculous."

"A consensus among the Religious Right on any kind of theocratic government is inconceivable." A Greek Catholic himself, he says that "if this country ever became the evangelical Protestant theocracy that is supposedly our hidden agenda, I would be on the first boat out." He would maintain the constitutional "separation of church and state, with the state respectful toward all religious beliefs but itself adhering to or enforcing none."

To distance himself and cultural conservatism further from the self-isolating beliefs of Fundamentalists, Weyrich endorses the view that "the case for cultural conservatism can be made in wholly secular terms." Of course, whether a person's approach is religious or secular, the values supported must be "traditional," for it is the traditional values that are "functional."

## The Program

The program associated with social conservatism is odd in that the various items are not obviously coherent—do not obviously fit together in one neat package. Wide agreement exists on a set of core issues and then different spokesmen press different supplementary issues as well—the same issues, in many cases, as are pressed by conservative conservatives, economic conservatives, or even libertarians. The obvious question is whether God put the package together.

One commentator expresses skepticism on this point. He takes the view that unnamed right-wing leaders, facing the problem of mobilizing support for right-wing stands on economic matters, decided that as a matter of strategy they ought to focus first "on social issues that have emotional appeal," the alleged thought being that once people are recruited or aroused by appeals relating to emotional issues they can also be induced to help out on other kinds (Higgins 1980, 108).

The policy issues that social conservatism emphasizes are those relating to (1) the family; (2) religion and the schools; (3) race, immigration, and multiculturalism; (4) free enterprise and welfare, (5) nationalism, and (6) crime and community.

### THE FAMILY

The social conservative view is that the family is a divinely ordained institution, to be protected and upheld. It should be based on marriage, and divorce should be difficult. The traditional role of women, and traditional attitudes toward sexual morality, should be preserved. Abortion is unacceptable, and homosexuality and pornography are abominations. Through tax policies and in other ways, government should seek to strengthen the family as an institution.

Currently, questions pertaining directly to marriage and divorce do not get much attention. With the ERA on the back burner, questions about the role of women are not especially prominent. Nevertheless, the prevailing view is that the husband should be the breadwinner and the wife the homemaker, nurturing children. Government has no business subsidizing arrangements for daytime child care, for this encourages women to work outside the home and neglect their children. Neither should government draft women into the armed forces. If they volunteer (and social conservatives seem reconciled to the possibility), they are to have assignments compatible with their nature and are not to be sent into combat. Children are the responsibility of parents and are not to be conceded rights that weaken parental authority.

Like many others, including many progressive liberals, social conservatives are troubled by sexual freedom and birth out of wedlock, especially where teenagers are involved. They generally want to maintain or restore the principle that premarital sex is morally wrong. If sex education is offered in the schools (and many social conservatives oppose it), it must be abstinence based. The emphasis must be on the immorality of sex, not on its naturalness, let alone its possible pleasures. Condoms are not to be distributed, nor is anything else to be done that might suggest public acceptance of violations of approved moral standards. "It is difficult to say which is more maddening," says one observer, "the teenagers who can't or won't exercise restraint or the adults who step in to make sure they don't have to."

A possible alternative to the above position, or a supplement to it, is to emphasize the potential costs of premarital sex. Birth out of wedlock threatens to blight the lives of young mothers, condemning them to long-term dependency on the government. And if ways can be found to compel dead-beat dads to provide child support, irresponsibility with respect to sex might be made less attractive. These are propositions that are likely to be acceptable to people endorsing different political ideologies, but social conservatives do not give them as much attention as they give to teenage sex. I should add, however, that social conservatives, like most others, accept the policy of granting governmental support to unwed mothers (AFDC, Medicaid, etc.), although the suggestion is made that those who are still teenagers should get aid only if they live with their parents.

Ever since *Roe* v. *Wade* (1973), the fight against abortion has been at or near the top of the social conservative agenda. A series of questions get negative answers: whether or in what circumstances abortion should be legal; whether federal funding should be available to indigent women for abortions; whether, even where abortions are legal, teenage girls should be permitted to obtain them without parental consent; whether abortions should be performed in military hospitals; whether the importation of the French RU-486 pill should be permitted; whether the use of fetal material for research should be legal; whether doctors and clinics receiving federal funds should be free to provide information or counseling relating to abortion; whether abortion clinics, personnel working in such clinics, and women going to the clinics for abortions should be protected against harassment and other interference; and whether the United States should give financial support to international programs that in any way might support or encourage abortions.

I cannot argue all the questions here, but focus on the first of them, whether abortion should be legal. The nature of the argument, as I have already suggested in chapter 5, depends in part on how the question is put. Those who are pro-life generally ask when life begins, which means that the answer necessarily has an element of the arbitrary in it, for the sperm and the egg were both alive prior to conception and were produced by human beings who were also alive; arbitrary or not, the usual answer is that life begins with conception, some saying that conception occurs when the egg is fertilized and others saying that it occurs when the fertilized egg implants itself on the wall of the uterus. In any event, given "life," the assertion is that it must not be taken. As Jesse Helms puts it, "God's law condemns the taking of innocent life." This being a matter of faith, or of divine revelation, no room is left for reasoned argument.

Those who are pro-choice generally ask not when life begins but when a person or a human being comes into existence. These are the terms in the Constitution and in the international covenant on human rights. The Constitution says that no "person" is to be denied the equal protection of the laws, and the covenant says that every "human being" has the inherent right to life. Again the answer to the question has an element of the arbitrary in it, but history shows widespread agreement that, at least for legal purposes, a person or a human being comes into existence only when a live birth occurs. This leaves the organism in the womb—whether zygote, embryo, or fetus—without status or protection.

The above ways of asking the question ignore the fact that the organism in the womb changes remarkably during the period of gestation. What begins as a fertilized egg ends up as a fully formed fetus ready to be born. Those who are pro-life tend to ignore the fact of change and to speak of the killing of babies or of protecting unborn children, whereas in fact what is usually involved is simply a zygote (a fertilized egg) or at most an embryo.

The questions posed above also ignore the rights and interests of the pregnant woman and of society. Many pro-life persons are willing to permit an abortion if the pregnancy resulted from rape or incest, or if it seriously threatens the life of the pregnant woman, but not otherwise. Pro-choice persons go further, offering some such arguments as the following: The organism in the womb is a parasite, sapping the pregnant woman's energy and perhaps making her sick. It impairs or destroys her capacity to be self-supporting and her enjoyment of equality of opportunity, and the burden continues after the baby is born—a burden that she may literally be unable to bear. Just as the moral obligation to sacrifice for others or go to their rescue has limits, so does the obligation of the pregnant woman to sacrifice for the organism in her womb. Moreover, just as she has a right of self-defense against persons who attack her or impose burdens on her, so does she have a right of self-defense against the zygote or embryo, if not also against the fetus, in her body. Further, to make an abortion illegal is to fasten a special limitation on her that men do not suffer and is therefore to deny her the equal protection of the laws. And it is not necessarily in the interest of society to have a baby born to a mother who is unable to give it proper care.

Apart from those who argue passionately over the abortion issue are those who would put it into the background and focus instead on the problems that arise once babies are born—that is, on the proper care and upbringing of infants and children. Representative Barney Frank evidently had these problems in mind when he commented that "those who oppose abortion are pro-life only up to the moment of birth."

President Clinton couches essentially the same thought in broader terms. The problem that he has with so much of the Religious Right, he says, is that "so many of them seem to believe that their number one obligation is to make whatever they think is wrong illegal, and then not worry about what kind of affirmative duties we have to one another."

Attitudes toward homosexuality come close to being as strident as attitudes about abortion. They are based on the view that homosexuality is both threatening to family values and morally wrong. Pat Buchanan is among those who speak out: "A visceral recoil from homosexuality is the natural reaction of a healthy society wishing to preserve itself. A prejudice against males who engage in sodomy with one another represents a normal and natural bias in favor of sound morality." Buchanan denounced Mayor David Dinkins of New York for offending and insulting Irish Catholic traditionalists "by prancing with sodomites" in a St. Patrick's Day parade. Social conservatives generally opposed Clinton's move in the direction of removing discrimination based on sexual orientation in the armed forces. Falwell speaks of "homosexuals who have chosen a perverted lifestyle," but says that Fundamentalists do not oppose civil rights for them. It goes without saying that social conservatism opposes the view that homosexual couples who live together in a long-term stable relationship should be recognized as a family, and still more it opposes the formal recognition of marriage between homosexual persons. So-called alternative lifestyles are not acceptable.

In Oregon in 1992 Fundamentalists succeeded in getting a referendum on a proposed constitutional amendment. If adopted, the amendment would have barred the state from recognizing "sexual orientation" or "sexual preference" as a basis for establishing quotas, granting minority status, or engaging in affirmative action. It would have barred the use of public funds at any level of government "to promote, encourage, or facilitate homosexuality, pedophilia, sadism or masochism." And, regardless of good grammar, it would have required state agencies, including the public schools, to "assist in setting a standard for Oregon's youth that recognizes homosexuality, pedophilia, sadism and masochism as abnormal, wrong, unnatural and perverse and that these behaviors are to be discouraged and avoided."

As with abortion, the issue is hotly debated. The basic question is whether, or to what extent, homosexuality is a matter of choice or a matter of biology. Recall Falwell's statement, quoted earlier, that homosexual persons have *chosen* a lifestyle and that this lifestyle is *perverted,* and note that assumption in the Oregon measure that homosexuality is *unnatural.* The view is open to question. The alternative view is that people range along a scale from those who are fully heterosexual through those who are bisexual to those who are fully homosexual; the overwhelming numbers, of course, are on the heterosexual end of the scale. Those anywhere near the bisexual portion of the scale can perhaps be said to have a choice, but whether the others do is an unsettled issue. Homosexual persons themselves overwhelmingly take the view that theirs is a biologically determined orientation, not a "preference" or a matter of choice. If this is true, then the Oregon measure is in about the same category as a measure that condemns left-handedness as unnatural and perverse.

Another approach to the problem appeals to the principle that people should have liberty as long as they do not harm others. On this basis, homosexual persons qualify for liberty—are entitled to be left alone. With rare exceptions, they are consenting adults whose conduct does no harm, so why should society interfere? Recall the question raised in chapter 5 whether gays and lesbians are not *persons* entitled to the equal protection of the laws.

The Oregon measure associates homosexuality with pedophilia, sadism, and masochism. The assumption that these various behaviors belong in the same general category is curious. In pedophilia a child is the sexual object of an older person, with the distinct possibility that the child may be harmed psychologically, if not also physically. The terms *sadism* and *masochism* are hopelessly vague, but *sadism* at least denotes harm to someone else. Thus in the Oregon measure homosexuality, which is ordinarily harmless, is linked with other behaviors that are intrinsically harmful, raising the question whether the effort was to condemn homosexuality on a guilt-by-association basis.

Of those who voted on the Oregon proposal, 57 percent voted no, but it is almost as significant that 43 percent voted yes. In fact, Fundamentalists in Oregon demonstrated so much political strength in the Republican Party that others, including the party chairman, speak of splitting off and forming an independent party.

Social conservatives regularly denounce pornography and governmental subsidies for offensive art. Pat Buchanan is among the more colorful spokesmen on the point. He bewails "the damage that 30 years of judicial activism have done to this wonderful country. By breaking down all local barriers to filthy speech and dirty books, the Supreme Court permitted America's popular culture to be converted into a public sewer, in which some of the world's worst pornographers now contentedly swim." He denies that there is a "constitutional 'right' to befoul the airwaves any more than there is a constitutional right to pollute our rivers.... Polluted ideas have caused greater injury to mankind than polluted water, and the marketplace of ideas is in greater need of watching than the marketplace of goods." He condemns the National Endowment for the Arts for subsidizing artists whose work he regards as blasphemous. Phyllis Schlafly takes a similar line, saying among other things that "cities must have additional means of protecting their citizens against the public display of moral garbage."

These attitudes do not necessarily call for any curtailment of *political* speech. A reasonable argument can be made that the First Amendment should be interpreted to permit the curtailment of nonpolitical speech in pursuit of a compelling public purpose. To social conservatives, and to some others, the protection of family values is such a purpose.

Michael Schwartz calls for "Tax Reform for Family Survival." "Strong family life," he argues, "requires a secure economic foundation," and tax policies can shore up that foundation. He points out that the income tax code of 1948 provided for a deduction of $600 per dependent. The tax reform of 1986 raised the figure to $2,000, but if it had been raised to keep up with inflation it would now be $6,000. Schwartz would make it $6,000, and would double the deduction for a baby in the tax year of its birth. In addition, he would make various other tax expenditures for the benefit of families with children (Lind and Marshner 1991, 214–15, 221–24).

Those arguing for such changes point out that in a number of respects federal tax policies have either been antifamily or have at least failed to give support to the family. Tax policies make it advantageous for a couple to refrain from marrying. They in effect subsidize mothers who get jobs outside the home, doing nothing comparable for mothers who are full-time homemakers. On top of this, welfare policies give more support to the poor who are unmarried or the divorced than to those who are married.

## RELIGION AND THE SCHOOLS

Issues relating to religion came to the fore in the 1960s when the Supreme Court ruled out prayer in the public schools and when this led to the proscription of other activities supportive of religion, such as the posting of the Ten Commandments in classrooms. The issue was important in leading religiously oriented social conservatives to decide that they must seek to influence public policy. It was among the issues that Reagan came to stress. He called for a constitutional amendment to permit voluntary school prayer. More generally, he said that we must "allow God back into our classrooms. He never should have been expelled in the first place."

Difficulties with the Internal Revenue Service added to the reasons for social conservatives to become politically involved. Partly to circumvent the ban on school prayer, and even more to circumvent the requirement of racial integration, a number of communities established private schools. And Bob Jones University, a Fundamentalist institution, attempted to maintain segregation as a matter of freedom of religion. They all then faced a ruling of the IRS that schools flouting public policy on the racial issue were not entitled to tax exemption, a ruling that to them was evidence of humanist harassment. Although this issue helped stimulate Fundamentalist involvement in politics, it has lost its prominence. I revert to it below.

Apart from prayer in the schools, social conservatives face the more fundamental question of control over the schools, and the Free Congress Foundation is explicit both about its goal and about its strategy: it wants "the complete separation of school and state." That is, public education should be brought to an end and all schools should be private schools. Granting that this is not an immediately practical goal, the foundation calls for incremental steps. School choice is high on the list of possible steps, with tax dollars following students to the school of their choice, whether the school is public or private. The private schools would presumably include church schools, although social conservatives disagree on the question whether church schools should accept money from the government. Some say yes, arguing that it is unjust to deny the benefit of the tax funds to parents who want their children to have a religious education. In contrast, some say no, arguing that government money would be a "poisoned chalice," leading to governmental regulations and controls. Charter schools are also favored, chartered and financed by government but freed from most governmental controls.

Describing such incremental steps, the Free Congress Foundation warns against complacency. School choice and charter schools are not to be regarded as a "fulfilling substitute for the real thing (privatized education)."

Social conservatives disagree about taxing in order to support public education. In a book on *Cultural Conservatism,* Raphael Kazmann takes the stand that taxation for this purpose, like taxing in order to support the various entitlement programs, such as AFDC and social security, amounts to stealing and thus violates the Eighth Commandment. In contrast Patrick Taylor, writing a different chapter in the same book, recommends that state governments should levy taxes sufficient to enable them to waive tuition and fees in publicly supported colleges and universities for students who meet certain standards but who otherwise could not attend (Lind and Marshner 1991, 132–34, 141, 259).

Fundamentalists among the social conservatives seek not only a right to choose among schools but also various rights relating to what is taught. They want to be able to veto assignments in books offensive to them. As already indicated, they want either to ban or to control the nature of sex education. And some of them make an issue of teaching Darwin's theory of evolution. Pat Robertson, for example, bewails the fate of a law that Arkansas enacted in 1981 (when Frank White and not Clinton was governor) requiring public schools to teach "scientific creationism" alongside evolutionary theory. The courts declared the measure unconstitutional, an action that Robertson describes as "unfair to the rights of the majority and disastrous to the future of this nation."

### RACE, IMMIGRATION, AND MULTICULTURALISM

In 1957 the conservative *National Review* took up the question "whether the White community in the South is entitled to take such measures as are necessary to prevail, politically and culturally, in areas in which it does not predominate numerically" and gave what it described as a "sobering answer": "Yes." It held that it is "more important for any community, anywhere in the world, to affirm and live by civilized standards than to bow to the demands of the numerical majority." Not that the white community should insist on permanent supremacy. Its problem was "to equip the Negro—and a great many Whites—to cast an enlightened and responsible vote." But until the Negro was so equipped, the "claims of civilization supersede those of universal suffrage."

Falwell confesses that in his earlier years his attitudes on race reflected his southern upbringing. He preached against the civil rights bill of 1964, regarding it as a "terrible violation of human and private property rights," and he maintained a segregated church. But then "God's still small voice" told him that racial segregation was wrong and he switched his position. He now calls for a society in which "no minority is exploited or discriminated against, where every race, color, or creed has equal access to justice and opportunity." But he does not emphasize the issue, not even mentioning it in his "Agenda for the 1980s"—his program for the Moral Majority (Neuhaus and Cromartie 1987, 113–15).

In contrast, Paul Weyrich regards "the quota issue" as a "potent one for conservatives," and he thought it foolish of Bush to sign the Civil Rights Act of 1991, which was a "quota bill." Cultural conservatives outside the ranks of the Fundamentalists generally share Weyrich's view, and some go beyond it.

The most extreme view that I have encountered denounces the idea of racial equality. "As a result of exhaustive tests," William Massey claims, "it is almost universally agreed that ... the races can be ranked in intelligence as follows: Whites and Orientals, American Indians, Hispanics and American blacks, in that order" (Massey 1992a, 31). Liberals, who believe in the equality of the races, are fanatics who go on to believe "that the inevitable and proper course of human evolution leads ultimately to a world government based on the brotherhood of man." This belief is dangerous, all the more so because of the innocence of the motives involved (Massey 1992b, 39–40). Massey leaves it to readers to guess what status and rights he would concede to the less intelligent races.

Issues relating to "multiculturalism" are not clear cut, partly because the term is vague. I have already discussed the subject briefly in chapter 5. Diane Ravitch makes a useful distinction between "pluralistic" and "particularistic" multiculturalism (Ravitch 1990). Pluralistic multiculturalists, although recognizing cultural differences, emphasize an overarching common culture and seek an accommodation among the different groups. Particularists think that no common culture is possible or desirable and want to emphasize cultural distinctiveness.

Social conservatives seem to assume that multiculturalism is necessarily particularistic, and they are against it. Thus Hilton Kramer describes multiculturalism as an "ideology of racial, ethnic, and sexual separatism," championed by the "radical Left." Richard John Neuhaus speaks of the "multicultural fevers that have seized upon almost the entirety of the American academy" and says that they "reflect an explicit and rancorous rejection of the core beliefs and institutions" of the nation. According to Russell Kirk, the multiculturalist prescription is "poison, ... animated by envy and hatred.... It is well to learn much about distant cultures, ... but to neglect or to repudiate the central and pervasive British culture in America would be to let the whole academic and social enterprise fall apart." Similarly, William Bennett, asking why it is important to study, value, and defend Western civilization, responds by saying that "it is ours. It is the culture in which we live." Moreover, he asserts, it is good.

The fear is that multiculturalism portends special status and rights for racial and ethnic groups, the acceptance of a flood of immigrants, and reduced pressure on immigrants to learn English. Troubles are envisaged for the United States analogous to those of Canada or, still worse, Lebanon and Cyprus. This is the background of the view of Thomas Fleming that "for the most part, multiculturalism is a war against the culture of the West and the institutions of American life."

In 1991 David Duke campaigned for the governorship of Louisiana. He lost, but his campaign led Samuel Francis to make an analysis that relates to multiculturalism. According to Francis, the Duke campaign provides an "obituary for the kind of issues mainstream conservatives have long espoused," centered on small or limited government and free-market policies. The real issues of the future, according to Francis, have to do with "the awakening of a people who face political, cultural, and economic dispossession." The threat of dispossession comes from quotas, affirmative action, race norming, civil rights legislation, multiculturalism in schools and universities, welfare, busing, and unrestricted immigration from the Third World; and allegedly it was Duke's success in playing on resulting fears that won him votes from "the entire range of Louisiana's white middle class." His campaign points the way toward "a new popular nationalism [making] plain that the threat to American national identity is only in part ethnic but also cultural, economic and political." The issue of the future, then, is not the size of the government but control over it, and "cultural destruction and dispossession" may or may not occur, depending on who controls (Francis 1992, 8–9).

Immigration is mentioned above. In the main, those who write on behalf of social conservatives are hostile to it, on the basis of both economic and cultural considerations, especially because so many of the immigrants are non-European in origin. The economic consideration is that so many of the immigrants become costly to American taxpayers: They go on welfare, need health care, commit crimes, and burden the schools. According to one claim, illegal immigrants alone consume 25 percent of California's budget for social services, and governments at the various levels spend half a billion dollars a year incarcerating criminal aliens. The view of George Kennan is cited that immigrants from the Third and Fourth worlds threaten us with levels of overpopulation and poverty matching those of the countries from which the immigrants come, and that the inability to resist immigration is "a serious weakness, and possibly even a fatal one."

To social conservatives the cultural consideration is even more important than the economic. The assumption is that immigrants adulterate the national culture. Instead of dispersing into English-speaking communities and assimilating, they tend, when they come in large numbers, to congregate in one area, such as Miami or Southern California, and then preserve their own language and culture. Moreover, where black immigrants are in question, the racial consideration comes to the fore, the symbolic question being whether a million Zulus would assimilate as readily as a million people from Ireland or Italy.

"At the root of the growing concern about immigration," says a writer in *National Review*, "is the public's sense that their country is being dramatically transformed without their consent." Pat Buchanan expresses the dominant attitude: "Since 1967 a floodtide of immigration has rolled in from the Third World, legal and illegal, as our institutions of assimilation—public schools, popular culture, churches, disintegrated.... We are changing irrevocably from a First World nation into the Brazil of North America: 'The combined forces of open immigration and multiculturalism constitute a mortal threat to American civilization.'" And Samuel Francis declares that "the main thing Americans must do to preserve their civilization and the ethnic base on which it is founded is to stop immigration, especially from countries that do not share the ethnic and cultural heritage of the historic core of this nation."

Some social conservatives take a different line on immigration.

The thought is that the "aliens among us" are not really the immigrants but the urban and mainly black underclass, the civil rights "overclass" (also largely black), homosexuals, and a considerable portion of the chattering class. The main threat to the culture stems from these groups. In contrast, immigrants, far from being really alien, the argument goes, tend to be strongly oriented toward religion, family values, and the work ethic, which suggests that we can look to them to save the culture that domestic groups are either failing to support or actively undermining. Immigrants, according to this view, are to be welcomed as "cannon fodder in the cultural war."

### Free Enterprise and Welfare

The current emphasis of social conservatism is on the issues described above. Nevertheless, other issues get some attention, such as free enterprise and welfare.

The free-enterprise system is uniformly endorsed, with alternatives, such as communism and socialism, excoriated. According to LaHaye, the "concepts [of] free enterprise, private ownership of land, and capitalism ... emanated from biblical teaching." Moreover, they have produced "the greatest good for the largest number of people in history" (1980, 39). One of his reasons for denouncing humanists is their "consistent hostility toward Americanism, capitalism, and free enterprise," and their call for socialism. To him, communism and Marxist socialism are associated with the idea that religion is the opium of the people and thus with atheism; and they lead to what Falwell calls "shared poverty."

Attitudes toward welfare are more ambivalent, although preponderantly negative. Pat Robertson's position is suggestive. He does not explicitly oppose governmental efforts on behalf of welfare, but says that "what we want for our families and our neighbors must come from within ourselves.... The problems of poverty, inequality, and injustice are problems of the human spirit. And federal spending, even without limits, will never create a truly great society." The American Coalition for Traditional Values goes farther, asking for the termination of "social programs that, it is believed, only increase the dependency of the poor." And Jesse Helms treats programs of the New Deal, Fair Deal, and Great Society collectively as an "onslaught ... for redistributing the wealth that rewards the indolent and penalizes the hard-working." To him, "the greatest antipoverty agency of all time is a business that turns a profit" (1976, 11, 41).

Michael Lienesch explains such negative attitudes by speaking of a dual covenant that emphasizes God's grace, but—more to the point in this context—also requires good works; and the requirement of good works leads to the Protestant ethic emphasizing personal responsibility, discipline, and hard work, with economic success treated as evidence of moral virtue and poverty as evidence of moral failure. It is indolence and vice that lead people onto welfare rolls (1983, 74).

Jerry Falwell puts in a dissent without giving it much emphasis. He speaks of Fundamentalist preachers who warn against the social gospel on the ground that it focuses on the welfare of the body as opposed to the welfare of the soul, and he goes on to describe this as "an excuse to ignore Christ's call to feed the hungry and heal the sick.... Today's Christian community must preach the Gospel clearly and at the same time put its faith into practical action on behalf of all those who suffer." He wants to "struggle to bring justice, equality and a fuller measure of mercy and generosity through our free enterprise system. The exploitation of workers, the misuse and abuse of power and wealth, the unequal and discriminatory distribution of profits should have no place in America's practice of capitalism."

He looks forward to a society in which "no one needs to be poor, hungry, or afraid" (1987, 352, 371–72). And Paul Weyrich wants government to "ensure care for the helpless" in accordance with Christian social doctrine (Whitaker 1982, 53).

## NATIONALISM

Social conservatives differ on issues of foreign policy, although the pronounced tendency is toward national patriotism and hostility to anything suggestive of "one-worldism." Among the reasons leading LaHaye to denounce humanists is the belief that they are willing to "sacrifice national benefits to international unity." They are socialist one-worlders first and Americans second. They even vote to increase American financial support for the United Nations. It is they who think that "patriotism is the last refuge of scoundrels" (LaHaye 1980, 72–77).

Pat Buchanan is the most extreme of those stressing nationalism, making a major point of the principle of "America First" and insisting on isolationist and protectionist policies. "The battle for the future is on between New Age globalists and old-fashioned patriots, between those who believe America must yield up her sovereignty to a New World Order and those who believe we must preserve the Old Republic.... America cannot afford to be bailing out every bankrupt regime on Earth and pulling everybody's bacon out of the fire." In contrast to Buchanan, Falwell says little about foreign affairs, except that he asks for strong support of Israel and the Jewish people everywhere.

Writing about the New Right, Samuel T. Francis names nationalism as its best known characteristic—a nationalism that requires the rejection of cosmopolitanism and abstract universalism, which are too much identified with the idea of the brotherhood of man and with egalitarianism and which call for a "relativization of identities," that is, a blurring of distinctions based on race, ethnicity, and nationality. The attitude is akin to LaHaye's rejection of one-worldism.

### CRIME AND COMMUNITY

As noted in the preceding chapter, conservatives of all sorts emphasize the importance of being "tough on crime" and belabor liberals for being soft. Liberals allegedly blame not the criminal but the conditions that breed crime, and so they seek social reform; in contrast, conservatives blame the criminal and seek to make his arrest surer and his punishment swifter and perhaps more draconic. Prisons should be built accordingly, even if it costs more to keep a person in prison than it would to send him to college and even if the person sent to prison is thereby assured a higher standard of living than he enjoys when he is free. More than a fourth of those being sent to prison are drug pushers.

Support for capital punishment has come to be symbolic of toughness, and some even speak of extending it to additional crimes. Thomas Fleming, for example, wants to extend capital punishment to rape, armed robbery, kidnapping, and arson; and he urges that nonviolent criminals be required to wear "some badge of shame" and that the pillory be used once more. The paradox is that so many who are adamantly pro-life are also adamant supporters of capital punishment.

Libertarians, be it recalled, would legalize drugs and thus reduce the problem of crime, whatever the other social implications might be.

The concern of social conservatives for community is a concern for localism and for decentralized institutions—for family, neighborhood, school, church, and local government. Whatever tends to weaken these institutions is to be deplored. The attitude has contributed, at the one extreme, to opposition to busing, the belief being that the preservation of the neighborhood school is more important than the achievement of racial balance. At the other extreme it has contributed, for example, to opposition to the creation of the Department of Education on the ground that this would "increase federal intervention and bureaucratic humanist regulation over public education." Jesse Helms expresses the belief that government begins with the individual and proceeds to the family, the ultimate government being the dominion of God. Somewhere in between is the state, which follows "the utterly erroneous belief that the civil government should take precedence over the family, the church, and every other form of social organization."

Samuel T. Francis gives a summary of the New Right position that also fits social conservatism. He calls for a

> Domestic Ethic that centers on the family, the neighborhood and local community, the church, and the nation as the basic framework of values.... In place of the hedonistic, pragmatist, relativist, and secularized cosmopolitanism of the present elite, the New Right should expound without compromise the ideals and institutions of the American ethos: hard work and self-sacrifice, morally based legislation and policies, and a public commitment to religious faith. (Whitaker 1982, 78)

# Chapter 12

# Progressive Conservatism

THE EXPRESSION *progressive conservatism* may look like an oxymoron, but it is used. Canada has a Progressive Conservative Party, and in the United States Jack Kemp describes himself as "a radical, bleeding-heart progressive conservative" (1992b, 1; cf. 1990b, 2).

In a sense, all conservatives want progress, just as liberals do. A recent book on *The Conservative Movement* declares that "a distinctive feature of the contemporary American Right is its emphasis on progress: moving beyond the past toward a future of unlimited material opportunity and social improvement" (Gottfried and Fleming 1988, vii). But conservatives differ in their conception of progress and how to achieve it. Reagan wanted progress in the form of general economic growth; benefit for the poor, if any, would come indirectly. His supporters could say that he operated on the theory that a rising tide lifts all boats, and his opponents could say that he relied on trickle-down theory. Kemp favors general economic growth too, and (like Reagan) he wants to get it by supply-side methods, mainly by cutting taxes (1990a, 1; Hood 1992, 42–43). But when he speaks of progressive conservatism, his thoughts are on the problem of poverty. He wants to make a more determined and direct attack on it than Reagan favored. It is Kemp's variety of progressive conservatism to which this chapter is addressed.

Kemp is not alone in his concern for poverty. Various other Republican leaders strike many of the same notes, for example, Newt Gingrich, Dan Quayle, and Vin Weber. So does George F. Will, in *Statecraft as Soulcraft*. And several persons connected with the Heritage Foundation, a conservative think tank, fit within the category. Stuart Butler and Anna Kondratas have written a book, *Out of the Poverty Trap, A Conservative Strategy for Welfare Reform* (1987). Although progressive conservatives distinguish themselves from other conservatives mainly by their concern for poverty, they have additional special concerns. I note them toward the end of the chapter. For the most part, however, the chapter describes what might be called *The Conservative War on Poverty.*

## The Need for Governmental Action

Recalling Reagan's statement that we fought a war on poverty and poverty won, James Pinkerton, who served in the Bush White House, goes on to say, "I prefer to think of the past few decades as a lost *battle,* not a lost war.... "

Stuart Butler, who is mentioned above and who is associated with the Heritage Foundation, also rejects the view that the war is over and has been lost. "The Gipper," he says, "could be clear and eloquent on cutting taxes, or on defending America. But when it came to dealing with poverty, he mumbled." To Butler, "mumbling" on the issue is unacceptable. Conservatives "must realize that they have no alternative but to declare an assault on poverty. If they don't, they will forever be on the moral and intellectual defensive" and will thus be at a disadvantage in political competition (Butler 1989, 27). Butler and Kondratas speak of "a consensus that has been remarkably constant across time and place [on the] principle that a civilized society is duty-bound to provide sufficient assistance to those who are infirm, disabled, or otherwise unable to support themselves to reach a minimum acceptable standard of living" (1987, 51).

Adam Meyerson of the Heritage Foundation speaks in the same vein. "Voters throughout the world continue to support a large government role in health, education, and social insurance; generous aid to the needy; and strong safety and environmental regulation.... The spirit of the age ... seems to favor some sort of welfare state...." (1989, 66). He adds that "the reflexive hostility to government of so many conservatives must ... be abandoned." He thinks it consistent with the idea of freedom if people "gather together and make decisions through governments of their own choosing." Vin Weber voices similar thoughts in explaining why he abandoned his earlier stand as "a strict libertarian." He speaks of "activist conservatism," and thinks that "activist conservatives" are becoming stronger on the Republican side in Congress.

George Will has similar thoughts. In *Statecraft as Soulcraft* he expresses regret that American conservatives are "caught in the web of their careless antigovernment rhetoric," saying that they are "partially

immobilized by their uneasy consciences about government power."
He speaks of "social goals for a conservative welfare state." He wants
a welfare system that "supports rather than disintegrates families,"
and he urges state action such as provision of prenatal care to enhance
equality of opportunity.

Kemp may not agree entirely with Will, but he does agree with
the general thrust of the above statements. Implicitly he rejects Reagan's view that government is the problem, not the solution. He says
that "in a democratic society, people are going to demand problem-
solving by government."

Perhaps more important, Kemp insists that governmental action
include a "war on poverty." He considers this "a moral and political
imperative." "We cannot politically or morally condone the existence
of the level of poverty, despair, homelessness, and joblessness that all
too often grips this Nation" (U.S. Congress 1991, 309–10, 324). He
wants conservatives to "become the vanguard of a crusade to end the
scourge of poverty." Every person, he says, should have "the opportunity to achieve his or her capacity.... All of our nation's people should
have the opportunity to share in the blessings of freedom, democracy,
and equality of opportunity." He says he was thrilled when Bush
asked him to be secretary of housing and urban development, for this
gave him "the opportunity to make HUD and its programs into models of 'progressive conservatism' in action" (1990b, 2).

I need not comment on the fact that, in calling for a war on poverty, Kemp follows in the footsteps of Lloyd George and Lyndon
Johnson. He has this in common with progressive liberals, and it es-
tranges him from some other conservatives. One of them disparages
him as "a supply-side millenarian who imagines limitless possibilities
of social uplift through the exercise of centralized state power."

## Empowerment

Kemp wants to wage the war on poverty by *empowering* people, and
other progressive conservatives join him in pushing this theme—most
notably William Bennett, Jeane Kirkpatrick, and Vin Weber. They
have established an organization that they call *Empower America*.

The meaning given to *empowerment* will come out more fully in
what follows, but we should note right off that the idea is similar to
the progressive liberal idea that it is important to give worth to liberty—important to think of people having liberty only when they can
make choices. Progressive conservatives join progressive liberals in

wanting to arrange affairs so that people have opportunity and choice. As noted, the idea is that every person should have "the opportunity to achieve his or her capacity." Jobs, education and training, housing, nutrition, health, self-esteem and self-discipline, and the internalization of values important to social life are all potentially involved. Progressive conservatives and progressive liberals would agree on the above.

Where they disagree is on methods. Kemp would *empower* by various methods, but above all by cutting taxes. He is a supply-sider, identified with the Kemp-Roth tax cut of the Reagan administration. He finds "the cornerstone of growth" in a "crucial insight" reflected in Laffer's curve. The "insight," discussed in chapter 10, is that government can get as much revenue, or more, from lower tax rates, for lower rates will stimulate entrepreneurial activity, produce economic growth, and expand the total amount of income and wealth to which the taxes apply (Kemp 1979, 10). Kemp plays on this theme endlessly. He wants to cut taxes especially in enterprise zones, to be discussed below. Apparently he would cut them no matter how low they already are.

William Bennett, joined with Kemp in *Empower America,* puts less stress on tax cuts and enterprise zones as the solution to the problem of poverty. He speaks of a "culture of poverty" and of the need for a work ethic and its associated values. Where Kemp looks to supply-side economics for solutions, Bennett is more inclined to look toward social conservatism and the Religious Right. But, perhaps to broaden his appeal, Kemp too has written of the "moral foundation" of capitalism and of the need to strengthen the family, the church, and the neighborhood, and he has joined in releasing an *Empower America* platform that includes planks designed to appeal to both economic and social conservatives (1993a, 578–79).

## Enterprise Zones

As suggested, enterprise zones are Kemp's favorite method for creating jobs. As secretary of housing and urban development, he thought of the zones mainly as urban, but they can also be rural. Kemp has been championing the idea of such zones for many years, and Reagan and Bush both asked Congress to provide for them; but then, fearing criticism about taxes, Bush vetoed a bill in which Congress responded. The zones in operation in 1992 (more than 1,500 of them) had all been established under state rather than federal laws. Clinton signed into law a bill calling for the creation of six urban and three rural "empowerment zones" on an experimental basis, plus a number of "enterprise communities"; Kemp opposed the bill on the ground that it gave government too large a role.

An enterprise zone is an area of concentrated poverty where government takes special action to stimulate the creation of jobs. Tax concessions of one sort or another are by far the most important kind of special action, but the states creating the zones provide for other kinds too, such as loans granted on especially favorable terms, guarantees of loans obtained from banks, improvements in the infrastructure, and better police protection.

Kemp advances two main themes in championing enterprise zones. The first is that people in poverty are like people everywhere, not belonging to a distinctive culture that makes them unattractive as employees or impossible as entrepreneurs. They will respond to economic incentives just like everyone else. "Our inner cities are overflowing with human capital, an untapped reservoir of human creativity" (1992a, 4). "Most Americans—rich and poor alike—share the same values, hopes, and dreams." It is necessary to "recognize the dignity and potential of every person in America" (1992b, 3).

The second theme concerns taxes. Kemp harps especially on the capital gains tax, arguing that if it is eliminated entrepreneurs will come forward within the zones, creating new enterprises and the related jobs. He denies that his main object is to attract investors into zones who otherwise would invest elsewhere.

Critics make several points. First, they claim that the enterprise zones in existence have had only modest success, giving scant basis for confidence in them. Kemp's response is that the tax concessions that the federal government can offer will make a significant difference.

Second, critics are skeptical about the personal qualities of residents of zones of poverty, wondering how many of them could be effective as entrepreneurs or even desirable as employees. The comment is that enterprises set up in the zones might well go outside them to recruit their workers.

The third argument is that tax concessions are unlikely to matter much—that taxes constitute so small a proportion of the total costs of a business that concessions are unlikely to swing decisions. Those wanting to create or expand a business are more likely to locate it where the relevant circumstances are favorable rather than, for example, in a rundown and decaying central city where it cannot be assumed that residents will have characteristics making them attractive as employees.

The fourth argument assumes that the main purpose of enterprise zones is to attract businesses that would be established elsewhere in the absence of tax concessions. This assumption leads to the point that if an enterprise zone program does work, it may have little net effect, for one community's gain is likely to be another community's loss. Moreover, problems arise when a business just inside the zone competes with a business just outside it, one getting advantages denied to the other. And, at least in the short run, tax breaks for one group of people necessarily mean increased burdens for others, a greater deficit, or an intensified budgetary squeeze.

The proposal to make a reduction or elimination of the capital gains tax the major inducement is especially controversial. The Bush administration made an issue of the reduction or elimination of this tax everywhere, not simply in enterprise zones, but Congress (controlled by Democrats) said no, and it was unwilling to make an exception for enterprise zones. Moreover, in many eyes the fact that the deficit mounted so monstrously given the tax cuts of the Reagan period suggests caution about regarding tax cuts as the proper weapon for the war on poverty. In addition, the effects of a reduction in the capital gains tax, if any, are not realized until a property is sold, and thus in the absence of a sale the reduction does not provide the quick benefits that new or expanded businesses are likely to need. Critics suggest that if any kind of tax break is employed to stimulate the creation of jobs in enterprise zones, one focusing on investments would be more promising than one focusing on capital gains. The Clinton program relies mainly on wage credits, reducing payroll taxes.

Critics of Kemp's plan to wage a war on poverty through enterprise zones also raise the question whether other strategies may not be more effective. The critics would begin with prenatal care and add other programs relating to nutrition, education, training, health, and the inculcation of proper values with the hope of giving people pride in themselves and making them more employable. And they might add special measures to assure law and order and a more attractive infrastructure in the zone in question. As noted in chapter 10, David Riemer would have government provide community-service jobs to all in need of employment; and he would expand the earned income tax credit.

The problem for libertarians and most conservatives is that these alternative strategies make for "big government"—that is, for "tax and spend" policies and for an expansion of the bureaucracy. Along with lower taxes, Kemp wants reduced spending.

Even some who favor enterprise zones criticize Kemp for relying unduly on tax concessions. Thus the executive director of the American Association of Enterprise Zones comments that "not once in all these years have I heard a HUD spokesman suggest that redevelopment planning might be more complicated than simply offering tax breaks," and he goes on to regret HUD's "utter disinterest" in rebuilding streets, upgrading security, and improving services, attributing this disinterest to a "preoccupation with supply-side theories."

## Housing

Just as Kemp identifies progressive conservatism with urban development through enterprise zones, so he identifies it with attacks on the housing problem of the poor. The federal government has involved itself in this problem since the time of the New Deal, extending its involvement now and then through new legislation. Its activities take a number of forms: constructing low-income housing, managing such housing or providing for management by private firms or by the tenants themselves; giving the poor vouchers or certificates that they can apply toward the payment of rent in either public or private housing; and selling public housing to residents or groups of residents. When tenants take over the management of a project, it is ordinarily through a corporation or a cooperative that they form, and then either the corporation or the cooperative may become the buyer of the housing project. Individual tenants may buy the dwellings that they have been renting. Low-income families sometimes become "homesteaders." For a nominal sum, perhaps only one dollar, a "homesteader" buys and promises to rehabilitate a governmentally owned dwelling that has been standing vacant and that probably has been vandalized.

Kemp selected some of the features of the established federal housing program and added others, putting them together in a program that he called HOPE: Home Ownership and Opportunity for People Everywhere. The counterpart of hope for people everywhere was a hope that the role of government could be reduced. Kemp wanted to transfer management to the tenants or to private contractors. He wanted to sell government housing to the corporations or the cooperatives formed by tenants, or to individual families. He wanted to promote sales in a number of ways: pricing the properties below the market level, guaranteeing loans made by private institutions, crediting rent money toward a down payment when it did not need to be used to make repairs, raising the ceiling on the permissible assets of those on welfare to $10,000 to permit them to save up more for down payments, allowing individual buyers to convert IRAs into down payments without tax penalty, issuing vouchers and certificates not only for the payment of rent but also for payments on a mortgage loan, and promoting homesteading. He also proposed assisting low-income families who want to move away from areas where poverty is concentrated. To him, homeownership was "the most basic form of empowerment," and HOPE was "the cornerstone of a new effort to empower the poor." HOPE attempted "to replace the cycle of poverty and dependency with the ladder of opportunity" (U.S. Congress 1990b, 361).

Kemp's enthusiasm and optimism are not universally shared. Congress funded his programs at a far lower level than he recommended. Lawrence Mead, a political scientist who describes himself as a conservative, says that empowerment as a basis for anti-poverty policy tends to presume exactly what is questionable—that "the poor can be competent managers of their own lives. If poor adults behaved rationally, they would seldom be poor in the first place."

On the other side, Jeffrey A. Tucker, a conservative of a different sort, attacks the proposal to allow those on welfare to build up increased savings on the ground that this will reduce the incentive to get off the welfare rolls and lead to a vast expansion of the numbers on the rolls. The latter charge reflects an assumption that eligibility for welfare would come to include all those with savings below the permissible limit. Tucker also complains that costs to the government in connection with the sale of public housing are exorbitant and that, anyway, sales "do not really institute formal ownership at all" since restrictions are imposed on reselling. The restrictions are designed to prevent those who buy on extremely favorable terms from making windfall profits through a quick resale. The usual device is a second mortgage covering the difference between the sale price and the fair market value. No payments are made on the second mortgage, and a certain percentage of it is forgiven with each successive year of ownership.

## Welfare Reform

In addition to calling for enterprise zones and homeownership, *empowerment* also calls for reforms in the welfare system. In fact, Newt Gingrich speaks of bringing the welfare system to an end. A 1992 memo signed by Kemp, Gingrich, and others speaks of governmental programs that are "well-intentioned but misguided, ... entrapping the poor in poverty, robbing them of their dignity, and sentencing them to a life of despair" (Kemp et al. 1992, 683). The rhetoric employed provides a basis for arguing that "welfare" should simply be terminated, but progressive conservatism in fact does not go this far. It seeks reform.

The problem is difficult, and it is easy to be misled by statements concerning it. The "welfare" system includes a number of different programs serving different categories of people, making generalizations about it suspect. Progressive conservatives who condemn the system are not ordinarily thinking of social security, and perhaps not even of Medicare, programs that cover those over a certain age regardless of their income level. What they ordinarily have in mind are means-tested programs (mainly AFDC, Medicaid, food stamps, SSI, and general assistance) providing benefits for the poor. And among the poor the critics focus on nonworking able-bodied adults—a small proportion of the total. The critics tend to forget that two-thirds of the poor are persons who are not expected to be self-supporting—children, the elderly, or the severely handicapped; and they tend to forget that approximately a quarter of the poor have jobs but do not earn enough to get above the poverty level.

Whoever shapes welfare programs faces a series of dilemmas that we have already encountered in connection with criticisms of programs identified with the New Deal and the Great Society; and it is in the nature of a dilemma that no entirely satisfactory solution is available. One dilemma is how to make aid available to able-bodied adults without undermining their motivation to be self-supporting. The general assumption is that the aid must be sufficient to make subsistence possible, but many jobs pay no more than that. So why should a person shift from welfare to a job? Further, those who are on the AFDC rolls are also entitled to Medicaid and food stamps, a bonus they lose if they go to work. And those who try to be self-supporting face costs that those on welfare avoid: the cost of travel to and from the work site, the cost of child care, costs due to taxes, costs of clothing appropriate for the job.

A second dilemma is how to stimulate and maintain the incentive of people to become better off while telling them that they will be dropped from the welfare rolls when they succeed. To keep on giving aid after incomes and assets have risen above a certain level is to confer an undue advantage—at the expense of taxpaying neighbors whose incomes may also be limited. But to cut people off the welfare rolls when their incomes and assets rise to a certain point is to penalize ambition. Further, how can encouragement to save money for education or for a down payment be reconciled with low limits on the assets that welfare recipients may hold?

A third dilemma is how to make aid available without undermining the family. Why should a woman marry if the support she gets from welfare is approximately as good as what a husband could provide? Why not maintain a relationship with a man without marriage, perhaps in the same household, in which case she can continue on welfare and he can continue on his job? For those already married, how can an aid program be managed so as to not to contribute to the breakup of the family? If a husband cannot provide adequate support, but if his wife and children could get aid in case he abandons them, he may think it his duty to move out, and if a woman cannot get Medicaid for herself or her children as long as she is married but could qualify if she were divorced, she may see divorce as a solution to her problem.

A fourth dilemma is how to provide support for infants and children without promoting irresponsibility on the part of mothers and fathers and without encouraging out-of-wedlock births. If the parents of a teenage daughter know that the government will save them from having to support a grandchild, how much will that affect their determination to influence her behavior? If the teenage girl herself (or, in truth, any woman) knows that the government will support her and her child, how much more likely is it that she will become pregnant? If a teenage boy or man knows that he can father a child without having to support it, how much more likely is it that he will become a father? And how much more likely is it that a second, third, and fourth child will be born if welfare payments go up with each birth? Surely government aid does something to accentuate the problem, but if you try to induce parents to be more responsible by withholding or minimizing aid, you condemn infants and children to a bad start in life.

A fifth dilemma applies especially to single-parent households: how to promote the work ethic and the idea of self-support and at the same time promote the loving care of children in the home.

Whatever horn of these dilemmas anyone picks, critics can always say that a different choice would have been better. I have already noted Kemp's stand that people on welfare should be permitted to build their assets up beyond the level heretofore permitted in order to become homeowners. He and others also want to make somewhat larger incomes tax exempt and to raise the tax exemption for dependents. Almost everyone favors cracking down on dead-beat fathers, requiring that a certain portion (a fourth?) of their income go for child support. In addition, progressive conservatives join with others in supporting several reforms. They support "learnfare," including a policy of reducing welfare payments to parents who fail to see to it that their school-age children actually attend school. They support "workfare," a policy of requiring able-bodied adult beneficiaries of aid to follow a course of action designed to help them become self-supporting. The requirement may be that they attend school or take training or gain work experience, the suggestion being that mothers of young children (children under three?) should be exempt.

In *Out of the Poverty Trap* (1987) Butler and Kondratas have additional suggestions. In their view, parents should be obliged to take more responsibility for the sexual behavior of their teenage children, including responsibility for the support of grandchildren. And their rule would be to require teenage mothers to stay with their parents rather than set up separate households on the basis of governmental aid. They would impose a lifetime limit of four years on eligibility for AFDC. And they would try to shift the burden of aid insofar as possible from the government to families and communities. They would cancel or amend various regulations that limit income-producing activities, for example, occupational licensing restrictions, building codes, and prohibitions of homework.

Given all the suggested changes, however, most of the dilemmas associated with welfare remain. No one has yet found out how to make welfare for the able-bodied fully compatible with the work ethic. And no one has yet found out how to provide for children without giving aid to an able-bodied parent.

## Education

Progressive conservatism includes a call for changes in the field of primary and secondary education, agreeing to a considerable extent with the social conservatives, although presumably for different reasons. Butler and Kondratas think that "private schools consistently outperform public schools"—without asking whether the difference may be due more to the nature of the families from which the pupils come than to the nature of the schools. "We shall never come to grips with poverty in America," they say, "until we deal with the disaster area of public education." Teachers should give more attention to the problem of "inculcating basic values and transmitting culture" and should insist on higher academic and disciplinary standards. Parents should involve themselves more fully in the schooling of their children and should be able to choose the school, public or private, that their children attend, government providing tuition tax credits and vouchers when private schools are chosen.

A manifesto of *Empower America* also endorses school choice, specifically including private, religious schools among those that may be chosen. The aim is to give the educational system some of the characteristics of a market, those schools surviving that develop and maintain attractive programs. If tax credits and vouchers end up supporting religious schools, and if school choice facilitates white flight from schools in which minorities are heavily represented, so be it.

The journal published by the Heritage Foundation carried in article in 1991 that focuses on Texas but has wider implications. The article urges Texas to "invest more in human capital."

> A strong conservative case can be made for increasing the size and scope of Texas's public sector where long-term economic benefits demonstrably exceed short-term costs to the state's taxpayers. Education, public health and safety, malnutrition, mental health, and adult illiteracy would appear to be priority areas for carefully targeted increases in government spending.... The state's "less is more" approach, perhaps appropriate to a rural, agrarian economy, simply is not capable of meeting the needs of a would-be modern industrial state.

The article puts special stress on the need for "increased educational outlays" tied to statewide programs for school choice and the "alternative certification" of teachers.

## Health Care

Rather than try to describe progressive conservative attitudes on health care by examining the current debate, I will focus on the treatment of the subject in the book by Butler and Kondratas cited above: *Out of the Poverty Trap.* "Whether conservatives like it or not," Butler and Kondratas say, "the shifting consensus in America now believes that adequate health care is an item, like food, education, and decent shelter, that this society must guarantee to its citizens." Their position is that conservatives should "stop trying to deny the inevitable and instead seize the initiative." If they do not, liberals will control the decision and bring about a massive extension of the welfare state.

What Butler and Kondratas want in connection with health care is an emphasis on the market and the responsibility of individuals, but they nevertheless assign important roles to government. In the first place, mainly through Medicare, government has already made commitments that must be honored. In the second place, government must attack what I call the free rider problem. Free riders are people who could afford to take out health insurance but fail to do it, with the result that they become burdens on their neighbors or on the government if they have bad luck or if their lifestyle leads to a need for health care. In the third place, government must see to it that insurance companies fix premiums without discriminating against bad risks. And in the fourth place, government must provide for the indigent.

Emphasis on the market means emphasis on competition, assured in several ways. Employers who offer health insurance as a fringe benefit can have health providers bid competitively for the job. Health maintenance organizations (HMOs) can compete for the patronage of individuals. And medical doctors can maintain walk-in clinics offering outpatient care.

Government is to outlaw free riding by requiring people who can afford it to carry health insurance; and it is to outlaw discrimination against people who are bad risks in any of several ways. For example, when large numbers are involved—as when the insurance covers workers in a big factory—the requirement can be that all workers be covered regardless of the risk in individual cases. When small numbers are involved, or when insurance is taken out by individuals, insurance companies can be required to enroll bad risks in numbers proportionate to their share of the good risks in a state. Further, all these arrangements are to provide in one way or another for health care during retirement years so that, as time goes on, Medicare can be phased out. The health insurance system is to be supported by tax expenditures in that premiums are to be tax deductible.

As to the problem of the indigent, Medicaid or the equivalent remains the solution for the indefinite future. And to make it less likely that people will refuse to take a job because they will thereby lose their eligibility for Medicaid, Butler and Kondratas would have government issue vouchers to those going off welfare—vouchers that can be used in paying for medical services. "In those cases where a person does not earn enough to put sufficient aside, or where an elderly person faces medical costs that he or she could not have been expected to insure against, then it is humane and legitimate for government to step in as the last resort—the final insurance underwriter." Self-protection is a social obligation, but when it is impossible or unreasonable, government should step in.

As if to establish themselves along with Kemp as "bleeding-heart conservatives," Butler and Kondratas say that "clearly a rich and civilized country like the United States has to find a better way to provide long-term care for its senior citizens than to require them first to reduce themselves to penury." More generally, they say that the resources of the federal and state governments "should always be there to underwrite our commitment as a society to those who genuinely need help." But they also say that "it is time to demand that Americans take real responsibility for their actions rather than rely on the welfare state to take care of all problems."

Butler and Kondratas do not discuss the question of the constitutionality of the requirement that people buy health insurance and that insurance companies accommodate bad risks without discrimination. The legislation that they propose would surely lead to a battle in the courts, but the odds are that the legislation would be sustained.

## Nonpoverty Concerns

Although usually discussed in the context of a concern for poverty, some of the proposals described earlier have wider ramifications. The proposals relating to education and health care have obvious ramifications extending beyond the poor, and so do some of the proposals relating to taxes—for example, the proposal that the income tax deduction for dependents be substantially increased. And progressive conservatives address some issues that have no special relevance to the problem of poverty.

In 1991 *Policy Review,* published by the Heritage Foundation, printed the answers of a number of conservative leaders to the question "What should be the ten most important foreign and domestic policy priorities for the conservative movement in the 1990s?" For the most part, the answers suggest either classical or reactionary conservatism (economic or social), but a few should probably be classified as progressive.

Among the few are two that mention environmental concerns. One of the respondents says that we must "preserve our land, water, and air," and he calls on conservatives to "halt their retreat from the environmental debate." Then, in harmony with the idea of limited government, he calls for "policies that place the burden for repairing environmental damage on polluters, not on innocent taxpayers." And another respondent says, "Of all the major areas of public policy, environmental policy is the place where conservatives are intellectually and organizationally the weakest.... Perhaps most important, it is essential for conservatives to recognize that environmental questions are above all moral questions. There are deep affinities between efforts to conserve nature and efforts to conserve the best values of civilization.

The biblical principle of stewardship ... has great potential to become the dominant environmental philosophy...."

A few of the answers speak of the problem of civil rights. Jack Kemp, for example, says that he "can think of no other idea so clearly consistent with progressive conservatism as the extension of equal human and civil rights to all Americans" (1990a, 5). Elsewhere Kemp has objected to references to "black crime" and to fears that whites may feel in totally black neighborhoods. His point is that crime is not to be identified with blacks but with economic and family circumstances, and that fear is felt not so much in black neighborhoods as in dangerous neighborhoods. Kemp is set on building a coalition that includes the poor and minorities, especially blacks.

Some of the answers speak of political centralization/decentralization, but as HUD secretary, Kemp was necessarily championing action by the federal government. Moreover, it is difficult to see how the problems of welfare and health could be dealt with effectively without major federal involvement. Nevertheless, according to Stuart Butler, "a core element of a conservative War on Poverty must ... be to give the fullest possible rein to the creative juices of state government" (Butler 1989, 28). And beyond political decentralization is an emphasis on "rebuilding America's communities." They are to be rebuilt in part by simply reducing the role of the federal government and in part by methods already described: empowerment, enterprise zones, tenant management or ownership of housing, and so on. Bush espoused the idea in speaking of "a thousand points of light"—points where local initiatives are taken to solve problems that otherwise might be left to the federal government.

Following the defeat of Bush in the 1992 election, Kemp organized a Republican Conservative Leadership Caucus dedicated to five principles: individual freedom, traditional family values, free enterprise, strong national defense, and personal responsibility. No doubt the concerns are genuine. The striking feature of the list is that the problem of poverty is not mentioned, at least not explicitly, and every kind of conservative can find something that is appealing among these principles.

## Big Government?

Kemp's name has appeared on a list of "big government conservatives." He denies that he belongs on the list. "I'm a limited government conservative," he says. Testifying before a congressional committee in 1991, Kemp listed eight features of what he called Bush's "growth and empowerment agenda," but which the context suggests is his own agenda. Seven of the eight features call explicitly for some kind of concession relating to taxes, and the general thrust of the eight is toward a reduction in the role of government. Although some of the eight features relate to Kemp's notion of a war on poverty and thus would not have been on Reagan's list, the methods of action proposed are all methods that Reagan and other economic conservatives could easily endorse (U.S. Congress 1991a, 322). A memorandum that Kemp signed in 1991, along with Gingrich, Weber, and others, called for "economic growth through lower taxes, less intrusive government, and more open trade," a formula that Reagan could applaud (Kemp et al. 1992, 682). And Kemp denounced Clinton's proposal for health care reform, saying that it "masks the largest power grab by the federal government in recent history."

I see no reason to question Kemp's statement that he is for limited government, and I assume that other conservatives who join him in a concern for poverty are for limited government too. Even when Butler and Kondratas propose that government impose requirements relating to health insurance on individuals and insurance companies, their object is to avert more extensive governmental involvement. Not only are progressive conservatives for limited government, their progressivism is limited too. Apart from their determination to attack the problem of poverty and apart from their stands on a few other issues, they fit congenially with other conservatives, mainly with economic conservatives.

# Chapter 13

# Neoconservatism

CONSERVATIVES characteristically look back to a better time when a wrong turn was made, and want somehow to regain or restore what was lost. They differ in identifying the wrong turn, some placing it in medieval times or before, some placing it in the eighteenth or nineteenth century, and some placing it in more recent times. On this standard, neoconservatism is of recent vintage—a reaction to wrong turns made in the 1960s and early 1970s. That is, a reaction to wrong turns relating to the Great Society program, to Vietnam, to communism and the Soviet Union, and to associated cultural developments.

Neoconservatism is not an organized movement, and it has no agreed platform or credo. Two of its leading analysts even deny that it is an ideology, speaking of it instead as a mood or a tendency. It is identified with a group of persons of whom Irving Kristol and Norman Podhoretz are probably the most widely known. Kristol is the author of *Two Cheers for Capitalism* (1978) and *Reflections of a Neoconservative* (1983), a columnist for the *Wall Street Journal,* and editor or publisher of the *National Interest* and the *Public Interest.* Podhoretz is editor of *Commentary.* Others sometimes named as neoconservative (correctly or not) include Elliott Abrams, Ken Adelman, Edward Banfield, William Bennett, Peter and Brigitte Berger, Midge Decter, Nathan Glazer, Jeane Kirkpatrick, Seymour Martin Lipset, Joshua Muravchik, Richard John Neuhaus, Michael Novak, Richard Perle, Richard Schifter, the late Aaron Wildavsky, and James Q. Wilson. Other names might be added, but the group is noted more for its intellectual and political influence than for its size. Several of those named are associated with the American Enterprise Institute. Lipset, Wildavsky, and Wilson are former presidents of the American Political Science Association.

Some of those named above were once Trotskyists, Stalinists, or otherwise on the far left—a background that helps explain their record of intense and unqualified hostility to communism and the Soviet Union. The counterpart is that neoconservatives are identified with support for what they think of as liberty and equality of opportunity, support for democracy and capitalism, and patriotic opposition to any disparagement of the United States. At the same time, some neoconservatives—Kristol most notably—are anguished by the fact that respect for individual liberty is widely taken to preclude, or at least strictly limit, social or governmental action on behalf of the moral values essential to the development and preservation of a good society.

## Hostility to Communism and Support for Western Values

In the earlier chapters on liberalism and conservatism I have not mentioned hostility to communism and socialism, or to the Soviet Union, believing it best to postpone the subject until later. But this policy of postponement runs into a problem here because that hostility, and a corresponding support for liberty, equality of opportunity, democracy, and capitalism, are such important features of neoconservatism.

The crucial point concerns the reasons for, and the intensity of, the hostility—a point that Norman Podhoretz illuminates in appraising Henry Kissinger's policies as national security adviser and secretary of state. Podhoretz credits Kissinger with never doubting that the Soviet Union was expansionist and therefore a threat, but holds that Kissinger nevertheless misjudged the nature of the threat. Along with Nixon, he "saw the Soviet Union as a nation-state like any other, motivated by the same range of interests that define and shape the foreign policies of all nation-states." Moreover, Kissinger allegedly took a similar view of Communist China and of the various smaller countries that were under communist control. They were all nation-states like others, pursuing national interests. Bargains could thus be struck with them, and accommodations made, more or less as with noncommunist states. And détente was possible.

To Podhoretz, this was a terrible mistake. Communist rulers were more like Hitler than like the kaiser. They had unlimited ambitions, seeking to revolutionize the world and presenting a barbaric threat to civilization. Any accommodation with them would be treacherous, leading people on our side to relax their guard while communists found devious ways to turn the accommodation into gain. To be sure, communist rulers might no longer really believe in Marxism-Leninism, but they were *objectively* its prisoners, having no other basis for claiming that their rule was legitimate. Even if they dreamed of simply trying to maintain the status quo, they could not make this their actual aim, for they knew that this would mean political suicide. So they were a mortal threat. It was even a mistake for Kissinger to try to play communist governments off against each other—for example, to support Tito's Yugoslavia or to play "the China card"—for the assumption had to be that communists everywhere were untrustworthy and evil. The struggle in which we were engaged was a principled struggle, a moral struggle, and not simply a matter of competing interests (Podhoretz 1981, 39).

The attitude applied to domestic as well as to international politics. American communists, and communists in Western Europe and Central America, were no more to be trusted—no more to be found acceptable in any way—than those in the Kremlin. And it was vital to limit and combat the influence of liberals and others who failed to understand the true nature of the threat. Irving Kristol made this clear in an article published long before the term *neoconservatism* came into use, in which he used the attitudes of Joseph McCarthy as a standard against which to judge liberals. McCarthy, he said, was "unequivocally anti-Communist," while "spokesmen for American liberalism" were not. These spokesmen were too inclined to regard communism as simply a leftist political movement rather than a mortal threat, too inclined to join or cooperate with communist-front organizations, and too inclined to ignore or excuse the horrors of Stalinism.

Whether Kristol was entirely fair is another question. The "spokesmen for American liberalism" whom he named no doubt count as liberals, but whether they count as spokesmen for other liberals is doubtful. They were academic and religious figures. Kristol did not name any political leaders as liberal spokesmen (Kristol 1952, 229–36).

Hostility to communism includes hostility to totalitarianism. And the counterpart of these various hostilities is support for individual liberty, equality of opportunity, democracy, and capitalism. Neoconservatives take the meaning of the first two of these values for granted, not probing into the question. To them, liberty is what exists in the absence of governmental restraint, and equality of opportunity is what exists in the absence of discrimination. The distinctive feature of the support that neoconservatives give to democracy and capitalism is the emphasis that they put on their attitudes. Where many others take democracy and capitalism for granted, neoconservatives put their concerns front and center—as when Kristol entitled his book *Two Cheers for Capitalism.* He gave it two cheers for the usual reasons, mainly the emphasis that capitalism gives to liberty and opportunity. The entrepreneur and the free market are instruments of progress, potentially benefiting everyone.

Support for capitalism necessarily includes sympathy and support for capitalists. Thus Kristol writes for the *Wall Street Journal* and has won respect in monied circles. In 1975 he had a hand in popularizing supply-side economics, publishing a seminal article on the subject in his journal, the *Public Interest,* and later endorsing supply-side economics himself. His endorsement centers on the usual theme that taxes should be reduced, but he seems more embarrassed than some other supply-siders by his inability to describe criteria for determining when taxes are too high and what their level should be (1981, 52).

## Hostility to Egalitarianism

Although neoconservatives support the idea of equality of opportunity, they oppose what they call egalitarianism. Aaron Wildavsky expresses the opposition in *The Rise of Radical Egalitarianism* (1991). His definition of "radical egalitarianism" is broad, referring to any effort to reduce or eliminate distinctions. He thinks that "people who wish to diminish distinctions among other people and those who empathize or sympathize and support them" have gained in influence. "Everywhere one looks—or so it seems to us—one finds people trying to diminish distinctions." His concern is with many sorts of distinctions—of income and wealth, of status and authority, of right and wrong.

The attack on distinctions of income and wealth, he says, manifests itself in demands for more governmental action on behalf of welfare and redistribution, more "state-sanctioned positive discrimination to increase equality of results," more environmental expenditures, and fewer property rights. It also includes demands for "greater equality of condition so as to reduce disparities in power." Egalitarians "see government as a vastly expanded compensatory mechanism whose purpose it is to make up for past inequalities." Implicitly, the attack is on some of the features of Johnson's Great Society program, on which I comment below.

The attack on distinctions of status and authority manifests itself, among other ways, in feminist demands for equality between the sexes. Feminism, according to Wildavsky and a number of other neoconservatives, threatens to destroy the family and is therefore to be opposed. Similarly, what Wildavsky sees as demands for equality of condition are anathema, for they put equality ahead of liberty and are blind to the fact that hierarchy is natural and necessary.

Wildavsky does not elaborate on the theme concerning right and wrong, saying only that egalitarians seek "the diminution of distinctions that once separated moral from immoral behavior." His general conclusion is that egalitarianism undermines "every major integrative institution" and enables "disintegrative movements" to flourish. The integrative institutions that he names are "political parties, trade unions, mainstream churches, the presidency," and the disintegrative movements are "single-issue special interest groups, charismatic religions, candidate-centered political movements, a critical press."

Wildavsky's book is impressionistic, tendentious, and polemical, marshaling little testimony or evidence to support the assertions made. The question is whether much of what he attacks is not in the strawman category. Moreover, his attack includes a glaring contradiction in the attitudes expressed toward government—a contradiction either in Wildavsky's impressions or in the alleged thinking of "radical egalitarians." On the one hand, these egalitarians are said to view government as a major instrument for reshaping society, and on the other hand they are said to want to undermine government on behalf of voluntary associations.

Irving Kristol, too, is concerned about egalitarianism. It originates, he thinks, not in the working class but in the "new class," the "professionalized classes of our modern bureaucratized societies." These professionalized classes, including professors, affluent journalists, and, in general, people who regard themselves as intellectuals, "are engaged in a class struggle with the business community for status and power." "Professors are genuinely indignant at the expense accounts which business executives have and which they do not." But since it would be in poor taste for professors and other members of the new class to pursue their private interests openly, they rationalize these interests in terms of the public good, claiming at the same time that bourgeois society is based on a deficient conception of that good (1978, 177, 179).

The rationalization of private interests in terms of the public good takes form in an ideology centering on the idea of equality. The members of the "New Class of self-designated 'intellectuals' ... pursue power in the name of equality." To illustrate the importance assigned to equality, Kristol cites John Rawls, attributing to him the view that "a social order is just and legitimate *only* to the degree that it is directed to the redress of inequality" and Kristol holds that among liberals this thesis "is not considered controversial."

Kristol himself is scornful of what he regards as the Rawlsian idea that it is more important for government to redistribute income and wealth than to promote economic growth for the potential benefit of all. He denounces "an intelligentsia which so despises the ethos of bourgeois society, and which is so guilt-ridden at being implicated in the life of this society, that it is inclined to find even collective suicide preferable to the status quo" (1978, 183).

He also points to other evils allegedly associated with an emphasis on equality. That emphasis assumes a "powerful consensus" about the nature of the common good, and it leads to an expectation that government will act on the basis of that consensus, discriminating against those who stand in the way. It explains why "so many liberal thinkers find it so difficult to detest left-wing (i.e., egalitarian) authoritarian or totalitarian regimes." And similarly, it explains why liberals ("true believers in justice-as-equality") dislike a free society, with all its inevitable inequalities (1978, 191–92).

In Kristol's view, a liberal society—that is, a liberal society of the sort he would approve—is one that is based not on a powerful but on a weak consensus. In such a society,

> there is nothing like near-unanimity on what the "common good" is, who contributes to it, or how. There is not utter disagreement, of course; a liberal society is not—no society can be—in a condition of perpetual moral and political chaos. But the liberty of a liberal society derives from a prevalent skepticism as to anyone's ability to know the "common good" with certainty, and from the conviction that the authorities should not try to define this "common good" in any but a minimal way. (Kristol 1978, 191)

In other words, government should be limited, pursuing only limited aims.

One gets the impression from reading both Wildavsky and Kristol that they exaggerate the emphasis that even leftist liberals give to the idea of equality. It is as if they are projecting onto others extreme views that they themselves held before migrating from the left to a neoconservative position. They do not cite any liberal political leaders who hold the views they denounce. For that matter, they cite very few "liberal spokesmen" of any sort. They make assertions, provocative but largely unsupported.

As noted, Kristol does cite the philosopher John Rawls, but only very briefly. Rawls puts himself in a vulnerable position by holding, in his Second Principle, that "social and economic inequalities are to be arranged so that they are ... to the greatest benefit of the least advantaged.... " Contrary to what Kristol says, the statement has led to controversy. The question is whether Rawls would really want to reject an inequality if the greatest benefit goes to the next-to-the-least advantaged, or, for that matter, if benefits go to almost anyone without harming others. Rawls himself does not stick consistently to the view that inequalities must be to the *greatest* advantage of the least advantaged, usually saying only that they must be to their advantage, which would permit the *greatest* advantage to go to others (Rawls 1971, 303).

This conception—that inequalities should be to the general advantage—is similar to the Aristotelian view that Kristol cites and approves: "a just and legitimate society is one in which inequalities—of property, or station, or power—are generally perceived by the citizenry as necessary for the common good." My own impression is that liberals are more inclined toward this view than toward the view that Wildavsky and Kristol attribute to them.

Egalitarianism is a vague concept, lending itself to confusion unless words are carefully chosen. It may refer to the constitutional requirement that all persons should enjoy the equal protection of the laws. It may refer to the idea of equality of opportunity. It may refer to a desire to reduce the gap between the rich and the poor, or simply to a desire to prevent that gap from widening. It may refer to leveling, that is, to a desire that all workers should have equal incomes. And other meanings are possible—the most sweeping being the meaning that Wildavsky accepts, calling for the reduction and elimination of most kinds of distinctions.

Problems naturally arise when authors denounce "egalitarianism" without specifying clearly what they mean. Perhaps they think they are being clear when they denounce the pursuit of "equality of results" or "equality of condition," but that is an illusion. For example, enjoyment of the equal protection of the laws and the enjoyment of equal incomes are both "results" in a sense, but it is scarcely to be assumed that a desire for one implies a desire for the other. Similarly, the existence of equality of opportunity and the existence of a gap between the rich and the poor are both conditions, but again a judgment about one does not necessarily extend automatically to the other. Given the fact that "results" and "conditions" may be of many different kinds, it is not helpful to assert or assume that a search for equality of results or equality of conditions is necessarily bad.

## The Welfare State

Neoconservatives do not propose to abolish or dismantle the welfare state. Like the progressive conservatives, they accept the need for governmental action on behalf of welfare, but they do not like some of the action that the federal government has taken and they want reform. Kristol speaks of Johnson's War on Poverty as one of the "disasters of our age." To give money to the poor is to demean them. To draw a line between the poor and the nonpoor is to create resentments. And to provide welfare that is withdrawn when people improve their condition is to put them in a poverty trap (1978, 235–36).

In further condemnation of the welfare state as it has developed, Kristol blames it for various social pathologies: higher rates of crime, juvenile delinquency, drug addiction, teenage pregnancy, and alcoholism. He also condemns it for being socially divisive, "setting American against American—class against class, race against race, ethnic group against ethnic group." It leads to "a high rate of taxation that frustrates economic incentives, and an inexorable decline in productivity and economic growth.... This in turn results in collective impoverishment." Moreover, the subject of welfare reminds him again of egalitarianism, which he thinks was basic to the War on Poverty and which he therefore denounces (1978, 237, 242–43; 1983, 244). At the same time, as indicated below, he accepts egalitarianism of a sort in assigning welfare functions to government. He does not want disparities of income to be so extreme that some are left to starve.

Note that Kristol's targets are the means-tested programs such as AFDC and Medicaid, not insurance-type programs such as social security and Medicare. In fact, describing early opposition of the Republican Party to social security as "idiotic," he castigates Republican administrations for not showing concern for the elderly (1978, 133).

Although denouncing means-tested programs, Kristol does not walk away from the problem of poverty. He grants that "people need governmental action of some kind if they are to cope with many of their problems: old age, illness, unemployment, etc.," and that we have a moral obligation to "provide a safety net for those unable to participate fully in the economy." The task is not to abolish the welfare state but to create one that is consistent, to the largest possible degree, with traditional American virtues. "It is idle," he says, "to talk about returning to a 'free enterprise' system in which government will play the modest role it used to." What he wants is a "conservative welfare state" (1978, 30, 126–27; 1981, 51).

Underlying Kristol's position is the assumption that "poverty is abolished by economic growth," so his prime emphasis is on that growth. But he himself implicitly grants that the word *abolished* is too strong. Poverty remains despite economic growth, and the problem needs to be attacked directly as well as indirectly. Kristol wants to get as much mileage as possible out of the principle that "people should be allowed to keep their own money—rather than having it transferred (via taxes) to the state." But he wants to guide them in the use of their money by giving them tax deductions when they spend it in specified ways. For example, make medical insurance premiums tax deductible, and even life insurance premiums. He also speaks of the possibility of "a mixture of voluntary and compulsory insurance schemes—old age insurance, disability insurance, unemployment insurance, medical insurance" (1978, 127, 247; 1983, 89, 122).

But what of people who have little or no money in the first place? Here Kristol hesitantly mentions "universal" as opposed to means-tested programs. He treats free public education, social security, and Medicare as successful "universal" programs and wonders whether the principle of universality should not be extended, for example, to children's allowances and to some form of national health insurance. He attacked Reagan's domestic policies as miserly, and he suggested that the Reagan administration raise social security payments so that it could proudly claim that it had abolished poverty among the elderly. How he reconciles these proposals concerning welfare with supply-side demands that tax rates be cut he does not say (Lipset 1988, 36; Kristol 1985, 36).

With respect to views about the welfare state, an obvious similarity exists between neoconservatism and progressive conservatism; more strictly, an obvious similarity exists between the views of Irving Kristol and the views of Jack Kemp. In fact, Kemp is quoted as saying, "Irving Kristol shaped my consciousness to recognize the necessity of the welfare system, or the safety net. It is absolutely incumbent upon a society to organize itself collectively and share whatever is necessary to make sure that people survive" (Blumenthal 1986, 186).

Midge Decter's question concerning welfare focuses on the relationship between individual and collective responsibility. The "center of the controversy between so-called conservatives and so-called liberals," she says, is "whether people are to be appropriately rewarded or penalized for their actual conduct." A related question concerns the extent to which the need for help stems from the conduct of specific individuals and the extent to which it stems from circumstances beyond their control.

## Defending America

Describing the circumstances leading people to become neoconservatives, Norman Podhoretz harks back to the late 1960s when "anti-
Americanism ... had virtually become the religion of the radical
movement in which we ourselves had actively participated in the earlier years of the decade."

> Somewhat to our own surprise, we found that we simply could not
> stomach the hatred of "Amerika" that increasingly pervaded the
> New Left and the counterculture. And this revulsion led to a process
> of reflection and reconsideration that gradually brought us to a new
> appreciation of the virtues of the American political system and of
> its economic and social underpinnings.
>
> So profoundly affected were we by this new appreciation that we
> have been devoting ourselves ever since to defending America
> against the defamations of its enemies abroad and the denigrations
> of its critics at home.
>
> Almost every idea espoused by the neoconservatives relates back
> to this central impulse to defend America against the assaults of the
> left.

Writing in 1989, Podhoretz took the view that "there is still no true
sense among liberals, and still less among those to their left, of the
amazing success of the American system" (1989, 56–57).

In 1991, a few months after the end of the war against Iraq, The
Nation published the responses of a number of people to the question
"What is patriotism?" The answers were of different sorts. Some of
them reflect the disparagement of America to which neoconservatives
(and many others) object: American achievements are so entangled in
shame that it would be presumptuous to take pride in them. If we
could come face to face with our past honestly, we would have little
basis for national pride. The Iraq war was a "crime against humanity.... Many nations today threaten their neighborhoods and the
world's environment, but none with such violence as ours." The "awful truth [is] that American imperialism is a knife at the world's
throat, and ... our public life has the moral tone one would expect to
encounter at a convention of armed robbers." "Sleazy politicians wrap
themselves in the flag and use patriotism to cover up their sins.... "

I cite these responses to indicate the kind of attitude to which I
presume the neoconservatives were reacting. They are leftist attitudes,
but the names of those quoted are not prominent in political life; none

are known to me as liberal political leaders. Jesse Jackson's response included no such disparagement; neither did the response of Mario Cuomo.

## Virtue

As noted earlier, Kristol gives capitalism two cheers. He cannot give it three because of a glaring shortcoming: it assumes that people are moved by their own interests and passions and makes no provision for the virtues or values essential to a good society. It relegates the problem of virtue, the problem of moral values, to "the area of personal concern, whether of the isolated individual or of voluntary associations of individuals." It neglects "the life of the mind, the psyche, and the spirit" and makes no provision for a "community of mutual love" (1978, x–xi).

Such laments occur again and again in Kristol's writing. He acknowledges the claim of Mandeville's *Fable of the Bees* that public benefits flow from private vices, but the claim does not comfort him. Our society, he says, is relentlessly breeding more and more people "whose private vices in no way provide public benefits to a bourgeois order." What we need is the right set of solidly established and publicly supported moral values.

The problem, as Kristol sees it, is traceable to liberalism, for "a liberal society is necessarily a secular society, one in which religion is mainly a private affair." Liberalism insisted on the disestablishment of religion, which led to a diminution of religious faith. And the problem is accentuated by the liberal-individualistic tendency to reject the authority of tradition. Faith and tradition, when they were powerful, called for distinguishing between liberty and license, with the implication that liberty is to be exercised only in ways that advance the good and that license is to be avoided. Faith and tradition also tended to lead people into stoical resignation in the face of deprivation and frustration—tended to lead them to accept the inequalities to which a free market inevitably leads (1978, 63, 138–39).

Now that faith and tradition are weakened, people are confused. Liberty and license are no longer distinguished. Even those who benefit from the system seek profit in ways that undermine it—for example, by selling magazines, sponsoring television shows, or distributing movies that celebrate the immoral. And people are less inclined to be stoical when they believe that their problems are open to solution. They demand governmental intervention on behalf of distributive justice. Or, worse, they turn nihilistic, refusing to take any values seriously, and switch to a counterculture that includes drugs, crime, and scorn for both sexual restraint and the family.

Secular humanism, which Kristol calls both a form of atheism and a quasi religion, developed along with secular rationalism as the role of faith and tradition declined, but it is an inadequate substitute. It excludes the transcendental. It denies the existence of the God-given. It glorifies "what F.A. Hayek calls 'constructivism,' the self-confident application of rationality to all human problems, individual and social alike." And it has failed. It "has been unable to produce a compelling, self-justifying moral code.... All the major philosophical as well as cultural trends [have begun] to repudiate secular rationalism and secular humanism in favor of an intellectual and moral relativism and/or nihilism" (1991, 23; 1992a, 49).

Given the declining influence of the religious and moral tradition and the inadequacy of secular humanism, Kristol sees decadence —that is, the lack of any answer to the question "what do we do after we have bettered our condition?" He sees "millions of spiritually sick people shopping around for a patent medicine of the soul." Social pathologies and discontents increase with affluence, the emphasis being placed "on the pleasures of consumption rather than on the virtues of work.... The purpose of politics becomes the maximum gratification of desires and appetites, and the successful politician is one who panders most skillfully to this 'revolution of rising expectations'" (1978, 253; 1983, 175).

Kristol illustrates the neglect of virtue and the emphasis on the material by noting that "the law insists that an 18-year-old girl has the right to public fornication in a pornographic movie—but only if she is paid the minimum wage." And he comments that "the current version of liberalism, which prescribes massive government intervention in the marketplace but an absolute laissez-faire attitude toward manners and morals, strikes neoconservatives as representing a bizarre inversion of priorities."

According to Kristol, the situation is both indefensible and fraught with danger.

> Who wants to live in a society in which selfishness and self-seeking are celebrated as primary virtues? Such a society is unfit for human habitation.... It is preposterous to think that the mass of men will ever accept as legitimate a social order formed in accordance with the laws of the jungle.... Can men live in a free society if they have no reason to believe it is also a just society? I do not think so. My reading of history is that, in the same way as men cannot for long

tolerate a sense of spiritual meaninglessness in their individual lives, so they cannot for long accept a society in which power, privilege, and property are not distributed according to some morally meaningful criteria.... I conclude that man cannot accept the historical accidents of the marketplace—seen merely as accidents—as the basis for an enduring and legitimate entitlement to power, privilege, and property. (1978, 85, 262–63)

Kristol is horrified by Machiavelli and by "the awful things men do in their lust for power." Had Machiavelli even accepted "the code of the Graeco-Roman writers (who did not believe in divine judgment either) he would at least have indicated how awful these things were.... But instead he declared that an honest and enlightened man had no right to regard them as awful at all" (1983, 127).

So far, according to Kristol, "the moral and spiritual heritage of Judaism and Christianity" have reduced the evil consequences of secularism and the neglect of moral values. "For many generations," he says, "capitalism was able to live off the accumulated moral and spiritual capital of the past. But with each generation that capital stock was noticeably depleted, had to be stretched ever thinner to meet the exigencies of life." It is thus a wasting asset, and the great threat is that it will be swept away by "the hurricanes of twentieth century nihilism." Nihilism is a greater threat than socialism (1978, 66; 1983, 117, 168).

Kristol does not credit "conservatives" with an answer to the problem. In fact, he berates them for failing "to articulate any coherent set of ideals and to suggest a strategy for achieving them," which puts them in the position of being, or seeming to be, "mindless defenders of the status quo, if not of privilege."

Kristol makes one specific suggestion himself, although not elaborating on it in any detail. He wants censorship—a liberal rather than a repressive censorship. For example, let those with a serious interest in an obscene play see it, but under some kind of regulation that excludes the general public. He grants the difficulties of drawing a line between the permissible and the impermissible.

Beyond that, his prescriptions are vague. Writing on "America's Mysterious Malaise" (1992b, 5), he speaks appreciatively of economic progress and the "successful creation of a Welfare State," but then points to unexpected evils attending these achievements: increased criminality, more teenage pregnancies, more abortions, drug addiction, the creation of a dependent, self-destructive "underclass," and the contempt of citizens for their governments and politicians—all suggesting to him that we are edging glacierlike toward a crisis. When this crisis comes, he thinks that it may be resolved by the development of "some kind of 'post-modern' politics, one that distances itself from the very building blocks of modernity—rationalism, secularism, science, technology, and representative government."

The question is whether Kristol's "post-modern" politics will not be very much like the politics that he has been favoring all along—a kind that he describes as waging a war on poverty, that is, on spiritual poverty. "That war on [spiritual] poverty is the great unfinished task before us. The collapse of socialism, along with the vindication of a market economy, offers us a wonderful opportunity to think seriously about such an enterprise. Only such an enterprise can ensure a capitalist future" (1992a, 51). He seems to want to give new life to beliefs that were once held and then widely abandoned. Not that he can prove these beliefs to be sound. "One accepts a moral code on faith. . . . Pure reason can offer a critique of moral beliefs but it cannot engender them."

But the faith need not be blind. It can be guided by the belief that our "ancestors, over the generations, were not fools and that we have much to learn from them and their experience." He commends traditional bourgeois values: "a willingness to work hard to improve one's condition, a respect for law, an appreciation of the merits of deferred gratification, a deference toward traditional religion, a concern for family and community, and so on." And he calls for "civic virtue": "the willingness of the good democratic citizen, on critical occasions, to transcend the habitual pursuit of self-interest and devote himself directly and disinterestedly to the common good."

Kristol has an encouraging word for religious conservatives. "Today it is the religious who have a sense that the tide has turned and that the wave of the future is moving in their direction. . . . Their numbers are growing, as is their influence. They are going to be the very core of an emerging American conservatism. . . ." The counterpart is that, in Kristol's view, secularism is declining, and this signifies the decline of liberalism too (Kristol 1993a).

James Q. Wilson (1985) has concerns similar to Kristol's. Wilson calls for the "rediscovery of character." Pointing to the fact that over recent decades illegitimacy rates have been rising and that higher and higher proportions of those eligible for AFDC have applied for it, getting something for nothing, he doubts that the explanation is to be found in economic incentives. Instead, attitudes have changed: it is a question of character. So is the greater willingness to engage in deficit financing a question of character, people being readier than in earlier times to seek a good life for themselves at the expense of their children and grandchildren. And the problem of crime itself is also at bottom a question of character. Thus government must involve itself in character formation, seeking to promote the private virtue on which the public good depends.

Wilson also concerns himself with the "moral sense" (1992). His argument is that "people everywhere have a natural moral sense that is not entirely the product of utility or convention."

This moral sense is "not a strong beacon light," but "a small candle flame, casting vague and multiple shadows, flickering and sputtering in the strong winds of power and passion, greed and ideology." Implicitly the argument is that both a public and a private interest exist in fanning the flame, with moral reasoning employed to "take up the incomplete task of moral development."

William J. Bennett focuses explicitly on religion. Our afflictions, he says, are primarily moral, cultural, and spiritual. "The enervation of strong religious belief ... has demoralized society." The chief problem we face is spiritual impoverishment, and the solution depends on spiritual renewal. The importance of politics has been greatly exaggerated. We must return religion to its proper place and give respect to those who are serious about their faith. Religion "provides society with a moral anchor—and nothing else has yet been found to substitute for it. Religion tames our basest appetites, passions, and impulses. And it helps us to thoughtfully sort through the *ordo amoris*, the order of loves." "If we have full employment and greater economic growth—if we have cities of gold and alabaster—but our children have not learned how to walk in goodness, justice, and mercy, then the American experiment, no matter how gilded, will have failed" (Bennett 1994a, 1994b).

Mentioning Bennett in this chapter, I am implicitly classifying him as a neoconservative, but some of his attitudes also fit with those of social conservatives. And in *Empower America* he is associated with Jack Kemp, a progressive conservative.

## Neos and Other Conservatives

Are neoconservatives conservative? Some other conservatives deny it, describing neoconservatives as impostors. They are "opportunists" and "interlopers" (Bradford 1986, 15; Gottfried 1986, 20). "It is splendid when the town whore gets religion and joins the church. Now and then she makes a good choir director, but when she begins to tell the minister what he ought to say in his Sunday sermons, matters have been carried too far" (Tonsor 1986, 55). The charge is that neoconservatives are welfare state liberals and cultural modernists and thus not genuine conservatives.

Of the various responses to the charge, that of Dan Himmelfarb is most interesting (Himmelfarb 1988). He points out that the neoconservatives acquired their separate identity beginning in the 1960s when what he calls a counterfeit liberalism developed. Up to then, "genuine" liberals had been strong in American political life. Franklin D. Roosevelt, Harry Truman, and John F. Kennedy had been progressive in their domestic policies and vigorously anticommunist in their foreign policies. But then "counterfeit" liberals came to the fore, shifting to the left, especially in matters relating to race and communism. Counterfeit liberals favored kinds of affirmative action—most notably, quotas—that deny equality of opportunity; they wanted to repress hate speech; and they regarded anticommunism as more of a threat than communism. They carried the day with the nomination of George McGovern for the presidency. But "genuine" liberals refused to make the shift to the left and came to be known as neoconservatives.

These neoconservatives differ from paleoconservatives (that is, from conservative conservatives and social conservatives) in various ways. Neos base their principles solidly on the Declaration of Independence and the subsequent American tradition, whereas paleos locate their roots in the medieval and ancient world. Neos revere the Founding Fathers because they were liberals in the best sense: champions of individual rights and liberties, popular government, spiritual equality, and cultural and religious pluralism. Paleos revere them too, but for a different reason; the significant point to the paleos is that the Founding Fathers were champions of the Christian tradition and defenders of the religious heritage of Western civilization. Neos believe in equality of opportunity and think of affirmative action as a perversion of the ideal. Paleos also object to affirmative action, but again for a different reason: they think of it not as a perversion but as an extension of the ideal of equality which they do not accept in the first place. Neos are anticommunist out of a concern for freedom, capitalism, and democracy, but paleos are anticommunist out of a concern for religion, tradition, and hierarchy. Neos distinguish between good and bad liberalism, but paleos think that all liberalism is intrinsically flawed, "primarily because it is a secular and egalitarian tendency, insufficiently respectful of tradition." Since neos accept the liberalism of an earlier time as good, Himmelfarb suggests that they should perhaps be called paleoliberals. They stand in opposition both to the (Old) Right and the (New) Left.

# Chapter 14

# Foreign Policies

**T**HIS CHAPTER differs in approach from all the preceding chapters. As the title indicates, the focus is now on foreign policies rather than on an ideology. That is, the chapter is organized around issues and prescriptions rather than underlying guiding principles.

The shift in focus has an element of the arbitrary about it. I might have said something about prescriptions concerning foreign policies in each of the preceding chapters. I did not do so because, first, the ideologies I have described relate mainly to domestic politics, making it both reasonable and feasible to analyze them within that framework. None of them puts foreign policy issues first. They all get their identity primarily because of their approach to domestic politics, and they are clearer and more coherent, and more distinct from each other, in prescribing for domestic politics. People who divide up ideologically in one way with respect to domestic politics may divide up differently with respect to foreign policies. Further, the terminological muddle is especially great with respect to foreign policy issues, making separate treatment desirable.

I start with this last problem: the terminological muddle. Then comes an analysis of attitudes toward communism and the Soviet Union. I recognize, of course, that communism has collapsed and the Soviet Union has broken up, but attitudes relating to them have played a prominent role, sometimes a crucial role, in giving an ideology its identity; and knowledge of the past is important to an understanding of the problems created by the collapse and breakup. Finally comes a focus on other general issues and an examination of ideological prescriptions relating to them. The prescriptions focus variously on (1) diplomacy, international law, and international organization; (2) human rights and democracy; (3) isolationism, "America First," and the national interest; and (4) the question of a new world order.

## The Terminological Muddle

Robert O. Keohane identifies three schools of thought on the foreign policies of states: Marxist, realist, and liberal (Dunn 1990, 165). None of the ideologies described in this book champions Marxism, so I exclude the Marxist school of thought from consideration. The very fact that the other two are called realist and liberal is a tip-off to a problem, for the intimation is that liberals are unrealistic and that no one is conservative.

Nevertheless, Keohane's choice of terms correctly reflects current practice, confusing as it is. Discussion of foreign policy issues does tend to be in terms of realism and liberalism. *Realism* generally assumes that the focus should be on states, not on individuals or on nongovernmental associations; that states pursue their own interests, with special emphasis on short-run interests; that these interests are overwhelmingly of a self-regarding sort, relating, for example, to sovereignty, freedom of action, security, power, domestic prosperity, and so on; and that the world is threatening, with foreign governments pursuing their selfish interests in potentially aggressive ways. The inclination is to stress the evil in men and to put the worst possible construction on the words and actions of foreign governments, especially those deemed potentially hostile. Realism thus prescribes distrust of foreigners, skepticism about the value of all things international (for example, international law and diplomacy, the United Nations, the World Court, and foreign aid), and cynicism about the idea of an international community and human progress. Politics is a struggle for power, and the fragile basis for peace is a balance of power. To get peace, you prepare for war. After World War II, Hans Morgenthau made himself the prototypical realist by championing the theme that in foreign affairs the United States should be guided by its interests, defined in terms of power.

In contrast, as used in this context, *liberalism* reflects idealism. It assumes that the focus should be on states, of course, but it is also concerned about individuals and nongovernmental associations—as evidenced, for example, by an emphasis on individual liberty, democracy, and human rights. It is hopeful that, although states pursue their interests, they will define those interests in an enlightened way and pursue them cooperatively, giving due regard to the interests of others. It is inclined to emphasize diplomacy, international law, and international organizations and is thus willing to work toward a reduction of the significance of sovereignty. It is hopeful about the development of a global community characterized by freedom to trade and travel and by cooperation for the common good. It urges that the rich and powerful give aid and perhaps make other concessions to the people of the developing world so as to reduce economic and other disparities. It necessarily acknowledges the need for national defense and thus for armed establishments, but is inclined to think that realists exaggerate foreign dangers and inclined to hope that such dangers as exist can be countered by political and economic means. It looks toward a world in which war and the threat of war recede into the background, making possible the reduction and limitation of armaments, if not complete disarmament. The counterpart is a fear that measures taken by one state to enhance its security may be seen by other states as threatening and thus accentuate the very dangers they are designed to counteract.

Note that the above definition of *liberalism* differs from the definitions employed in discussions of domestic politics and thus is a source of confusion. It would be clearer if those who speak of realism in international affairs would contrast it with idealism and skip any reference to liberalism. A few authors seem to sense a problem and seek to solve it by giving *liberalism* a meaning applicable to domestic politics, even if this is not the meaning that they in fact employ. Thus Doyle says that "what we tend to call *liberal* resembles a family portrait of principles and institutions, recognizable by certain characteristics—for example, individual freedom, political participation, private property, and equality of opportunity—that most liberal states share" (Doyle 1986, 1152). And Hoffmann defines *liberalism* as "the doctrine whose central concern is the liberty of the individual: both his or her freedom from restraints and constraints imposed by other human beings ('political liberty in this sense is simply the area within which a man can do what he wants') and his or her freedom to participate in a self-governing polity ... " (Hoffmann 1987, 395). The problem is that such definitions have little relevance to foreign policies, and the authors who advance them tend in practice to assume other definitions that they do not acknowledge, still less spell out. Hoffmann, for example, forgets about the definition quoted above and treats *liberalism* as the opposite of either *realism* or *authoritarianism,* depending on circumstances. None of the authors dealing with international politics acknowledges the existence of any kind of *conservatism* as a counterpart of *liberalism.*

The terminological confusion leads to such statements as the following by Keohane: "Conservative economists find the international order favored by liberalism congenial" (Dunn 1990, 190). And according to Doyle, Ronald Reagan advanced a "liberal claim" and "joined a long list of liberal theorists" (Doyle 1986, 1151). The man who was proud to call himself a conservative and who heaped scorn on the "L-word" would be astounded. The confusion extends into the writing of Irving Kristol, who uses *liberal* as an epithet applying to anything that he dislikes about foreign policy.

As if to add to the confusion, Rudolf Rummel writes of "Libertarianism and International Violence" without showing any awareness of the definition of libertarianism used in this book. To him, libertarian states are "those emphasizing individual freedom and civil liberties and the rights associated with a competitive and open election of leaders" (Rummel 1983, 27–28).

## Anticommunism and the Soviet Threat

Liberals and conservatives of different sorts have all been anticommunist and, until it broke up, fearful of the Soviet Union. It was Truman, a liberal, who enunciated the Truman Doctrine. He and his secretary of state, Dean Acheson, played prominent roles in building up NATO against the Soviet Union. Truman ordered American intervention in Korea to defeat communist aggression. Kennedy announced as president that he was a Berliner and faced Khrushchev down in the Cuban missile crisis of 1962. He and Lyndon Johnson were principally responsible for the effort to stop communism in Vietnam.

At the same time, the more extreme views have been on the conservative side. The background is one of fundamental distrust of liberals, with conservatives thinking of liberals as inclined toward socialism, wanting an activist government that redistributes the wealth and is thus "committed to a secret emotional complicity with communism." According to conservatives, liberals are too indulgent, too tolerant, too incapable of distinguishing between good and evil, "too broadminded to take their own side in an argument." Liberals are thus "unfit for leadership in a free society and intrinsically incapable of offering serious opposition to the communist offensive."

Given such attitudes, conservatives tended to condemn Franklin Roosevelt for some of the agreements he made at Yalta and to condemn Truman for the "loss of China." John Foster Dulles, before he became Eisenhower's secretary of state, called not simply for "containing" communism but for rolling it back. Most of the different sorts of conservatives supported McCarthyism—named for Senator Joseph McCarthy, who in the early 1950s accused various agencies in the executive branch of the federal government of allowing themselves to be infiltrated by communists, crypto-communists, or fellow travelers. A spy fever gripped the country at about the same time, focusing largely on the revelations of an ex-communist, Whittaker Chambers, and on Alger Hiss, who went to prison. The mildest and most pervasive of the claims was that liberals were "soft on communism."

McCarthy was so irresponsible in some of his charges that many people all along the political spectrum came to denounce him. Eventually the Senate itself adopted a resolution formally rebuking him. But since he was without question anticommunist, those who opposed him—and by extension all those who thought that the anticommunist agitation and propaganda had gone too far—came to be denounced as anti-anticommunist; and liberalism suffered from this charge more than conservatism.

The conservatives who favored limited government—that is, the economic conservatives and a substantial portion of other conservatives—faced a dilemma with respect to the Soviet Union. How could they achieve or maintain limited government while building up and maintaining a strong military establishment? The obvious answer was that they could not do both. And their hostility to communism and fear of the Soviet Union were intense enough that, in the main, they chose military strength. They would accept greater governmental involvement in the economy, higher taxes, and even the denials of liberty that conscription involved, if necessary, to defeat communism. And they would insist on domestic vigilance, including the vigilance of the FBI, to counteract the domestic threat of communism.

It was not only that they wanted defense against the Soviet Union and action to prevent the spread of communism. They also sought to roll back and eventually defeat communism in the Soviet Union. Thus a 1964 statement of the American Conservative Union denied that permanent coexistence with communism was either desirable or possible. Permitted to have its way, communism would enslave the world. In the face of such a threat, the United States should not satisfy itself with a defensive posture; instead, it should exert "relentless pressure" to advance the frontiers of freedom. Barry Goldwater expressed similar attitudes, and so did Pat Buchanan. According to Buchanan, "the only way to bring true peace to mankind is to eliminate the root cause of the century's struggle, the Communist Party of the Soviet Union. Containment is not enough" (P. Buchanan 1988, 365).

Attitudes of this sort have been central to neoconservatism, as indicated in the preceding chapter. Thus Norman Podhoretz wrote in 1981 that the conflict between the United States and the Soviet Union was a clash between two civilizations—or, more accurately, between civilization and barbarism. Communism was the single greatest threat to liberty on the face of the earth. The invasion of Afghanistan, which had begun in 1979, indicated that the Soviet Union had "moved into a dynamically expansionist or imperialistic phase." The threat was analogous to the one that Hitler had posed—a mortal threat to the United States and the West in general. And safety was not to be sought by dividing communists against each other, for example by playing the "China card" or supporting Titoist Yugoslavia. The enemy was communism in whatever country it was found and must be combated everywhere through an activist foreign policy (Podhoretz 1981, 31, 39–40; 1982, 24).

Although progressive liberals were anticommunist, they did not go to the same extreme as conservatives did. The fact is illustrated by McGovern's campaign for the presidency in 1972. Insofar as foreign affairs were concerned, his preoccupation was not with the Soviet Union or communism but with the war in Vietnam—a war that he had opposed from the beginning. He saw no good reason to "fight to the bitter end against a tiny band of peasant guerrillas in the jungles of little Vietnam." Our involvement in the war was "a moral and political outrage," "the saddest chapter in our national history." His first act, if he became president, would be to order the termination of all acts of force in all parts of Indochina and to inaugurate an orderly American withdrawal. He was, nevertheless, "deeply committed to a strong military," believing that "we must always be strong enough to prevent any threat to our security" (McGovern 1974, 105–10, 115).

President Carter likewise refused to view the Soviet Union and communism with the same degree of alarm as most conservatives. He declared in 1978 that he had "no fear of communism and no inordinate concern" about it. He was "not preoccupied with the Soviet Union." He favored détente, with both the United States and the Soviet Union exercising restraint and honoring their agreements meticulously. His aim was to "convince the Soviet Union of the advantages of cooperation" (*Public Papers* 1978, 1:978, 1053).

To conservatives and neoconservatives, these attitudes were naive, and the Soviet Union followed policies that seemed designed to prove them right. Not only did it invade Afghanistan, thus seeming to declare to the world that it was willing to use war to extend its revolution, but through Cuba and otherwise it extended aid, including military aid, to leftist movements (communist or partly communist) in various countries, including El Salvador and Nicaragua. On top of this, as another source of trouble for Carter, Islamic fundamentalists in Iran seized the members of the American diplomatic mission in Teheran and held them hostage.

Reagan, when he became president, accepted the neoconservative appraisal of the danger and appealed for a rapid and extensive buildup of American military power. He would confront the "evil empire" and be steadfast in "the struggle between right and wrong and good and evil." He would not be soft on communism (*Public Papers* 1983, 1:364).

Reagan demonstrated his attitude in 1983 when he ordered U.S. troops into Grenada to overthrow a Marxist government there. Although the action tended to be supported by various sorts of conservatives and condemned by liberals, it was over too quickly for a major political struggle to occur.

The bitterest battle of the time between liberals and conservatives was over policies toward El Salvador and Nicaragua. In El Salvador a right-wing regime faced left-wing guerrillas trying to overthrow it. In Nicaragua the guerrillas (the Sandinistas) came out on top, but then *contras* rose up in counterrevolution. Progressive liberals in the United States generally favored a hands-off policy with respect to these struggles, believing that they were mainly domestic, that prior U.S. interventions were at least in part responsible for them, and that their outcome was "of almost total inconsequence" (Moynihan 1990, 127). In contrast, the various kinds of conservatives, including Reagan, were more inclined to view the struggles as evidences of Moscow's effort to extend communism and to hold that victory for the anticommunists was an absolute imperative.

With respect to Nicaragua, the issue concerned support for the *contras*. According to Reagan, they were "freedom fighters," struggling not simply to free Nicaragua from Moscow's control but to establish democracy. Reagan described "the core of our foreign policy [as] protecting the security of the United States while advancing the cause of world freedom and democratic rights." That the United States should do this was the Reagan Doctrine. According to liberals, in contrast, the *contras* were reactionaries who had little domestic support and who would restore something like the dictatorship that had been overthrown. To liberals, the claim that the *contras* and other right-wing groups in Central America would promote democracy was so obviously ridiculous that it had to be hypocritical.

The result was that liberals in Congress—mainly Democrats—prohibited the use of U. S. funds for aid to the *contras*, but some government officials around Reagan, presumably reflecting his views and wishes, were so passionate in their anticommunism and so fully convinced that the Nicaraguan regime was both communist and a danger to the United States that they circumvented and violated the law. Their attitude was similar to the attitude of left-wing terrorists and right-wing death squads in various Latin American countries who self-righteously used murder as a political weapon. When individuals believe that they know beyond doubt both what is good for the country and that the achievement of this good is overwhelmingly important, they tend to feel that they have a patriotic dispensation to violate any rule of law or morality that stands in the way.

Whether the Reagan administration also violated international law in intervening in Grenada and in aiding the *contras* (especially in mining Nicaraguan ports), and whether Bush later violated international law in invading Panama, is a matter of hot dispute—a dispute in which ideologies shatter. People sharing the same ideology with regard to domestic issues come out against each other on the foreign policy issue. Thus Daniel Patrick Moynihan, who classifies himself as a liberal, argues that the various acts of intervention violated international law and deplores "evidence that the United States is moving away from its long-established concern for and advocacy of international legal norms of state behavior" (1990, 176). But some liberals, some neoconservatives, and some conservatives disagree.

Moynihan himself names a respected "certified liberal," Lloyd Cutler, who disagrees with him at least on the Panama issue. Charles Krauthammer, who is known as a neoconservative, also disagrees, dismissing international law with contempt (1989, 44–50). Jeane Kirkpatrick, generally described either as a progressive conservative or a neoconservative, and Robert Bork, generally described as a conservative, both take international law seriously but defend the various acts of intervention as legally permissible (Bork 1989/90; Kirkpatrick 1984). Whatever an impartial jury would decide, it is clear that the conservative Reagan administration was not concerned enough about the law to stay clearly within it.

After the fact, Irving Kristol, the blue-ribbon neoconservative, endorsed a different line with respect to Nicaragua. Instead of supporting the *contras* against the Sandinista government, he would have given Nicaragua an ultimatum: "Either you Finlandize yourself or we invade." Since Finlandization implied no further acceptance of Soviet aid, Kristol assumed that, under his formula, the United States would have invaded. It did not matter if the invasion violated our obligations under the UN Charter; in fact, Kristol deplored any mention of the UN Charter in connection with such an issue (DeMuth et al. 1987, 46). He was contemptuous of the United Nations, which he regarded as "an organization bent on delegitimizing, eventually destroying, the state of Israel" (Kristol 1984, 26). Implicitly he was also contemptuous of international law. To him, the subordination of American foreign policy to "the authority of international organizations [is an] idea of liberal internationalism [and] is dead." Kristol saw a "new and more assertive nationalism" developing in the United States.

Most liberals and some conservatives came to the view long ago that the United States made a mistake in intervening in Vietnam and was wise to withdraw, but other conservatives are so passionate in their anticommunism that they disagree at least in part: whatever they think of the wisdom of the original intervention, they denounce the withdrawal. Embarrassed by the fact that Republicans arranged the withdrawal, they resort to circumlocutions. Thus Pat Buchanan says that "the Establishment ... lacked the mental stamina and moral courage to see that war through to victory. Vietnam was liberalism's last great adventure, and greatest debacle" (1988, 316). Note that the tragedy of Vietnam is attributed to liberalism, not to the more passionate form of anticommunism. Kristol shares this view, attributing our intervention both in Korea and in Vietnam to "liberal internationalism."

Different explanations attend the collapse of communism and the breakup of the Soviet Union. Margaret Thatcher makes the bold statement that "Ronald Reagan won the Cold War.... He had a little help—at least that's what he tells me. But that imperishable achievement will be seen by history as belonging primarily to him." Bill Clinton's comment is that "the notion that the Republicans won the Cold War alone reminds me of the rooster who took credit for the dawn." Charles H. Fairbanks, Jr., sounds two different notes. On the one hand, he treats the collapse of communism as "the greatest affirmation of conservative principles since the miscarriage of the French Revolution," and on the other hand, he says that the Soviet system, "sick for many other reasons, finally died by suicide." John Maynard's view is that "socialism collapsed in the USSR under its own weight.... The Soviet Union ... collapsed because of the inherent failure of socialism and the self-deception which made its socialist rulers unable to see the fatal flaws of their own system." Myron Rush stresses "the key role of chance and personality in the fall of communism." Had not the role of the dice brought Gorbachev to power, the USSR would still exist. And Paul Weyrich credits the collapse to a spiritual revival in the Russian people and perhaps in the Kremlin itself. Historians will be debating this issue for decades to come.

Before becoming undersecretary of state in the Clinton administration, Strobe Talbott wrote an article entitled "Rethinking the Red Menace." He said that "for more than four decades, Western policy has been based on a grotesque exaggeration of what the U.S.S.R.

could do if it wanted.... Scenarios for a Soviet invasion of Western Europe have always had a touch of paranoid fantasy about them." Where the West thought the Soviet Union was strong, it was in fact weak. The upheavals of 1989 in the Soviet Union demonstrated that "the conventional wisdom that has largely prevailed over the past 40 years" had been wrong and that those who had taken a less alarmist view of Soviet capacities and intentions had been right. The Soviet system went into meltdown "because of inadequacies and defects at its core, not because of anything the outside world has done or not done or threatened to do" (Talbott 1990).

The collapse of communism and the breakup of the Soviet Union pose a special problem for conservatives. Not that any variety of conservatism loses its *raison d'étre;* all varieties have additional features in their platforms that will continue to attract support. But nevertheless one basis for their appeal is gone. And what is more important, a basis for cooperation among conservative groups is also gone. Bush's defeat in 1992 is generally ascribed to the poor state of the domestic economy, but the fact that he could not appeal to anticommunism and to fear of the Soviet Union surely played a role. And it will be harder in the future for conservatives to get together in a coalition such as the one that Reagan was able to form.

In the above, I follow the widespread practice in speaking of the collapse of communism. Some speak of its death. This ignores the fact that communists rule in China, which means that they rule over nearly a fifth of the human race. Chinese communists attracted the condemnations of the world when they suppressed the Tiananmen demonstration of 1989, and their alleged use of prison labor leads to agitation for the restriction of imports from China. In an article in the *Conservative Review,* Jack Wheeler claims that "Red China is a major potential threat to the future peace of the world, and already enslaves more people than the Marxists in the Kremlin ever did," and he wants the United States to adopt a strategy aimed at the liberation of China (Wheeler 1992, 25, 27). But, on the whole, communism in China is accepted with relative equanimity. Perhaps it is because the Chinese communists are switching to a market economy. Perhaps it is because they have not so far appeared to be threatening.

## Diplomacy, International Law, and International Organization

Those taking an internationalist approach to foreign affairs tend to emphasize diplomacy, international law, and international organization. I have already described some of the relevant attitudes in describing the terminological muddle and the dispute relating to communism and the Soviet Union, but need now to focus on them.

Underlying the internationalist approach is the assumption that the United States has no real choice but to be concerned about the world environment in which it operates. We want that environment to be congenial to our purposes. At the minimum it should not seriously obstruct our pursuit of those purposes, and at best it should facilitate our achievement of them.

In pursuing our purposes we must be sensitive to the fact that other states have purposes too, some compatible and some incompatible with ours. This dictates concern not only for the purposes that various states pursue but also for the methods that we and they employ.

The prescription to which these considerations lead is internationalist, with internationalism denoting the view that the United States should play an active role in the world, supporting the United Nations and other international organizations, respecting international law, opposing aggression, seeking the limitation of armaments, promoting human rights and democracy, extending foreign aid, favoring the reduction of barriers to trade and travel, and, in general, looking toward the development of a closer-knit international community. The view is not exclusively identified with any one ideology. Progressive liberals are most likely to share it, but so do some conservatives and neoconservatives.

The need for diplomacy (i.e., for communication with other states) is obvious and generally agreed. International law and international organizations, however, get different appraisals, as indicated by the descriptions given above of the "liberal/idealist" and "realist" schools of thought.

Internationalists want to emphasize both international law and international organizations. The assumption is that orderly relationships among states are desirable and that law and organization provide the most promising basis for such relationships. After all, law and organization are vital to the domestic political order, so why should we not look to them to promote international order as well? True, they have not been entirely successful, but internationalists are not necessarily utopian. They know that just as crime, riots, revolutions, and civil wars occur within countries, so are comparable outbreaks to be expected among countries. What the internationalist hopes for is improvement, not utopia—improvement taking the form of wider and firmer agreement on the purposes it is permissible to pursue and the methods it is permissible to employ in international relationships. And, in addition, wider and firmer agreement on the kinds of actions to take to encourage and enforce respect for law.

I speak here in vague terms. The most difficult question concerns enforcement action. The Charter of the United Nations authorizes such action but does not require it. Sentiment has been building up for a rule against any effort to change international boundary lines by force, but it would be too much to say that a corresponding sentiment exists about the enforcement of the rule. President Bush decided to take military action against Iraq when it committed aggression against Kuwait, and he got majority support in Congress. But the case for action was specific to the circumstances: access to oil was at stake, and so was the security of Israel. It is too much to suppose that Bush was responding to the principle that the United States should take armed action against any aggression anywhere.

Serbian aggression in Bosnia (even if it is classified as genocidal) does not so clearly threaten American interests and thus produces a weaker and more divided reaction. Aggression by one of the states of the former Soviet Union against another is still less likely to induce the United States to go to the aid of the victim. And experience in Somalia will surely make the country hesitate about pursuing even humanitarian missions abroad if there is any significant prospect that the role of the military will need to extend beyond the provision of police services. All of this suggests that internationalism is suffused with a lively concern for national self-interest, which is not surprising. In contrast to Bush, who told the United Nations what he wanted to do about Iraq and got its approval, Clinton satisfies himself, in relation to Bosnia, with doing "everything the UN [asks] us to do." Given the absence of a clear American interest, he does not assert leadership. Those who think that the United States should do more call this an abdication.

Nevertheless, internationalism persists. The acceptance of the North American Free Trade Agreement (NAFTA) and the conclusion of another round of negotiations under the General Agreement on Tariffs and Trade (GATT) in 1993 indicate that internationalism is dominant in the economic realm. In the political realm it calls, cautiously and hesitantly, for the development of international community. To the internationalist, order and stability are approximately as important in the international as in the domestic realm and must be sought in similar ways: through voluntary cooperation; through bargaining, involving both carrots and sticks; and through political processes and organizations for developing, adjusting, and enforcing the law.

Internationalism is not identified exclusively with any of the ideologies described in the preceding chapters, but it gets its support especially from the ranks of the progressive liberals.

## Human Rights and Democracy

Concern for international community, for world order under law, includes a concern for human rights. The Charter of the United Nations obliges all members to *promote* human rights, and more than half of the states of the world have ratified treaties requiring them actually to *respect* the rights named. But even if support for international law should include support for human rights, the obligation is in a special category because this particular development of international law is relatively new and the implications are still being worked out.

One of the surprises is that support for human rights is not narrowly ideological, but comes from conservatives of different sorts as well as from progressive liberals. This has not always been so. Beginning in 1949, conservatives led by Senator John W. Bricker took Truman's recommendation that we ratify the genocide convention as the occasion for a general attack on the whole idea. They held that treaties on human rights would infringe too much on our sovereignty, obligating us internationally with respect to essentially domestic matters. They objected to the fact that the Universal Declaration of Human Rights included rights of an economic and social sort; and supposing that treaties on human rights would do the same, they objected to "socialism by treaty." They objected that treaties, as the supreme law of the land, might change our constitutional arrangement, transferring powers from the states to the federal government, and Bricker championed an amendment to the constitution to make this impossible. The result was that Eisenhower and John Foster Dulles announced that the United States would abandon any effort to promote human rights by treaty, and for almost two decades thereafter American participation in the international movement for human rights was muted.

The situation began to change in the 1970s. First some liberals in the House, finding it intolerable that the United States was giving aid to governments that were grossly and consistently violating human rights, induced Congress to require that in such circumstances aid be cut off. Further, they induced Congress to require the establishment in the Department of State of a Bureau on Human Rights and Humanitarian Affairs, charged with monitoring the record of other states on human rights. The bureau in fact began publishing an annual volume on the human rights record of states all over the world.

Then in the 1970s the American ambassador to the United Nations, Daniel Patrick Moynihan, began speaking up on human rights. "It is for the United States deliberately and consistently to bring its influence to bear on behalf of those regimes which promise the largest degree of personal and national liberty.... We stand for liberty, for the expansion of liberty." He says that he and a colleague "changed the language of American foreign policy," making human rights "one of the organizing principles that define our interests and help to inform our conduct in world affairs." As if to illustrate the fact that concern for human rights fits with several ideologies, Moynihan says that nothing would have been more appropriate to the conservative President Gerald Ford than championship of the idea of human rights and that if Ford had taken the idea up it might have enabled him to win reelection in 1976.

Nevertheless, it was President Carter who, as Anthony Lewis put it, wove the issue of human rights inextricably into the foreign policy dialogue. Early in his administration he proclaimed that a commitment to human rights was "a fundamental tenet of our foreign policy," and he proceeded to exert pressure on various other governments on behalf of human rights, with actual or threatened reductions in aid as a major weapon. Moreover, by this time the General Assembly had adopted various treaties and conventions on human rights, most notably two covenants (one on civil and political rights and the other on economic, social, and cultural rights), and it had adopted a convention on racial discrimination. And the Organization of American States had adopted the American Convention on Human Rights. Carter arranged to have all four signed on behalf of the United States, and he referred them to the Senate, asking it to consent to ratification. He did not, however, make the matter a major issue, presumably fearing a Brickerite reaction on the part of conservative nationalists.

The principal negative reaction to Carter's general policy on human rights came from those absorbed in the struggle against communism and the Soviet Union, most notably from neoconservatives. Their question was how the promotion of human rights related to that struggle, and they saw two sources of distress.

In the first place, they feared that the promotion of human rights was weakening the West on the diplomatic/military front. On the one hand, we could not do much about human rights in the communist states since they were not receiving aid and since they seemed impervious to verbal remonstrances. On the other hand, in exerting pressures against noncommunist governments we were likely to be acting against a friend or ally. In Nicaragua pressures from the United States even contributed to the overthrow of a regime friendly to us and its replacement by a regime friendly to Moscow (Kirkpatrick 1982, 72). True, the governments friendly to us were likely to be authoritarian and guilty of violating human rights, but, the neoconservatives argued, their violations were relatively minor compared to those of communist governments, and, anyway, authoritarian governments were more likely than communist governments to evolve into democracies. So the championship of human rights was counterproductive in the struggle against communism and the Soviet Union.

Reagan himself endorsed this line of argument early in his first administration. He complained that Carter had been "selective," punishing pro-Western governments in the name of human rights while seeking détente with the Soviet Union. And Reagan nominated a person to be head of the human rights bureau in the Department of State who opposed any action to promote those rights abroad—a nomination that the Senate refused to confirm.

The second source of distress for neoconservatives, noted by Irving Kristol, was the belief that in championing human rights we were weakening ourselves on the political/philosophical front. To Kristol, the view that human rights include goals of an economic and social sort was suggestive of socialism, as it had been to Senator Bricker in the early 1950s. Not only did this view give greater potential strength to left-wing elements in American politics but it also strengthened communist governments; accused of violating civil and political rights, they could counter with the claim that they were doing more than capitalist governments for human rights because they were guaranteeing rights of a social and economic sort. For these reasons, the leading neoconservatives—and the Reagan administration—were ambivalent about international action to promote human rights.

Reagan's substitute was to proclaim that the United States would champion democracy in the world. He thus accepted a goal similar to Carter's without putting himself in Carter's shoes. Early in his first administration, speaking to the British parliament, he declared that freedom is "the right of all human beings," and he proposed to "foster the infrastructure of democracy, the system of a free press, unions, political parties, universities, which allows a people to choose their own way to develop their own culture, to reconcile their own differences by peaceful means." He therefore called for "actions to assist the campaign for democracy" (*Public Papers* 1982, 1:745). In switching the emphasis from human rights to democracy, Reagan made a kind of chicken-and-egg debate inevitable.

Among the measures taken on behalf of democracy under Reagan was the establishment of the National Endowment for Democracy. It is privately incorporated and governed by its own board but financed by Congress. The NED makes grants to institutes within the United States (the Free Trade Union Institute and institutes affiliated respectively with the Republican and Democratic national committees and the U. S. Chamber of Commerce), which in turn seek to promote democracy in selected foreign countries. Their policy is to give assistance and guidance to democratic organizations, but not to engage directly in partisan activities themselves (Muravchik 1991, 204, 207–14). The NED continues to function under the Clinton administration.

As in the case of support for an emphasis on human rights, support for an emphasis on democracy comes from people who differ in their domestic ideological outlook. Neoconservatives are divided. Joshua Muravchik has written a book on *Exporting Democracy: Fulfilling America's Destiny* (1991). He holds that we can simultaneously do good and serve our own national interests by making the promotion of democracy in the world a major foreign policy objective. Among other things, he believes that "democratizing the Soviet Union must be by far the highest goal of U.S. foreign policy." Carl Gershman takes a similar stand, arguing that support for democracy should be our "central purpose." "We have a unique opportunity to exercise leadership in supporting the progress of democracy, arguably the foremost political issue of our time. Our prestige and morale would inevitably suffer if we were to relinquish this responsibility." Michael Ledeen, writing in the conservative *American Spectator*, gloats at the thought that "we are on the verge of fulfilling our destiny as the leader and the inspiration of the Second Democratic Revolution."

Irving Kristol is skeptical. He grants that "it is in our national interest that those nations which largely share our political principles and social values should be protected from those that do not," but he speaks of the "futility" of efforts to "enhance democracy" abroad. His outlook is nationalist, not internationalist (Harries 1991, 63, 69).

Neoconservatives are not alone in advocating American support for democracy in the world.

Stephen Solarz, a progressive liberal, combines a concern for democracy with a concern for human rights: "In those countries that are not already democratic, we ought to condition the offer of U.S. assistance, other than that needed to meet pressing humanitarian concerns, on specific democratic reforms and real respect for human rights" (Solarz 1992, 25). And Clinton and Gore joined the chorus in their 1992 campaign book *Putting People First*: "We should promote democracy ... throughout the world." They promise to "pursue a foreign policy of Engagement for Democracy." They will attach conditions to foreign aid and launch a Democracy Corps with a mission like that of the Peace Corps. They will help the Soviet peoples build free political and economic institutions.

Warning notes are sounded. Supporting democracy abroad might involve greater burdens than it is prudent to assume. Further, it is possible that democratic elections may have unwelcome results. Ronald Steel speaks of the feeling of relief in Western chanceries when the Algerian military put a stop to an electoral process in which Islamic fundamentalists were heading toward victory. Although in principle good democrats must accept even the unwelcome results of elections, it is a question whether they need to allow democracy to be used for its own destruction. The International Covenant on Civil and Political Rights says no. It specifies that nothing in it implies for any group or person "any right to engage in any activity or perform any act aimed at the destruction of the rights and freedoms recognized herein."

In 1986, after repeated Senate hearings and prolonged debate, the United States finally ratified the Genocide Convention that Senator Bricker had been so determined to reject, and, more remarkably, in 1992 it also ratified the International Covenant on Civil and Political Rights, mentioned earlier. Ratification of the covenant is remarkable both because the obligations assumed are broader than those of the Genocide Convention and, even more, because it happened almost without notice. The Senate Committee on Foreign Relations voted unanimously to advise and consent to ratification, which means that both liberals and conservatives (including Jesse Helms) voted favorably; and little debate occurred in the Senate itself. President Bush ratified. And so insignificant did the action seem that the *New York Times* did not even report it. On the one hand, the action suggests the existence of a substantial consensus on the view that the United States should involve itself more fully in the international movement on behalf of human rights; and on the other hand it suggests that the experience of other countries with the covenant shows that it does not have as much effect on domestic policies as people of Senator Bricker's frame of mind once feared.

In some eyes, the stress on either human rights or democracy is too broad. Instead, the stress should be on the creation of a confederation of the West. Thus Charles Krauthammer looks toward the creation of "a super-sovereign West economically, culturally, and politically hegemonic in the world." He acknowledges that this goal is not far removed from the goal of promoting democracy in the world, but he wants the focus to be on the center, not on the periphery.

He thinks that "the unification of the industrial West [should be] the major goal of the democratic crusade rather than the conversion, one by one, of the Third World states." Nevertheless, if democratic Western countries became confederated and "hegemonic," the prospects of human rights and democracy in the rest of the world would surely be enhanced. Krauthammer acknowledges that the development of a confederation of the West "would require the conscious deprecation not only of American sovereignty, but of the notion of sovereignty in general" (Harries 1991, 11–13).

## Isolationism

Although internationalism, including support for human rights and democracy, has been running strong in the United States, isolationism and a concern for "America First" are also prominent. Libertarians, for example, are isolationist. Wanting no more than minimal government for domestic purposes, they have to favor limiting it as much as possible in international affairs. Believing that coercion against individuals is wrong, they have to oppose coercion at the international level.

Murray Rothbard, described in chapter 7 as an anarchocapitalist, provides an extreme illustration. If he had his way, he would not be satisfied with limited government but would have no government at all. Acknowledging that this is not a realizable goal in a visible future, however, he responded in 1978 to the question how a libertarian society in the United States would defend itself against the Russians. His response was to reject the assumption that the Russians might attack. A libertarian American society, he said, would not be a threat to anyone, and this would mean that "there would be little chance of any country attacking us" (Rothbard 1978, 1985, 237–38). The implication is that since that American Indians did not threaten Europe at the time of Columbus, and since Afghanistan did not threaten the Soviet Union in 1979, they were safe.

Quite apart from Rothbard, the 1991 platform of the Libertarian Party is isolationist. It asks for a "return to the historic libertarian tradition of avoiding entangling alliances, abstaining totally from foreign quarrels and imperialist adventures, and recognition of the right to unrestricted trade, travel, and immigration." It calls for "a drastic reduction in the cost and size of our total diplomatic establishment," including a withdrawal from the United Nations. It would bring home all American military personnel now stationed abroad and make the policy of nonintervention its guide in foreign affairs. It grants the possible need for defense against intercontinental missiles, but would provide for that defense on a purely national basis. Americans who travel, do business, or own property abroad would do so at their own risk; the government doing nothing to protect them or their interests (Libertarian Party 1993).

David Boaz of the Cato Institute takes a similar position. "It is time," he says, "to redefine American security interests as the protection of the life, liberty, and property of American citizens in the United States. It is not the role of the United States to police the world or to spread democracy at the point of a gun. We need to maintain our nuclear deterrent, but we should bring the boys home and significantly reduce the size and expense of the armed forces" (Boaz 1990, 9). Other writers associated with the Cato Institute describe NATO as obsolete. They want to "celebrate its success and enjoy the financial benefits of reduced military obligations" (Bandow and Carpenter 1990, 12).

Among those inclined toward libertarianism, the predominant reaction to the war against Iraq was hostile. The real purpose of the war, according to David Boaz, was not to punish aggression or to secure access to oil but to preserve the military-industrial complex. The collapse of communism and the Soviet Union had threatened that complex with severe cutbacks; more specifically, it threatened the careers of persons in the Department of State and in other agencies having to do with international affairs, so they could breathe a sigh of relief when Saddam Hussein invaded Kuwait. They could replace the struggle against communism with a quest for a new world order—a prescription for perpetual conflict. The true explanation for the war was to be found in the writings of the students of public choice (Boaz 1991, 1).

Some libertarians dissent from the above views. Although opposing coercion, they are troubled about the question what to do when someone else initiates it; and some of them come up with the conclusion that participation in war may be the lesser of two evils. Self-defense may be justified, and what actions should be regarded as threatening enough to call for defensive action is a matter of judgment and strategy (Robbins 1990).

Pat Robertson classifies as an isolationist, whatever the views of other social conservatives. In *The New World Order* (1991) he pictures virtually everything relating to foreign affairs as ominous. A "tightly knit cabal," consisting of people in the White House, the State Department, the Council on Foreign Relations, the Trilateral Commission, and "secret societies" among New Agers, threatens us with the elimination of national sovereignty and the establishment of a new world order under the domination of Lucifer and his followers. The cabal will set up "a world government, and world police force, world courts, world banking and currency, and a world elite in charge of it all." In the United Nations, the Third World "has already voted to take away by decree the wealth of Europe and America and give it to themselves," and world government would make something like this happen. "A worldwide IRS under a banking hierarchy would become the American citizen's worst nightmare," indulging in "financial bloodsucking." Laws enacted by Congress would be superseded by world government laws, and decisions of our courts would be overridden by decisions of the World Court. "Humanistic-occultic" leaders of a world government would see to it that it oppresses Christians and Jews. And so on. All this as pure assertion unsupported by evidence or reasoning. Robertson does not announce himself as an isolationist, but he sees nothing but evil and danger outside the United States. His attitude would change, of course, if "God's people [were] given their rightful place of leadership at the top of the world."

## America First

Pat Buchanan is the outstanding champion of the slogan "America First." In fact, his slogan is "America first, second, and third." He emphasizes nationalism, both political and economic. He wants the United States to pursue its national interests.

Buchanan expresses political nationalism in a number of ways. He would abrogate the mutual security treaty with Japan and pull American troops out of both South Korea and Europe. "If Germany and Japan are rich enough and powerful enough to steal our markets and buy up our greatest corporations, they are rich enough and powerful enough to start paying the full cost of their own defense." He would dissolve the Rio treaty and restrict the Monroe Doctrine to the north coast of South America and points north. At the same time, he thinks it both a strategic and a moral imperative that America remain the first military power on earth.

Describing the United Nations as "the greatest spy nest in history," he would require it and "all associated agencies" to move out of North America. Further, he would reconsider American membership in the United Nations, asking whether it advances the national interests of the United States. He opposed the war against Iraq, predicting that it would be "the last hurrah of the interventionists." He opposes a "globalist crusade" on behalf of democracy partly because he sees no compelling American interest that it would serve and partly because the cultural traditions of many other countries make democracy unsuitable for them. "The battle for the future is on," he says, "between New Age globalists and old-fashioned patriots, between those who believe America must yield up her sovereignty to a New World Order and those who believe we must preserve the Old Republic." Independence and freedom of action are his watchwords. With questionable consistency, however, during his campaign for the presidency in 1992 he spoke of the moral commitment of the United States to guarantee the security and survival of Israel and said that a Buchanan administration would honor that commitment.

With respect to the economic aspects of foreign policy, Buchanan holds that the country "ought to be led by tough economic nationalists who are out to make America first." He would phase out all foreign aid, pull out of the development banks, and make no new grants to the World Bank and the IMF. Although supporting the free trade agreement with Canada, he would not let America's unskilled go jobless while Mexico's unskilled get work. He says, "I don't view myself as a protectionist but as a trade hawk."

Samuel T. Francis, who classifies himself as an Old Right conservative, speaks of institutionalizing an America First foreign policy (1991, 9–11). "No treaty should be concluded or ratified that compromises or dilutes national sovereignty or requires changes in United States law and policy contrary to the constitution." The Bricker amendment should be revived and adopted. We should aim at a military force sufficient only to defend a limited security zone—perhaps the zone Buchanan suggests (above) for a revised Monroe Doctrine. Congress, not the president, should be supreme over foreign affairs, and lobbying on behalf of a foreign country should be a crime.

At the close of the section on communism, I mention Kristol's view that a new and more assertive nationalism is developing. Buchanan provides supporting evidence, and so do others on the right even if they do not employ "America First" as a slogan. Samuel T. Francis, cited above, speaks of "a new nationalism that insists on the military and economic pre-eminence of the United States, on international activism (and even expansionism) in world affairs, on at least some measure of protection for domestic producers, and on far more resistance to Third World arrogance, aggression, and barbarianism." He points to opposition to the Panama Canal treaty as evidence of this nationalism.

Irving Kristol too comes out in favor of the national interest as the touchstone of our foreign policy. He decries "Wilsonian liberal internationalism" both in its original version (the League of Nations) and in the more recent "chastened" version that includes foreign aid and efforts to promote democracy abroad. To him, foreign aid is "utterly discredited" in that it feeds "corruption, economic inefficiency, and political irresponsibility" in the receiving countries; I have already noted that he regards the effort to promote democracy as futile. He rejects isolationism. What is left is the pursuit of our national interest on a case-by-case basis.

The notion that the United States should pursue its national interest in foreign affairs has come up so much that it deserves a special comment. In a way, no one disagrees on the point. Every commentator agrees that we should be concerned for our interests. The question is whether this gives adequate guidance and whether we need to be concerned with anything in addition to our interests. Critics respond that the prescription is too vague and that, as usually interpreted, it is too narrow.

Those who champion the concept try to reduce its vagueness by supplementing it with additional prescriptions. As noted, Hans Morgenthau thought that the national interest should be "defined in terms of power," but that does little to help. Does it mean that we should go all-out in maximizing our power, without limit? If not, what does it mean? Others tend to speak of "direct" national interests, or (in effect) of short-run and self-regarding concerns, and they tend to disparage any "moralizing" about foreign policies. But suppose that it is in the direct, immediate interest of the United States that a particular foreign leader should die. Should we then use murder as a political weapon? Suppose that it is in our direct, immediate interest to flout a requirement of the UN Charter or of general international law. Should we therefore flout that requirement? Suppose that, as in the case of the Argentine attack on the Falkland Islands, no direct, short-run interest of the United States is at stake, but we know that future relationships with both Argentina and Britain will be affected by what we do or fail to do. Do we give priority to short-run considerations or long-run considerations? Suppose that American consumers can gain by importing goods produced by child labor abroad, and suppose that American taxpayers are better off if we ignore famine abroad. Many circumstances of these sorts indicate that the guidance we get from a concern for our interests is not clear.

The above questions serve double duty. They support not only the contention that the national interest is too vague a concept to be our sole guide but also the contention that it is too narrow. People who decide on foreign policy questions, or who influence the decisions, surely have consciences; and we want them to have consciences. Persons who are totally amoral in treating others may soon demonstrate their amorality in their treatment of you. Those who kill foreign adversaries may also start killing their domestic adversaries. Those contemptuous of international law may also become contemptuous of domestic law. Those callous about child labor abroad may lose any concern for the welfare of children at home. We certainly do not want a totally amoral society within the country, but we risk undermining the role of morality at home if we flout its requirements abroad.

Further, even if those in charge of foreign relations were totally amoral themselves, they would be subject (if they are in a democratic country) to democratic pressures. Voters are likely to be as concerned as others for "the national interest," but they are not likely to regard it as their sole guide, and leaders who earn a reputation for cynicism about law and morality in international affairs jeopardize their political careers. In any event, even the leaders who are cynical are likely to see an advantage to the country if it has a reputation for accepting the norms of international behavior and giving reasonable and equitable consideration to the interests of other countries. It may be in the national interest to have, or at least to appear to have, a concern for justice as well as for selfish advantage.

## Conservative Conservatism

Christopher Layne styles himself as a "real" conservative, in contrast to the neoconservatives. His "real" conservatism strongly suggests what I call conservative conservatism. Writing in the mid-1980s, he sought to distance himself from "global containment, recast as the Reagan Doctrine" (Layne 1985–86, 73), which he identified with the neoconservatives.

"Real" conservatives, according to Layne, distinguish between what is desirable and what is vital. Writing prior to the collapse of communism, he thought it desirable to save all Third World countries from communism, but not vital; contrary to the neoconservatives, we were not threatened by communism per se. For nationalist and other reasons, the communists of China and Yugoslavia were already following anti-Soviet policies. Anyway, the United States would bankrupt itself if it attempted to save all Third World countries, thus endangering what we seek to defend—"the vitality and strength of America's political and economic institutions." We cannot expect to mold the world in our own image, or even to have an ideologically congenial world. We ought to reduce rather than extend our overseas commitments, and cut government spending.

Russell Kirk expresses similar views. Offering a critique of neoconservatism, he speaks of people who "have been rash in their schemes of action, pursuing a fanciful democratic globalism rather than the national interest of the United States.... To expect that all the world should, and must, adopt the peculiar political institutions of the United States—which often do not work very well even at home—is to indulge the most unrealistic of visions" (1993, 179, 184). The object should be to "build on what is there rather than trying to replace it with something that is alien."A soundly conservative foreign policy should be neither interventionist nor isolationist, but prudent. The object should be the preservation of the "true national interest" (1993, 221).

Having noted the fact that Irving Kristol and Russell Kirk agree that the national interest should be the guide, I should call attention to a delicious bit of irony. Commenting on "some eminent neoconservatives" (who surely included Kristol), Kirk says that "not seldom it has seemed to me as if [they] mistook Tel Aviv for the capital of the United States" (1993, 180).

## A New World Order?

In 1991 the United States attacked Iraq, following its aggression against Kuwait. In announcing the attack President Bush sought to justify it not in terms of direct service to an immediate national interest but in grander terms. With implicit approval, he quoted statements by others: we did not act simply for "the price of a gallon of gas"; we acted because "a world in which brutality and lawlessness are allowed to go unchecked isn't the kind of world we're going to want to live in." And he went on with a statement of his own: "We have before us the opportunity to forge for ourselves and for future generations a new world order—a world where the rule of law, not the law of the jungle, governs the conduct of nations. When we are successful—and we will be—we have a real chance at this new world order, an order in which a credible United Nations can use its peacekeeping role to fulfill the promise and vision of the U.N.'s founders" (*Public Papers* 1991, 1:44).

Reactions to the war against Iraq varied. I have already cited the protests of writers associated with the Cato Institute, suggestive of isolationism. In contrast, the different sorts of conservatives generally supported the war, although not necessarily for the reasons that Bush gave. An article in *Policy Review,* published by the Heritage Foundation, thought it misleading for Bush to justify the action as a response to aggression when the United States has not responded similarly to acts of aggression elsewhere in the world. "Bush should be honest and direct and say that America cannot afford to let a man like Saddam Hussein sit on the world's oil lifeline, nor threaten U.S. and allied interests with chemical, biological, and nuclear weapons of mass destruction. These alone are sufficient reasons to drive Iraq out of Kuwait." The conservative journal *Human Events* opposed a land war against Iraq, holding that Bush should "stick with air war against Saddam." It commented further that the "cry for a 'new world order' sticks in the craw" of many on the right and protested the thought that the United States might become "the cop on the planet beat." Tom Bethell, in the conservative *American Spectator,* took the view that a policy of asking American taxpayers to rescue beleaguered foreign governments would be a disaster. It would be "liberal internationalism run amok."

Progressive liberals hesitated about declaring war against Iraq, many in Congress opposing, even if they supported the subsequent military action as a patriotic duty. Not that they necessarily opposed a response to Iraqi aggression, but they were more inclined to give economic sanctions a longer time to work.

It turned out that Bush had nothing in mind concerning a new world order beyond defeating Iraq. He had no additional proposal to make. He was plainly not prepared to act against any aggression anywhere.

With the disappearance of the Soviet threat, several conservative or neoconservative authors and journals have volunteered suggestions for the future. Most elaborate is the "Blueprint" issued by the Heritage Foundation (Holmes and Kosminsky 1992, 50–69). It lays down a number of rules and prescriptions, the gist of which is indicated by the following:

1. "The main purpose of America's foreign and defense policy is to protect the lives, liberty, and property of Americans." Although we have an interest in promoting Western values around the world, the first obligation is to people at home. We must do nothing for others that contradicts our own vital interests.

2. Nevertheless, "America must continue to play a global role, not out of altruism or moralism or a calling to leadership, but because only through an active and engaged foreign policy can

Americans hope to control their own destiny and thus ensure their hard-earned freedoms." The objective must be to "make the world safe for America."

3. As an aspect of the global role, we must protect our own land, sea, and air frontiers and must prevent any hostile power from dominating Europe, East Asia, or the Persian Gulf. And, with respect to nuclear weapons, we should adopt "tough new anti-proliferation measures."

4. Free trade is vital to our own prosperity, and free markets and democracy abroad are to be encouraged. We are to do this, however, only by economic and diplomatic means.

Burton Yale Pines served as editor of this Heritage "Blueprint." In an article of his own, he warns against "an ambitious foreign policy," for such a policy requires "big government," and "big government" threatens individual liberty. At another point, he speaks of what he calls the "bargain" after World War II in which conservatives accepted an expanded role for government in return for protection against the communist danger. Now, he says, with the Cold War over, the "bargain" is obsolete and the role of government can safely be reduced. We no longer need a "global" foreign policy, but should adopt specific policies for specific problems.

> For a conservative, the goal of foreign policy is not a successful crusade for democracy or for human rights or for spreading the American way of life. These are worthy ends for individuals and private organizations to pursue; they do not justify, however, the federal government deploying Americans in harm's way or even spending taxpayer money on them.
>
> For a conservative, the only legitimate goal of American foreign policy is the creation of a world environment in which America is left alone and at peace, in which America can trade and raise its living standards, in which Americans can expand their options and enrich their lives. (Pines 1991, 68)

An article by Paul Johnson provides a sharp contrast. After speaking of the long period of international peace that Europe has enjoyed and of the fact that all the countries of Europe are now democratic, Johnson dreams of spreading "this comparative and unprecedented felicity ... progressively to the rest of the world." He starts with a call for "the improvement and enlightened use of the United Nations idea." Germany, Japan, and perhaps India should become permanent members of the Security Council. Instead of playing a reactive and negative role (waiting to act until aggression has occurred, for example), the enlarged Security Council should try to ward off unacceptable developments by timely preventive action, usually police action; this would be "a giant step toward the realization of an international rule of law." The whole United Nations would be thought of in terms of contingency planning and crisis management.

Further, the United Nations, rejecting the assumption that all countries are ready for independence and capable of governing themselves, should put some of them (notably some of the countries of Africa) under trusteeship, that is, put them under the control of one of the more advanced countries, which would be internationally accountable for their policies. The duration of the trusteeships would vary with circumstances.

China, according to Johnson, should be more fully enmeshed in the international system, the aim being to "convert her from an international anomaly ... into a central pillar of the new global structure of order." Steps should be taken toward a global system of free trade and toward the rational use of the resources of the world. The fullest possible use of human talent should occur, and to make this possible, various measures should be taken to assure the education and physical well-being of the people of the world. "We are now posed on the verge of a great adventure in international political and economic coming together, which can turn the twenty-first century into the period when the first global society is forged."

Johnson's article appeared in the leading conservative journal, the *National Review* (Johnson 1992).

# Chapter 15

# Neoliberalisms

A S I HAVE SAID earlier, Reagan was so successful in heaping scorn on the "L-word" that it is widely regarded as a political albatross. Academics such as John Rawls are not deterred from accepting *liberal* as a label, and neither are some of those making policy recommendations (as in the pages of the *American Prospect)*, but those facing elections tend to avoid it. Some speak of neoliberalism, thus acknowledging a relationship to the liberal heritage while also distancing themselves from it. Implicitly or explicitly they are saying that liberalism needs to be modified. Some modify it without endorsing either the old or a new label. I am calling all of these current positions *neoliberal.*

The first section of this chapter asks whether progressive liberalism is in truth so discreditable that it needs to be abandoned. Then will come sections on "a neoliberal manifesto," "the end of equality," community, and the New Democrat.

## Is Liberalism Discreditable?

Although strongly influencing others against liberalism, Reagan never attempted to make a clear and coherent case for his views. He did not take up the various features of liberalism and assess them. Instead, he loaded the "L-word" with negative innuendo, making "tax-and-spend" the normal modifier of "liberal," blaming liberalism for welfare, and creating the impression that liberals are responsible for "big government" and "bureaucracy." In other words, he attacked liberalism with a caricature, and liberals let him get away with it, apparently not having a clear conception of the ideology that presumably guides them. Moreover, they tended to join in the debate at Reagan's level in speaking of "borrow-and-spend" conservatism. Both progressive liberalism and the various kinds of conservatism deserve more respectful treatment.

I do not attempt here to describe the characteristics of liberalism that would have permitted a more effective defense against Reaganism; they are treated in chapters 3 through 6. The features that I pick out to stress are those pertaining to individual liberty and equality of opportunity. The main point associated with individual liberty is that liberals are not satisfied to leave it as an abstract, empty concept. They want liberty to have worth, and want to use government in various ways to add to its worth. Freedom to sleep under a bridge is not enough.

The main point connected with equality of opportunity is similar. Liberals are not willing to define it simply as the absence of discrimination. A person with a broken leg scarcely has equality of opportunity in a race even if, like all the others, he has an open lane ahead of him on the track. And the person born into a poverty-stricken single-parent home scarcely has equality of opportunity in comparison with a person born into an upper-middle-class suburban home. To promote equality of opportunity, you need not only to eliminate discrimination but also, insofar as possible, to make up for special disadvantages, both those for which society is responsible and those for which the individual is not responsible. The ideal, as Rawls puts it, is that "those who are at the same level of talent and ability, and have the same willingness to use them, should have the same prospects of success ... irrespective of the income class into which they are born." To come anywhere near achieving this ideal, numerous kinds of action by government are essential. Left to itself, a free market is as likely to accentuate the problem as to contribute toward its solution.

Giving worth to liberty and enhancing equality of opportunity are grand goals, and liberals can well contend that they are not to be foresworn or neglected because of the ill-founded scorn implied in innuendo about the "L-word."

To be sure, these features of liberalism did not inspire the scorn. It costs money to give worth to liberty for millions of people; and it costs money to make equality of opportunity effective. And those with money do not like to have it taxed away for the benefit of others, particularly when the goals pursued are not clear. They are generally unaware of the fact that, by and large, they get more than do the poor from the federal government—for example, through the mortgage-interest exemption, to say nothing of social security and Medicare. The irony is that the economic conservatives who made "tax-and-spend" the normal modifier of liberalism ran up so monstrous a federal debt.

The association of liberalism with welfare strengthened the negative innuendo. Once liberalism is identified with welfare, it also comes
to be associated with the decline of the family, single motherhood, an
underclass, and long-term dependency, with blacks contributing disproportionately to the problems. In other words, welfare and therefore liberalism come to be associated in the minds of many with immorality and a rejection of the work ethic on the part of people whom
racists view as undeserving anyway.

In fact, most conservatives join liberals in accepting a need for
welfare; Reagan professed to be willing to provide it for the "truly
needy," who surely constitute a high proportion of the actual beneficiaries. And most conservatives support social security and Medicare
even while denouncing the "welfare state." Moreover, most liberals
join most conservatives in wanting changes in welfare and the "welfare state" so as to reduce the attendant shortcomings and evils. In
other words, the differences between liberals and conservatives on
welfare policies are scarcely great enough to explain or justify an
abandonment of liberalism.

Liberalism became the "L-word" too because of the idea that it
was identified with special interests. But special interests come with
government. As a dispenser of benefits and burdens, government inevitably attracts interest groups; and when government is democratic,
the activities of these interest groups are predominantly in the open.
To be sure, the greater the activism of a government, the greater the
role of special interests is likely to be, but it is naive and pejorative to
speak of "interest-group liberalism" without also speaking of "interest-group conservatism." Pressures from interest groups are bound to
exist, and in some degree to get responses; liberals and conservatives
may not be sensitive to pressures from exactly the same interests, but
sensitivity of some kind goes with conservatism as well as with liberalism.

Nevertheless, justifiably or not, few political leaders proudly call
themselves liberal. Either they reject any such label, perhaps claiming
that the traditional labels are obsolete, or they speak of neoliberalism.

## A Neoliberal Manifesto

Neoliberalism does not have an agreed meaning, an agreed history, or
an agreed program. President Carter is sometimes mentioned as a
neoliberal. So are two senators of the 1970s and 1980s—Gary Hart
and Paul Tsongas. A book entitled The Neoliberals appeared in 1984
(Rothenberg), and the next year another appeared explicitly advocat-

ing what it called neoliberalism (Peters and Keisling 1985). The second of these books includes "A Neoliberal's Manifesto" by Charles Peters, on which I focus.

According to Peters, neoliberals are still liberal, sharing agreement on numerous matters "from the protection of the environment to opposition to any form of racial, religious, or sexual discrimination." "We still believe in liberty and justice and a fair chance for all, in mercy for the afflicted and help for the down and out." But neoliberals want thoughtful rather than automatic responses to problems, not sticking strictly to the old ideological line. For example, "we no longer automatically favor unions and big government or oppose the military and big business." He illustrates what he regards as the new position by insisting on performance standards requiring that increases in productivity occur before increases in wages and salaries can be expected, and he denounces the managers of a failing company for taking "ridiculously high salaries" despite their dismal record. The implication is that wages and salaries should be proportionate to contributions to the public good rather than the capacity of trade unions or managers to rig things in their own favor.

The primary concerns of neoliberalism, according to Peters, are with community, democracy, and prosperity. He does not say explicitly what he means by *community*, but he apparently equates a concern for community with a concern for the public good. "We reject the Me Decade and the proliferation of special-interest groups.... We want a leader who will challenge us to rise above our personal and group interests when they conflict with those of the community." He deplores what he describes as "the liberal intellectual's contempt for religious, patriotic, and family values," although he presents no evidence relating to the extent of such contempt. He would permit silent prayer in the schools.

Peters's prescriptions for democracy are scant. He wants more politics, not less—more good people running for office and serving in the bureaucracy. He would open half of the government's civil service positions to political appointees, limiting these appointees to no more than five years of service; he would thus make political parties more responsible for what happens, bring "real-world experience" into government, and "send back into the ranks of the voting public people who have learned firsthand why Washington doesn't work."

As to the promotion of prosperity, Peters goes along with George Gilder and the economic conservatives in saying that his hero is "the risk-taking entrepreneur who creates new jobs and better products." Peters would give special treatment to stock issued to finance new plant and equipment, exempting it from the capital gains tax on its first resale. He would free the entrepreneur from "economic regulation that discourages desirable competition" while preserving regulations designed to protect the health and safety of the workers and the public. He would give workers a share in the ownership of the company, perhaps by paying them in part with stock. He would "encourage long-term growth rather than short-term profit." He would seek cooperative rather than adversary relationships in business and government, applauding when workers in a threatened company accept wage cuts to keep it alive. He would reduce what students of public choice call rent seeking, with so much talent (for example, the talent of lawyers and lobbyists) used unproductively. He would seek improvement in the public schools, and give government more freedom to fire civil servants and schoolteachers who are unable or unwilling to do the job. He would provide military manpower through a draft, thus reducing costs and mixing the social classes.

Most drastically, he would apply a means test to income-maintenance programs such as social security, veterans' benefits, and unemployment insurance, holding that "the country can't afford to spend money on people who don't need it." Oddly enough, he says nothing in this connection about tax expenditures (for example, the mortgage-interest exemption) that benefit the same class of people. And he makes no comment about the political storm that would surely be generated by a serious proposal to withdraw social security and pension benefits from people of the middle and upper classes.

Robert Kuttner's comment is that "in the end neoliberalism often seems only to reinforce the conservative impulses of our day."

## The End of Equality

The End of Equality (1992) is the title of a book by Mickey Kaus. The title is ambiguous. It turns out that Kaus wants to bring the pursuit of money equality to an end and to make social equality the new goal. "Money equality isn't what America is about. Social equality is." The central purpose of neoliberalism is to bring about the change. "We need to rip the house [of liberalism] down and build it anew on a more secure foundation." We need to abandon Money Liberalism for Civic Liberalism.

Money Liberalism, according to Kaus, focuses on income differences and seeks to reduce, even suppress, them. It dwells on the disparity between rich and poor, aiming at "fairness" through redistribution. But pursuit of this goal is misguided and gets us into difficulties, the most prominent of which relate to the give-them-cash approach to the problem of welfare. In taking this approach, liberals perhaps did not create the underclass with its single-parent family and its culture of dependency, but they were enablers; and they undermined the work ethic. The message of AFDC, according to Kaus, is: "Leave your man, or have an illegitimate baby, and the government will take care of you." And other aspects of welfare are not much better. Public housing projects are "among the most hellish places on earth." Further, Kaus accuses liberals of telling us that social justice means material equality, and so in effect telling us that we are doomed to live in an unjust society. Money equality is an impossible and destructive goal.

Instead of seeking money equality, we should seek social equality, which implies dignity and respect for everyone, regardless of income differences. The waiter and the diner should look each other in the eye with mutual respect. We can obtain social equality by restricting the sphere of life in which money matters and enlarging the sphere in which it does not matter. We should "focus on changing the attitudes and institutions that translate money differences, however large or small, into invidious social differences." We should emphasize the "non-economic sphere of life—a public, community sphere—where money doesn't 'talk,' where the principles of the marketplace (i.e., rich beats poor) are replaced by the principle of equality of citizenship." Civic Liberalism should prevail. "Civic Liberals would carve out a space free of capitalist domination, of domination by wealth." And we should identify "a value shared, by rich and poor alike, on which to build an egalitarian life. It seems to me there is only one real candidate: work."

According to Kaus, the "non-economic sphere of life," the community sphere, includes the public schools, attended by students of every income level and culture; publicly provided day-care centers; the streets, highways, transportation system, public buildings, and parks where people mingle in security; political campaigns and elections, conducted in such a way as to promote a sense of equal participation; a health-care system that treats rich and poor alike; the armed services, into which selected recruits are drafted without economic, cultural, or racial bias; or, if not the armed services, then a national service corps that mixes the classes in a common endeavor, with social equality as the main goal.

Social equality is to be nurtured in all the above spheres, but the main method of promoting it is to stress the work ethic. Every able-bodied adult should work. As noted in chapter 6, Kaus would have the government offer employment to every citizen over eighteen who wants it; no more handouts to the able-bodied. He would replace the welfare state with a "Work Ethic State," in which status, dignity, and benefits flow only to those who work but in which work is available for all. Further, Kaus would have the government supplement wages as necessary "to ensure that every American who works full-time has enough money to raise a normal-sized family with dignity, out of poverty." He grants that what he proposes would not be cheap, estimating that the extra cost would come to $43 to $59 billion a year. The proposal makes welfare seem more attractive because it is so cheap.

One basic question, perhaps *the* basic question, is whether Kaus is right in saying that liberals have in fact championed money equality in the sense of material equality and whether social equality should really be the paramount goal. Kaus does not deal carefully with either of these questions. In answering the first, he is careless with the facts and in answering the second he simply makes unsupported assertions.

With respect to money equality, Kaus says that its "most respected defenders ... deny they desire to go all the way, to pursue their goal until everybody makes the same amount or owns the same amount ... ," but at other points he refers to material equality as the liberal goal and speaks of liberal efforts to "suppress inequality of money." Actually all liberals who consider the question, and not only the most respected ones, deny any desire to go all the way toward economic leveling, else they would not be liberal. After all, liberalism concerns itself with liberty as well as with equality, and no one upholding liberty could think it compatible with even-Steven leveling. What liberals do, and all they can do compatibly with liberalism, is to concern themselves with the extent of the disparities. Kaus himself should be concerned with the disparities more than he is because the more extreme they are, the more they reduce or even preclude social equality. And the disparities pose a problem not only because of their implications for social equality but even more for their implications for the worth of liberty.

Liberty has worth for people in proportion to their ability to take advantage of it. For the poor, the uneducated, the unskilled, the sick, and those disadvantaged in other ways, its worth is limited or nonexistent. The ideal of the progressive liberal, as I see it, is not so much to achieve money equality or even social equality as to make it possible for all to take full advantage of their liberty, giving all effective equality of opportunity. People should not be prevented by circumstances beyond their control from achieving their potential. Within the limits of reason, the policy should be to help everyone be the best he or she can be.

I am influenced in this connection by Robert E. Lane, who writes of *The Market Experience* (1991) and concludes that we give evidence of not knowing our own minds: we grossly overemphasize money in explaining what motivates us. Money counts, of course, and counts heavily up to the point where a decent living is assured. But beyond that, what we are really after is not money, let alone money equality. What we are really after is the development and use of our talents and capacities as a basis for well-being and happiness. Making money does not correlate at all well with the achievement of these goals. Happiness is not a bank account.

Lane does not even mention social equality as a motivating value, and this is not surprising. Theoretically, social equality could be achieved in circumstances in which everyone is equally miserable. The waiter who looks the diner in the eye may nevertheless be unhappy, feeling that he has talents and potentialities that circumstances prevent him from developing and using. It is important, of course, that people use their talents in ways that do not subvert the common good and that preferably contribute constructively to it; and some kinds of attitudes on the part of others (contempt, for example) make it difficult to enjoy a sense of well-being and happiness. Thus the motivations that liberalism supports have a social aspect. But the promotion of social equality (or of any kind of equality other than equality of moral worth and equality before the law) is not plausible as a top-priority liberal or neoliberal goal.

Further, Kaus's assumption that any or all of the programs of the welfare state are manifestations of a pursuit of money equality is grotesque. The pitifully small sums of money given out to AFDC mothers, for example, cannot by any stretch of the imagination be explained by an alleged devotion to money equality. Various considerations operate, as indicated in chapter 6, but concerns relating to equality play a minor role if they play any role at all. The appropriate generalization is that people do not want money equality and do not expect social equality; and liberalism goes along with the people in these respects.

Kaus could shift his emphasis from social equality to the worth of liberty and still make the same policy proposals, especially concerning work. The sense of well-being and happiness is associated mainly with work, not with social equality. People develop their talents in order to qualify for work and then develop them more through work. Given a choice between different lines of work, people are at least as likely to base the choice on a concern for their happiness as on a concern for money. Those who work presumably benefit their employers, clients, or customers, but ideally they benefit themselves too, gaining pride and satisfaction from what they do. The liberal or neoliberal can thus join Kaus in promoting the idea of a work ethic state for reasons having more to do with the development and use of talents than with a desire for social equality. The problem is that many of those who get work through the operation of the free market resist the thought of paying taxes to help out those who do not.

## Community

I noted that the neoliberal manifesto calls for more emphasis on *community*. Both friends and critics of liberalism join in this call, which suggests that something is in fact lacking either in liberalism or in our understanding of it.

Discussion of the subject goes on at various levels from the academic-philosophic to the journalistic. The landmark philosophic contributions are those of John Rawls, Alasdair MacIntyre, and Michael Sandel. I have referred at several points to Rawls's *A Theory of Justice* (1971). The other book on which I comment is Sandel's *Liberalism and the Limits of Justice* (1982).

Rawls's theory of justice is individualistic. In his imagination, he assigns the job of working out the principles of justice to a number of individuals who are behind a veil of ignorance about the consequences of their decisions for themselves personally. Their choice is to focus on individuals and their rights, not on the family, the community, or the public good. They adopt the general principle that the rights of individuals take priority over practically all competing claims.

Sandel attacks this principle, wanting more emphasis on the community. Along with the rights of individuals, he wants to stress the good of the community, the public good. He does not offer a detailed prescription telling us exactly how to determine what the public good is, or what kind of an adjustment should be made between the rights of the individual and the good of the community, but he accepts the possibility that the public good should sometimes take priority over individual rights. His position is described as *communitarian*.

The first problem with Sandel's position is a minor one but should be mentioned. He takes his criticism of Rawls to be a criticism of liberalism, as if liberalism gets its complete and correct expression in Rawls. I do not quarrel with this in a major way, but I mention a qualification shortly.

The second problem with Sandel's position is that it fails to distinguish between kinds or degrees of individualism. Rawls's individualism is not of the rugged sort. His is not a devil-take-the-hindmost philosophy. On the contrary, he is concerned with the general well-being. Recall that, according to Rawls, inequalities are to be to the advantage of the least advantaged, and equality of opportunity is to be fair. In other words, Rawls wants liberty to have worth and wants equality of opportunity to be effective for everyone. His ideal, remember, is that "those who are at the same level of talent and ability, and have the same willingness to use them, should have the same prospects of success ... irrespective of the income class into which they are born." In other words, his is a caring kind of individualism that surely comes close to, if it is not the same as, what communitarians would prescribe.

This caring kind of individualism inspired the New Deal and the Great Society. Both mobilized resources of the community to help provide for those in some kind of need. And the measures against discrimination included in the Great Society program gave people who had been excluded from the community their rightful place in it.

The third problem with Sandel's position is that it ignores, just as Rawls himself ignores, generally accepted qualifications on individualism and individual rights. One kind of qualification is illustrated by the fact that, although everyone has a right to life, government has a right to conscript people and send them into battle where they may lose their lives. In other words, individual rights give way before compelling public interests. The principle applies not only in connection with national defense but in many other connections as well. You have a right to free speech, but you are not to shout "fire" in a crowded theater or harangue a crowd in circumstances that make your speech an incitement to immediate violence. The principle is that rights are conditional and not absolute; they are not to be exercised in such a way as to undermine a compelling public interest. People differ on the question how compelling a public interest has to be before it can be said to override an individual right, but the principle is firmly established in American judicial practice and is widely accepted elsewhere.

Another kind of qualification grows out of the fact that rights frequently conflict with each other. My right to swing my fist is limited by your right to keep your nose intact. My right to burn leaves in my yard is limited by your right to clean air. In other words, externalities associated with the exercise of a right may make limitations necessary. The adjustment between conflicting rights may of course be based only on a concern for the interests of the individuals involved, but in many cases it is based on concern for a public, community interest.

It would not be surprising if communitarians directed criticisms at ideologies other than progressive liberalism. Classical liberalism with its emphasis on *laissez faire* is a more likely target, and Spencerian social Darwinism and modern libertarianism are even more likely. Further, economic conservatism, with its emphasis on property rights, is as likely to lead to the neglect of community as the emphasis on other kinds of rights. But communitarians do not distinguish between the various kinds of liberalism and pay no attention to conservatism.

Not that progressive liberalism or any other ideology goes as far as it might in stressing community. This is the point that Amitai Etzioni makes in *The Spirit of Community* (1993). He wants us to turn away from the language of rights "to a language of social virtues, interests, and, above all, social responsibilities." He appeals to a moral sense more than to government and law. He wants to rely as much as possible on the family as an institution for instilling desirable rules of behavior and on gentle community pressures. Everyone should be more responsive to the values that make for a desirable social life. But Etzioni gives government a role in urging that the schools be used as instruments for the inculcation of the proper social and moral values; and unlike members of the American Civil Liberties Union, he would not be troubled if airline pilots were required to take routine drug tests and if motorists were stopped at sobriety checkpoints. In other words, he would put less emphasis on individual rights and more on the needs of the community.

## A New Democrat?

If you start with the assumption that Clinton and his administration are liberal, you quickly run into problems. In the first place, Clinton himself rejects the liberal label. Campaigning for the presidency and facing a statement characterizing the Democratic ticket as liberal, he said that this was a "load of bull we've been paralyzed with for too long." Later in the campaign he is described as seeking to counter a "Republican offensive portraying him as a leftist, tax-mad, big-government liberal." He sought to position himself instead as "a new kind of Democrat," "a 'third way' Democrat, neither of the left nor the right." The election should not, he said, be "about the stale, failed political rhetoric of the past." He sought to position himself as a "centrist."

In the second place, some of Clinton's policy positions do not fit well with progressive liberalism. Most prominently, he joins economic conservatives and others in criticizing welfare. He even goes them one better, promising to "end welfare as we know it." In contrast to conservatives who suggest a maximum of three or four years on welfare, Clinton commits himself to no more than two. Like Jack Kemp, he says he aims "to empower people, not entitle them." And he endorses the principle that if you don't work, you don't eat. Moreover, as if to distance himself from the traditional concern of progressive liberals for blacks and the poor, Clinton puts the stress on the middle class, and during the campaign of 1992 he conspicuously failed to cultivate the support of Jesse Jackson, the black leader. In fact, Clinton said little about race. An editorial in the *Nation* asserts that "Clinton has occupied Republican positions on almost every issue—crime, trade, the deficit, defense, welfare—so the G.O.P. has nothing substantive with which they can disagree." Another observation is that Clinton is "a political phagocyte—he swallows the germ of any competing idea, hoping he can neutralize the threat."

A rejection of progressive liberalism is also intimated in the report of a task force headed by Vice-President Al Gore. As president, Clinton asked Gore to make a "performance review" of the federal government and to recommend reforms. The report begins with the following statement:

> The federal government is not simply broke; it is broken. Ineffective regulation of the financial industry brought us the savings and loan debacle. Ineffective education and training programs jeopardize our competitive edge. Ineffective welfare and housing programs undermine our families and cities.
>
> We spend $25 billion a year on welfare, $27 billion on food stamps, and $13 billion on public housing—yet more Americans fall into poverty every year. We spend $12 billion a year waging war on drugs—yet see few signs of victory. We fund 150 different employment and training programs—yet the average American has no idea where to get job training, and the skills of our workforce fall further behind those of our competitors. It is almost as if federal programs were *designed* not to work ... We have spent too much money for programs that don't work....

The same highly critical attitude pervades the whole report. Focusing on the federal civil service, the report speaks of the involvement of forty-three persons in changing a light bulb, of six caseworkers from different agencies attempting to serve the same pregnant, teenage girl, of managers "hamstrung by rules and regulations" that go against

common sense, and so on. The report calls for greater decentralization, with the empowerment of state and local governments. It extols
the idea of "entrepreneurial government" emphasizing results and
customer satisfaction. It implicitly concedes that the federal civil service is bloated, calling for the elimination of 252,000 civil service posts.
No wonder that an official of the libertarian Cato Institute says that
"most of the text and proposals could have been written by the Reagan administration." The document does not suggest progressive liberalism.

For a time prior to his running for the presidency, Clinton was
chairman of the Democratic Leadership Council (DLC), which spon-
sors the Public Policy Institute (PPI). Presumably his political inclina-
tions are similar to theirs, although the precise extent of the agreement is uncertain. In any event, these Democratic agencies do not go
down the line for progressive liberalism. The DLC says that it is neither liberal nor conservative, but that it is both; and the PPI, in the
New Democrat which it publishes, sometimes uses language more
suggestive of the right than of the left. It emphasizes "robust economic growth" and deplores any emphasis on "old-style redistribution." It rejects "the tax-and-spend policies of the old Democrats." It
wants to reduce the role of the federal government, saying that "we
need to eliminate unneeded layers of bureaucracy, decentralize decision making, empower people not bureaucrats, increase accountability, and give citizens more choices in public services.... "

In one issue of the New Democrat, Will Marshall identifies
"America's basic political creed" with classical liberalism rather than
with progressive liberalism, and he speaks of the discomfort Americans feel with transfer payments and preferential treatment. He says
that the dominant ideas of both major parties have outlived their time
and that Americans are loath to choose "between Democrats' special
interest liberalism and Republicans' neocapitalism." He calls for a
"third way ... that rejects the old choice between big government and
weak government in favor of non-bureaucratic public activism that
empowers people and communities to solve their own problems." The
third way also "rejects the old choice between conservative neglect
and liberal entitlements, in favor of a new politics of reciprocity which
stresses the obligations that citizens owe each other and their country." He sees intimations of the new politics of reciprocity in "the conservative empowerment movement led by Jack Kemp and the Heritage
Foundation's Stuart Butler" (Marshall 1992, 5–6).

The comment of Jeff Faux in the liberal American Prospect is
that "those who carry the intellectual baggage for the DLC do not

curse the House of Liberalism and the House of Conservatism with equal fervor. For them, liberals are clearly the enemy." They are the enemy because of their alleged record of catering to "minority groups and white elites—a coalition viewed by the middle class as unsympathetic to its interests and its values" (Faux 1993, 21).

If the above were the whole story, one could scarcely conclude that progressive liberalism is alive and well in the Clinton administration. But the story has another side. Clinton and Gore both speak of "reinventing government," a term identified with the work of David Osborne, who focuses on the question of the role of government in promoting economic growth. Since Clinton and Gore use Osborne's language and have given him a post in their administration, the reasonable presumption is that they look favorably on his analysis and outlook.

In *Laboratories of Democracy,* as I indicated in chapter 6, Osborne inquires into the policies of state governments relating to economic growth. It turns out that these governments, whether controlled by Republicans or Democrats, rarely follow *laissez-faire,* hands-off policies. "While the Reagan administration was denouncing government intervention in the marketplace, governors of both parties were embracing an unprecedented role as economic activists." They set up funds to permit the investment of public money in entrepreneurial ventures. They sought to stimulate technological innovation. They invested in human capital by overhauling educational systems. They established boards on which business, labor, and government were represented to restructure labor-management relations. They helped existing enterprises to expand and helped new enterprises to start up. They helped look for markets abroad. They made a variety of tax concessions. Not that every single state engaged in every one of these activities, but most of them engaged in more than one.

Peter Eisinger has done research similar to Osborne's. His statement is that every single state has a Department of Economic Development or the equivalent, and he reports an estimate that 15,000 state and local officials are engaged in economic development activities as their primary responsibility (Eisinger 1988, 16).

The practices of the states lead both Osborne and Eisinger to speak of a partnership between government and business, not as a blue-sky proposal but as a description of what is going on. Whether what goes on reflects liberalism is a question. Osborne speaks of the need for a new "paradigm" to guide relationships between government and business. But the assumption of governmental activism in economic matters fits with progressive liberalism better than with any of the other ideologies described in this book.

A similar intimation comes from the writings of Robert Reich, who serves in Clinton's cabinet and whose friendship with Clinton dates back to the time when both were Rhodes scholars. Reich is a progressive liberal. He speaks of the "myth of the unmanaged market" and says that "every major industry in America is deeply involved with and dependent on government.... No sharp distinction can validly be drawn between private and public sectors within this or any other advanced industrialized country; the economic effects of public policies and corporate decisions are completely intertwined" (Reich 1983, 232–33).

Reich might stress the fact that government provides the stable legal order and regulates the monetary and financial system in which the economy functions. One need only look at the fate of Somalia, for example, to see what happens when government breaks down. What Reich in fact stresses is the role of government in developing human capital and providing the legal and physical infrastructure for the economy.

Reich's position is that human capital is the most important kind of capital. It resides in people—in their education, skill, experience, imagination, health, socialization to civic values, and devotion to a work ethic. The market alone, Reich points out, does not generate human capital; at least, it does not do it adequately. Ideally the family plays a crucial role in instilling most of the desired qualities, but especially with respect to education and training, government has come to the fore. Moreover, education begins (or should begin) earlier and lasts longer than was once the case. And it should include all the various branches of knowledge, those relevant not only to scientific and technological progress but also to the organization of people for productive effort.

Private firms can and do provide some of the education and training that is necessary, but what they have an interest in doing is limited. They provide only for their own employees, which means that separate arrangements are necessary for all others, including those too young to be employed. Further, what private firms do even for their own employees is likely to be limited by the fear that an employee, once trained, will transfer to a different firm. Theoretically, education might be left to the market and provided on a commercial basis, but this would so clearly be to the disadvantage of the poor, and would leave so much human talent undeveloped, that it gets few endorsements outside the ranks of the libertarians and the social conservatives. By almost universal consent, the responsibility belongs to government. And the responsibility takes on new urgency given the globalization of the economy, the increasing reliance on advances in knowledge, and the rapidity of change.

In addition to calling for greater governmental investment in education, Reich calls for greater investment in health and in the infrastructure. The thrust of his work, like the thrust of Osborne's work, is in the direction of an activist federal government, seeking partnership with business in the effort to promote economic growth. And activism on the part of government fits with progressive liberalism better than with any kind of conservatism.

I mentioned the Public Policy Institute, calling attention to attitudes that do not fit well with progressive liberalism. To balance the picture, I should also mention other attitudes. For example, an article in the *New Democrat* takes the stand that all firms over a certain size should be required to invest the equivalent of 1.5 percent of their payroll in training, with every employee entitled to a share of that training; and it says that "the government should limit benefits provided to wealthy Americans and paid for by taxes from moderate- and average-income families." Further, it calls for a sharp increase in governmental support for research and development. Another article describes voluntary national service as "the cornerstone of the DLC's New Democrat agenda." Such service "is a society-transforming idea. It replaces the two dominant, competing ethics of the 1980s—'every man for himself' on the one hand, and 'something for nothing' on the other—with a new ethic of reciprocal responsibility."

I cited Jeff Faux, who charges that those carrying the intellectual baggage for the DLC regard liberals as the enemy. Will Marshall's rejoinder is that New Democrats seek to adapt liberalism to "new realities" and to reconstruct it as a "progressive force." They "look beyond the left-right debate to a new synthesis that combines the valid insights from both sides in a new agenda for progressive reform." Instead of tax and spend, they would "cut and invest"—cut "unproductive federal spending" and invest in "education and job training, research and development, transportation, communications, and other public infrastructure systems."

Changes in the climate of opinion need also be noted in connection with the effort to determine in which ideological category, if in any existing one, Clinton should be placed. Reagan gave great popularity to economic conservatism, but he also stimulated a reaction, and the reaction was supportive of governmental activism. Although economists differ among themselves, a substantial number of them call for liberal policies. Thus James Tobin: "There is no more important cause for liberals, in my opinion, than to educate the nation to the importance of public investments and of the taxes to pay for them.... The cost of undiscriminating denigration of governments, politicians, and public servants and the need to restore government as an essential and effective instrument of progress are becoming more and more apparent" (Sears 1991, 62). Tobin goes on to speak of the need for greater governmental investment in education and health, in the infrastructure, and in the protection of the environment.

Alan Brinkley strikes a similar note:

> It is clear today that free-market capitalism does not, and perhaps cannot, alone create the preconditions of economic growth. The private sector is not equipped to sustain and improve the nation's most basic infrastructure. It has not been effective in creating a trained and educated work force. It has not reliably generated the new technologies upon which advanced economies have come to depend. These are, in other words, critical tasks in which the state must play a significant role (as it has in the past), or they will remain undone. (Brinkley 1993, 86)

Clinton himself, although taking some stands that put him to the right of center, takes others that are centrist and to the left of center. "I believe," he says, "that free enterprise is the engine of growth in America. We are fundamentally a conservative, private, capitalist free enterprise country." But far from treating government as part of the problem and far from wanting to reduce its role, he speaks of it as a partner with the private sector. He asks that the partnership "think about new approaches based on old values like work and faith and family and opportunity, responsibility, and community." He cites these "old values" again and again. "I am doing my best," he says, "to restore a sense of real community in this country." In his eyes *community* implies that "we have responsibilities to one another and ... we go up or down together" (*Weekly Compilation* 29:247, 678, 1659, 2503).

Along with repeated references to these values go repeated statements to the effect that "our goal should be to enable every person who lives in this country to live up to his or her God-given potential." Clinton makes this a prominent theme in his speeches, coming back to it again and again. Jack Kemp claims the same goal for progressive conservatism (as noted in chapter 12), but it is not a goal that fits well with any of the other ideologies described in this book.

Numerous policies of the Clinton administration fit with progressive liberalism. Soon after his inauguration, Clinton reversed the ban that the Bush administration had imposed on fetal tissue research. He signed the Family and Medical Leave Act, which Bush had vetoed. He restored American support for international programs aimed at restricting population growth. He appointed a defender of abortion to the Supreme Court. He signed the motor-voter bill, which most conservatives opposed, making it easier for people to register to vote. He sought a reduction in discrimination against homosexual persons in the military. He signed the Brady bill, a modest step toward gun control. He secured the establishment of a National Service Corps to provide greater opportunity for young people. He secured legislation relating to the college student loan program, lowering interest rates and changing the arrangements for repayment. In making appointments to federal offices, he conspicuously concerns himself with the representation of women and minorities. He secured an expansion of the earned income tax credit, contributing significantly to the reduction of poverty.

Of vastly greater importance, Clinton proposed reform in the national health-care system, asking for universal coverage and assigning a significant role to government. Public support for some kind of reform in the health-care system is so general that almost all those who face election or reelection, regardless of their ideology, give the idea some kind or degree of support, but still it is reasonable to classify the Clinton proposal as a manifestation of progressive liberalism. William Kristol takes this view, describing the health-care plan as "the centerpiece of contemporary liberalism's domestic agenda." According to Kristol, the plan "embodies many of the characteristics of contemporary liberalism—the amazing faith in government, the distrust not just of market forces but of normal people making decisions about their lives, the arrogance of taking over 14 percent of the economy and trying to shape it from Washington." Given this view, Kristol wanted the plan defeated as a means of "unraveling Clintonism and ... laying the groundwork of a counter-offensive on behalf of the conservative reform agenda" (W. Kristol 1994, 15).

One wonders whether Kristol would go along with David Frum's attack on Big Government in an article in the neoconservative journal, *Commentary*. In addition to denouncing the federal government for handling "the welfare function" in such a way as to increase the likelihood of personal misbehavior and destructive conduct, Frum bewails the fact that state governments ever began extending aid to higher education. He thinks that "the universities would be more wholesome places from the conservative point of view" if aid was denied. He acknowledges that in the absence of aid the proportion of Americans going to college would shrink, but that is quite acceptable to him. Nothing in what he says suggests any concern for the worth of liberty or the effectiveness of opportunity. He does not join Clinton in favoring policies designed to help people live up to their God-given potential (Frum 1994).

Clinton's approach to the welfare problem takes different forms. As noted earlier, he has secured an expansion of the earned income tax credit for those who have jobs, children in the home, and incomes below the poverty level. The credit is calculated as a percentage of the income earned, and those whose credit exceeds their tax bill get the balance in cash from the IRS. The aim is to lift people out of poverty, rewarding families and work at the same time and making work more attractive than welfare. The expectation is that some 25 million families will benefit. Clinton describes this as the most significant reform in twenty years relating to welfare.

In a sense, every effort to stimulate the economy should be regarded as an attack on the welfare problem. Deserving of special mention is the establishment of "empowerment zones" and "enterprise communities" in distressed areas, the aim being to create jobs and encourage economic development in them. Tax benefits are the principal instrument. The similarity with Jack Kemp's proposed enterprise zones is obvious, but Kemp opposed Clinton's plan as inadequate.

Other measures relating to welfare are yet to come. Reform of the health care system would presumably reduce or terminate the need to be on welfare as a means of qualifying for Medicaid. Clinton speaks of "empowering" people on welfare with the education, training, and child care they need for up to two years, so they can break the cycle of dependency. Moreover, Clinton speaks of creating community-service jobs for those not absorbed by the free market; and his advisers speak of shifting from "workfare," with work done in return for welfare, to work for wages. Such measures would cost more than welfare does now, and may or may not be practical in a political sense, but they fit with progressive liberalism. A White House aide is quoted as rejecting the thought that the proposed changes go against the interests of the poor. "If we can get day care, health care, and a jobs program for poor people by calling it 'welfare reform,' so be it."

The struggle over the North American Free Trade Agreement (NAFTA) raises a question that is resolved by considering the fact that both economic and ideological issues were involved. The economic issue was whether to put the emphasis on growth, accepting certain risks, or on the protection of existing jobs. The ideological issue was whether to reduce or maintain governmental intervention in the market. (Tariffs and other trade barriers are forms of intervention.)

In the upshot, those choosing growth, including Clinton, found themselves aligned with economic conservatives whose main motivation was to reduce the role of government. And Clinton found himself opposed by his usual allies, the trade unions, who opted for the protection of existing jobs. Although the bedfellows were strange, the choices do not indicate that Clinton should count as an economic conservative.

Conservatives themselves take this view. They regard Clinton as unmistakably a liberal. His program is said to be "simply tax-and-spend liberalism masquerading as an intellectually coherent economic policy. It is a program rooted not in scholarship, empiricism, or theory, but only in blind ideology—a belief in the absolute efficacy of government" (Moore 1993, 39). Another judgment is that Clinton "is an ideologue who denied his true intentions in order to win office." The core of his philosophy is said to be "a collectivist faith in the state as the source and fount of economic vitality and social health" (Stelzer 1993, 22). Edward H. Crane, more libertarian than conservative, says that "Clinton cloaks a leftist, egalitarian, redistributionist philosophy in the rhetoric of 'competitiveness' and 'reinventing government.' ... The Clinton administration may well be the first truly leftist administration in American history" (1993, 2).

Avowed liberals join conservatives in treating Clinton as a liberal, even if his liberalism is somehow different. Paul Starr speaks regretfully of the path that liberals took in the late 1960s leading them into the electoral wilderness. They had become identified with "an ethic of expensive entitlements [that] seemed to deny limits." It is time to shift to "an ethic that emphasizes prudence and responsibility as much as rights," and the intimation is that Clinton is doing precisely this (1991, 10). Robert Kuttner says that Clinton "has pretty much lived up to our suspicion ... that despite the down-home accents, the DLC baggage, and the anti-Washington rhetoric, he was a progressive fellow all along; and that in talented, self-confident hands liberal themes remain viable politics" (1993, 6).

Mickey Kaus's conclusion is different: "Clinton's pitch is state-of-the-art neoliberalism" (1992b, 21).

# Chapter 16

# Concluding Observations

T HIS BOOK is about ideologies as conceived by the intellectual elite, revealed by their writing, and not as conceived by the mass public, revealed by public opinion polls. This suggests the first purpose of the chapter: to see how the two conceptions differ. The second purpose of the chapter concerns the sources of disagreement about ideologies. Given reasonableness and intelligence, why do people not agree?

## A Comparison of Conceptualizations

The focus on conceptions advanced by the intellectual elite is dictated by the purpose of the book: to help you choose an ideology for yourself and to appraise the choices that others make. The assumption is that, for this purpose, it is best to focus on those who presumably have given the matter careful study and thought rather than on those who happen to be included in a sample and who respond without any special preparation to the promptings or questions of an interviewer.

Nevertheless, my effort to provide a basis for choice among ideologies includes a description of them. The claim through the book is that I am describing the various ideologies fairly, properly identifying their central features and the considerations that you need to take into account in deciding what to support and what to oppose. Thus it is potentially of some interest to check my descriptions against those that emerge from polling the mass public.

The most obvious difference is that I deal with more ideological positions, and describe them more fully, than the pollsters do. You could not get a clear description of public choice theory or of libertarianism from the results of polls, and I have seen nothing in those results that would enable you to characterize what I call conservative conservatism, progressive conservatism, or neoconservatism. Whether you could characterize economic conservatism or social conservatism is a question. Neither do the polls permit a clear distinction between classical and progressive liberalism. And they do not take up neo-liberalism.

In fact, with respect to political ideologies, the usual procedure in polling is to deal with just two categories, liberal and conservative. Other categories are rarely recognized. And the usual procedure is to lump all liberals and all conservatives together, perhaps with some recognition of degrees of difference within each category but not with any recognition of differences in kind.

Tom W. Smith summarizes the results in an article on "Liberal and Conservative Trends in the United States Since World War II" (Smith 1990). Focusing on questions that have been used year after year, he says that liberalism "has changed its emphasis and even some key tenets over time," and he speaks of the "old problem of the blind men and the elephant," but (with reference to domestic politics) he says that polling reveals "contemporary liberalism" to be:

> (1) reformist, opting for change and generally opposed to the status quo; (2) democratic, favoring a full extension of electoral rights; (3) libertarian [*sic!*], supporting civil liberties such as free speech and the right to protest; (4) regulatory and interventionist, backing the management of business and the economy by the government; (5) centralist, using the federal government to set and enforce national standards and regulate state and local governments; (6) humanitarian, favoring a social welfare system for the care and protection of society in general and the lower class in particular; (7) egalitarian, advocating equal treatment for all and perhaps equal conditions for all; and (8) permissive, tolerating and often approving of nontraditional life styles and practices (e.g., homosexuality, nudity, and the use of drugs).

This characterization of liberalism differs in major ways from mine. Nothing about Smith's summary suggests what seem to me to be central features of progressive liberalism: the desire to give worth to liberty, or to promote liberty defined affirmatively rather than negatively, and the desire to promote effective equality of opportunity for all. Whether the summary gives adequate recognition to issues concerning the capacity of collectivities for rational action and the usefulness of government in this connection is more debatable, but I think it leaves something to be desired.

Why the two descriptions of liberalism differ so much is a question. Perhaps my analysis is wrong. Perhaps my analysis and the results of polls are both correct, the elite view never having been communicated to the mass public. The elite view puts the emphasis on ultimate ends and grand strategy, which is not necessarily the emphasis either of those who formulate polling questions or of those interviewed.

Given this major difference between the two conceptions, they are nevertheless consistent with each other. The various beliefs that Smith mentions all fit within the framework of my characterization—with some qualifications. By my standards, Smith misuses the term *libertarian*. His statement that "perhaps" liberals advocate equal conditions for all is potentially misleading, depending on what the words mean; I know of no evidence that any noteworthy liberal writer seeks equal incomes for all. Although it is all right to say that liberals are inclined to *tolerate* nontraditional lifestyles and practices, no liberal leader whose writing I have seen expresses *approval* of homosexuality, nudity, or the use of drugs. In addition, I would make various relatively minor changes in Smith's wording, but otherwise, as I say, his characterization of liberalism fits within mine.

The more surprising difference relates to conservatism. Smith does not characterize it at all. He presents no list of the features of conservatism analogous to his list of the features of liberalism. Instead, he assumes, as the pollsters themselves apparently assumed, that conservatism is simply the polar opposite of liberalism: if you aren't a liberal, you must be a conservative. This means that the failure to call attention to central features of liberalism has a counterpart with respect to conservatism. More specifically, differences among the ideologies about the meaning of liberty and of equality of opportunity do not show up at all.

Further, like a number of others who write about polling, Smith speaks of "the liberal-conservative continuum" as if all liberals and conservatives can be ranged along the same scale, differing only in the degree to which they support or oppose the same set of propositions.

This contrasts with my findings. As you know, I divide conservatives into five categories (seven if you put the libertarians and the public choice theorists among the conservatives, which would be plausible). I assume that these conservatives are generally predisposed to cooperate with each other in politics against "liberals," but apart from that I cannot think of a single outlook that they all share.

Further, it is questionable whether "liberals" and "conservatives" should always be thought of as opposites. Alternative possibilities exist, among them that "liberals" and "conservatives" may have some of the same concerns but differ in the urgency they assign to them or the strategies to employ in pursuing them; and that they have concerns that are simply different rather than being opposites.

Whether these different conceptions of "conservatism" matter much depends on the purpose pursued. What is done through polling may be satisfactory if the purpose is to guide political candidates and officeholders and to predict the outcome of elections, but I would argue that it is not satisfactory if the purpose is to help those who want to select or develop an intellectually tenable ideological position. For this latter purpose, fuller and more thoughtful inquiry is essential.

## Sources of Agreement/Disagreement

Reasonable and intelligent people disagree in choosing among ideologies, and one of the questions is why. Part of the answer is obvious and banal, even though important, like the disagreement that stems from conflicting interests. Before dealing with this part, I want to mention considerations that are probably influential even if not so obvious.

Through this book I have repeatedly spoken of different conceptions of liberty and opportunity. Some adopt a negative definition of liberty: Liberty is what exists in the absence of governmental restraint. Others regard this negative definition as a mockery and go on to either of two affirmative views. One of these views is that liberty exists to the degree that people can take advantage of it in pursuing their ends. The other accepts the negative definition, but goes on to emphasize various policies, like public support for education, designed to give worth to liberty.

Given the fact that progressive liberals and the various kinds of conservatives all champion the idea of liberty, the difference in the definitions they employ leads them to make different prescriptions. If liberty is what exists in the absence of governmental restraint, the prescription is to cut down on the restraints; that is, reduce the role of government. If liberty is the capacity to pursue ends, the prescription is to expand that capacity by expanding the role of government. Much of the difference between liberals and conservatives can be explained in these simple terms.

Observations like those relating to liberty are also in point about the idea of equality of opportunity. To some, especially to most kinds of conservatives, equality of opportunity exists automatically in the absence of discrimination, so all government needs to do is to bring discrimination to an end. To others, especially to progressive liberals, the absence of discrimination is not enough; government must also take remedial action to make up for disadvantages resulting from earlier discrimination and from other circumstances beyond the individual's control.

Although I am explaining disagreements in part in terms of the definition of words, I hasten to acknowledge a problem: every element of an explanation needs itself to be explained. Why do some find a negative definition of liberty congenial while others insist on a positive definition? Why do some accept a restricted conception of liberty and of equality of opportunity while others insist on a broader conception? We have no evidence on this point. It is plausible to suppose that in some cases it is a matter of intuitive versus thoughtful choice. It is also plausible that people accept the definition that fits best with the values and interests they want to pursue. More on this below.

Ideological disagreements stem not only from different definitions but also from what I will call different conceptions of the factual situation—conceptions that in principle are subject to empirical checking. I have several "factual situations" in mind.

The first concerns the nature and characteristics of the poor. Two general models are widely accepted. One of them assumes the existence of an underclass, living in a culture of poverty, meaning that the people involved are lacking in character as well as in competence and skills. They are long-term dependents, undeserving. Perhaps they are drug abusers. The other model is that the poor are pretty much like everyone else, wanting jobs or better jobs, wanting to get ahead, possessing the characteristics that theoretically make self-reliance possible and perhaps possessing the necessary competence and skills, but somehow in need of special help. Perhaps they need additional training of some kind. Perhaps they are temporarily down on their luck and need to be tided over. Perhaps jobs are simply not available. Perhaps the available jobs pay so little that those who work full-time are still in poverty.

No doubt some of the poor fit each of these models, but the tendency is to choose between them, ideological outlooks and policy prescriptions correlating with the choice. Not that disagreements would disappear if only the true characteristics of the poor were ascertained, but they would surely be reduced.

The second factual situation relates to taxes. Supply-siders never seem to doubt that a reduction in taxes will make the tide rise, lifting all boats. Both the poor and the rich will gain. Whether the government will gain or lose in terms of revenue is a question on which supply-siders themselves disagree, some promising that revenue will go up and others gloating at the prospect that the government will be starved of funds and therefore forced to reduce its activities. Whatever the specifics of the supply-side theory, demand-siders (Keynesians) take a different view, and ideological disagreement is born.

A third factual situation relates to teenage pregnancy and unwed motherhood, the question being the extent to which they are properly blamed on the availability of AFDC payments. Some empirical evidence has been collected on the question, but not enough to make the answer a matter of fact rather than a matter of guess and argument; and policy disagreements ensue.

I speak above of "factual situations," but obviously the facts involved are not the kind that you can look up in an almanac. Research is called for, and the element of guess or judgment may never be entirely eliminated. This is all the more true of appraisals of government. Government is such a huge enterprise, engaging in so many activities and coordinating the behavior of so many people, that sweeping generalizations cannot be proved true or false, but this does not prevent people from making them. And, acting on the basis of impressions and guesses, they disagree. It is uncertain to what extent disagreements would be reduced if standards could be developed for judging public and private enterprises and then making studies of the extent to which the different kinds of enterprises meet the standards, but ideally this should happen.

The argument that disagreements stem from different conceptions of the factual situation can be made in broader terms: that disagreements stem in part from inadequacies in our knowledge. We do not know, at least not for sure, what proportion of the poor should be treated as moral delinquents living in a culture of poverty. Neither do we know just how the level of taxes relates to economic growth or what the relationship is between unwed teenage motherhood and the availability of AFDC. Nor do we know how private enterprises and government compare in getting things done right.

Lack of reliable knowledge leads to disagreement in other fields too. What is the relative prospective gain (or loss) from additional investment in education at the different levels? What is the relative gain (or loss) from investment in the infrastructure, including the information superhighway? If you want to reduce crime, what should be the relative emphasis be on changing the conditions that produce crime and punishing the criminal? If the emphasis is to be on changing the conditions, what are they, and what relative importance do they have? And so on. In handling virtually every problem of public policy, it is necessary to make decisions on the basis of inadequate knowledge about cause and effect, condition and consequence. And the more we have to depend on guesswork (judgment?), the more room there is for disagreement.

At the outset I spoke of banal points, and I now come to them. Given room for choice, people tend to believe whatever is most advantageous to them; and since what is advantageous to one person or group or class may be disadvantageous to another, disagreement follows.

The broader way to put this point is to say that people tend to adopt the ideology that best reflects and promotes their values and interests. The statement comes close to being a tautology because concern for certain values and interests is itself a central feature of ideologies. Values are conceptions of the desirable, and all ideologies include them. The achievement of the desirable is an interest, and all ideologies go in the direction of promoting interests. Once you have decided what values and interests you want to promote, you have gone a long way toward adopting an ideology.

Values and interests include the selfish and the self-regarding but go beyond it. As I noted especially at the close of chapter 8, people take political stands not only on matters in which they have a personal stake but also on matters in which their personal stake is remote if not nonexistent. The point is that political disagreements stem in part from the endorsement of clashing sets of values and interests of both a selfish and an unselfish sort. People are generally concerned about the public good, but they do not agree in defining it.

Differing sensitivities are closely associated with different values and interests. For example, those who put great stress on the creation of wealth are likely to be especially sensitive to the interests of the entrepreneur, and those who put great stress on enabling people to develop their talents to the fullest are likely to be especially sensitive to everything connected with education, including the problem of assuring everyone access to it.

Numerous influences are at work when people select the values and interests to endorse. As noted, their own personal advantage is one consideration but by no means always the decisive consideration. Social background plays a role—the influence of family, community, and social class. Special experience plays a role—the special experience of growing up in a particular decade, or the special experience that comes with identification with a particular enterprise. In some connections, religious conviction plays a role, perhaps a decisive role. And in other connections, ethnic or national identity and commitment play a role. In truth, the greater the role of faith or emotion in ideological choices, and thus the more limited the role of reason, the more likely it is that disagreements will be intense and difficult to bridge.

The only formula that I have to offer concerning ideological differences is that we ought to seek greater knowledge of several kinds: knowledge that makes us fully aware of the various ideological outlooks, including our own; knowledge that facilitates rational choice; and knowledge that tends to reduce disagreements and make differences less disagreeable.

At the same time, I would urge a hard look at the tendency to stress rugged individualism and to assume that greater income and wealth should be the paramount goals. I see no need to reinforce natural tendencies toward selfishness and greed. To be sure, a certain level of physical comfort and well-being is important, but the question is whether we know our own minds when we assume that satisfaction and happiness will increase proportionately with material success. It seems more likely to me that satisfaction and happiness will come more fully with efforts to develop and use our talents to the fullest and to help others do the same.

# References

Ahlseen, Mark. 1992. "The Economics of Affirmative Action," *Conservative Review* 3 (August): 18–22.

Armey, Dick. 1990. "Moscow on the Mississippi. America's Soviet-Style Farm Policy," *Policy Review*, no. 52 (Winter), 24–29.

Atwood, Thomas C. 1990. "Through a Glass Darkly. Is the Christian Right Overconfident It Knows God's Will?" *Policy Review*, no. 54 (Fall): 44–52.

Bandow, Doug, and Ted Galen Carpenter. 1990. "Preserving an Obsolete NATO," *Cato Policy Report* 12 (September/October): 1.

Barash, David P. 1992. *The L Word. An Unapologetic, Thoroughly Biased, Long-Overdue Explication and Celebration of Liberalism.* New York: Morrow.

Barfield, Claude E., and William A. Schambra, eds. 1986. *The Politics of Industrial Policy.* Washington, D.C.: American Enterprise Institute.

Barnes, Fred, and Grover Norquist. 1991. "The Politics of Less. A Debate on Big-Government Conservatism," *Policy Review*, no. 55 (Winter): 66–71.

Barry, Norman P. 1979. *Hayek's Social and Economic Philosophy.* London: Macmillan.

———. 1987. *The New Right.* New York: Croom Helm.

Bartley, Robert L. 1992. *The Seven Fat Years and How to Do It Again.* New York: Free Press.

Beiner, Ronald. 1992. *What's the Matter with Liberalism?* Berkeley: University of California Press.

Bennett, Willliam J. 1994a. "America's Cultural Decline Must Be Reversed," *Human Events* 50 (14 January): 12–14.

———. 1994b. "Revolt Against God. America's Spiritual Despair," *Policy Review*, no. 67 (Winter): 19–24.

Bergland, David. 1990. *Libertarianism in One Lesson.* 5th ed. Costa Mesa, Calif.: Orpheus.

Berlin, Isaiah. 1970. *Four Essays on Liberty.* New York: Oxford University Press.

Blumenthal, Sidney. 1986. *The Rise of the Counter-Establishment. From Conservative Ideology to Political Power.* New York: Times Books.

Boaz, David. 1990. "The Vision Thing," *Policy Review,* no. 52 (Spring): 9.

———. 1991. Editorial, *Cato Policy Report* 13 (January/February): 1.

Boaz, David, and Edward H. Crane, eds. 1993. *Market Liberalism. A Paradigm for the 21st Century.* Washington, D.C.: Cato Institute.

Bork, Robert H. 1989/90. "The Limits of International Law," *National Interest,* no. 18 (Winter): 3–10.

Borrus, Michael. 1992. "Investing on the Frontier. How the U.S. Can Reclaim High–Tech Leadership," *American Prospect,* no. 11 (Fall): 79–87.

Bozell, L. Brent. 1961. "Legal Libertine," *National Review* 11 (18 November): 340–41.

Bradford, M.E. 1986. "On Being Conservative in a Post-Liberal Era," *Intercollegiate Review* 21 (Spring): 15–17.

Brinkley, Alan. 1993. "Liberals and Public Investment: Recovering a Lost Legacy," *American Prospect,* no. 13 (Spring): 81–86.

Brookes, Warren T. 1993. "The National Press and the Statist Quo," *Cato Policy Report* 15 (September/October): 1, 9–16.

Buchanan, James M. 1975. *The Limits of Liberty. Between Anarchy and Leviathan.* Chicago: University of Chicago Press.

———. 1986. *Liberty, Market and State. Political Economy in the 1980s.* Brighton: Wheatsheaf.

———. 1988. *The Political Economy of the Welfare State.* Stockholm: Industrial Institute for Economic and Social Research.

———. 1989. *Reaganomics And After.* London: Institute of Economic Affairs.

Buchanan, James M., and Gordon Tullock. 1962. *The Calculus of Consent. Logical Foundations of Constitutional Democracy.* Ann Arbor: University of Michigan Press.

Buchanan, James M., Robert D. Tollison, and Gordon Tullock, eds. 1980. *Toward a Theory of the Rent-Seeking Society.* College Station: Texas A&M University Press.

Buchanan, Patrick J. 1988. *Right From the Beginning.* Boston: Little, Brown.

———. 1993. "The Coming Resurrection of the Republican Party," *Human Events* 53 (30 January): 86–87.

Burke, Edmund. 1966 (1790). *Reflections on the Revolution in France.* New Rochelle, N.Y.: Arlington House.

Butler, Stuart. 1989. "Razing the Liberal Plantation," *National Review* 41 (10 November): 27–30.

Butler, Stuart, and Anna Kondratas. 1987. *Out of the Poverty Trap. A Conservative Strategy for Welfare Reform.* New York: Free Press.

Carey, George W., ed. 1984. *Freedom and Virtue. The Conservative-Libertarian Debate.* Lanham, Md.: University Press of America.

Catholic Church. 1986. National Conference of Catholic Bishops. *Eco-*

*nomic Justice for All. Pastoral Letter on Catholic Social Teaching and the U.S. Economy.* Washington, D.C.: National Conference of Catholic Bishops.

Codevilla, Angelo M. 1993. "Big Green," *National Review* 45 (12 April): 60–63.

Cohn, Jonathan S. 1993. "Damaged Goods. Before Reinventing Government, Clinton Needs to Repair It," *American Prospect,* no. 13 (Spring): 64–70.

Coughlin, Richard M., ed. 1989. *Reforming Welfare. Lessons, Limits, and Choices.* Albuquerque: University of New Mexico Press.

Crane, Edward H. 1993. "Socialized Medicine vs. Patient Power," *Cato Policy Report* 15 (November/December): 2.

Cribb, T. Kenneth, Jr. 1990. "Conservatism and the Academy: Prospects for the 1990s," *Intercollegiate Review* 25 (Spring): 23–30.

Cross, Colin. 1963. *The Liberals in Power (1905–1914).* London: Pall Mall Press.

DeMuth, Christopher C., interviewed by Adam Meyerson. 1992. "Captain of Enterprise. Christopher C. DeMuth on the Business of Liberty," *Policy Review,* no. 60 (Spring): 10–19.

DeMuth, Christopher C., et al. 1987. *The Reagan Doctrine and Beyond.* Washington, D.C.: American Enterprise Institute.

Dicey, A. V. 1962 (1905). *Law & Public Opinion in England During the Nineteenth Century.* London: Macmillan.

Doyle, Michael W. 1986. "Liberalism and World Politics," *American Political Science Review* 80 (December): 1151–63.

Dunn, John, ed. 1990. *The Economic Limits to Modern Politics.* New York: Cambridge University Press.

Eisinger, Peter K. 1988. *The Rise of the Entrepreneurial State.* Madison: University of Wisconsin Press.

Epstein, Richard A. 1992. *Forbidden Grounds. The Case Against Employment Discrimination Laws.* Cambridge: Harvard University Press.

Falwell, Jerry. 1987. *Strength for the Journey. An Autobiography.* New York: Simon and Schuster.

Faux, Jeff. 1993. "The Myth of the New Democrat," *American Prospect,* no 15 (Fall): 20–29.

Ferejohn, John A. 1974. *Pork Barrel Politics. Rivers and Harbors Legislation, 1947–1968.* Stanford, Calif.: Stanford University Press.

Francis, Samuel T. 1991. "Principalities & Powers," *Chronicles* 15 (December): 9–11.

———. 1992. "The Education of David Duke," *Chronicles* 16 (February): 7–9.

———. 1993a. *Beautiful Losers. Essays on the Failure of American Conservatism.* Columbia: University of Missouri Press.

————. 1993b. "Race and Reality," *RRR Rothbard-Rockwell Report* 4 (March): 19–24.

Freeden, Michael. 1986. *Liberalism Divided. A Study in British Political Thought 1914-1939*. Oxford: Clarendon.

Friedman, Milton. 1962. *Capitalism and Freedom*. Chicago: University of Chicago Press.

————. 1976. "The Line We Dare Not Cross," *Encounter* 47 (November): 8–14.

————. 1991. "Say 'No' to Intolerance," *Liberty* 4 (July): 17–20.

————. 1991a. "The Great American Tax Debate. A Symposium," *Policy Review*, no. 56 (Spring): 53–59.

Friedman, Milton, and Rose Friedman. 1980. *Free to Choose: A Personal Statement*. New York: Harcourt Brace Jovanovich.

Frum, David. 1994. "It's Big Government, Stupid!" *Commentary* 97 (June): 27–31.

Gilder, George. 1993. "Wealth and Poverty Revisited," *American Spectator* 26 (July): 32-37.

Goldwater, Barry M. 1979. *With No Apologies*. New York: Morrow.

Goodin, Robert E. 1988. *Reasons for Welfare. The Political Theory of the Welfare State*. Princeton: Princeton University Press.

Gottfried, Paul. 1986. "A View of Contemporary Conservatism," *Intercollegiate Review* 21 (Spring): 18–21.

————. 1993. *The Conservative Movement*. 2d ed. New York: Twayne.

Gottfried, Paul, and Thomas Fleming. 1988. *The Conservative Movement*. Boston: Twayne.

Graham, Otis L., comp. 1971. *The New Deal. The Critical Issues*. Boston: Little, Brown.

Gray, John. 1992. "The Virtues of Toleration," *National Review* 44 (5 October): 28–36.

Green, Philip. 1992. "A Few Kind Words for Liberalism," *Nation* 255 (28 September): 309, 324–29.

Green, Thomas Hill. 1906 (1887). *Works*. Vol. III. *Miscellanies and Memoir*. Ed. R. L. Nettleship. New York: Longmans, Green.

*Green Book*. 1992. U.S. House. Committee on Ways and Means. *Overview of Entitlement Programs*. 102d Cong., 2d sess.

————. 1993. U.S. House. Committee on Ways and Means. *Overview of Entitlement Programs*. 103d Cong., 1st sess.

Greenleaf, W.H. 1983. *The British Political Tradition*. Vol. 1, *The Rise of Collectivism*. Vol. 2, *The Ideological Heritage*. New York: Methuen.

Greenstein, Robert. 1985. "Losing Faith in *Losing Ground*," *New Republic* 192 (25 March): 12–17.

Harpham, Edward J., and Richard K. Scotch. 1988. "Rethinking the War on Poverty: The Ideology of Welfare Reform," *Western Political Quarterly* 41 (March): 193–207.

———. 1989. "Ideology and Welfare Reform in the 1980s." In *Reforming Welfare. Lessons, Limits, and Choices,* ed. Richard M. Coughlin. Albuquerque: University of New Mexico Press.

Harrell, David Edwin, Jr. 1987. *Pat Robertson. A Personal, Religious, and Political Portrait.* San Francisco: Harper & Row.

Harries, Owen, ed. 1991. *America's Purpose. New Visions of U.S. Foreign Policy.* San Francisco: ICS Press.

Harrison, Bennett, and Barry Bluestone. 1988. *The Great U-Turn. Corporate Restructuring and the Polarizing of America.* New York: Basic Books.

Hayek, Friedrich A. 1944. *The Road to Serfdom.* Chicago: University of Chicago Press.

———. 1960. *The Constitution of Liberty.* Chicago: University of Chicago Press.

———. 1979. *Law, Legislation and Liberty.* Vol. 3, *The Political Order of a Free People.* Chicago: University of Chicago Press.

———. 1984. *The Essence of Hayek.* Edited by Chiaki Nishiyama and Kurt R. Leube. Stanford, Calif.: Hoover Institution Press.

———. 1988. *Collected Works.* Vol. 1, *The Fatal Conceit. The Errors of Socialism.* Edited by W.W. Bartley III. Chicago: University of Chicago Press.

———. 1991. *Economic Freedom.* Cambridge, Mass.: Basil Blackwell.

Helms, Jesse. 1976. *When Free Men Shall Stand.* Grand Rapids, Mich.: Zondervan.

Henderson, Rick. 1992. "Bewarin' o' the Greens," *Reason* 24 (August–September): 5.

Higgins, George C. 1980. "The Prolife Movement and the New Right," *America* 143 (13 September): 107–10.

Himmelfarb, Dan. 1988. "Conservative Splits," *Commentary* 85 (May): 54–58.

Himmelfarb, Gertrude. 1976. "What Is a Liberal—Who Is a Conservative?" *Commentary* 62 (September): 62.

Hoffmann, Stanley. 1987. *Janus and Minerva.* Boulder, Colo.: Westview Press.

Holmes, Kim R., and Jay P. Kosminsky. 1992. "Making the World Safe for America. The Heritage 'Blueprint' and Its Critics," *Policy Review,* no. 61 (Summer): 51–69.

Holmes, Stephen. 1991. "The Liberal Idea," *American Prospect,* no. 7 (Fall): 89–97.

———. 1993. *The Anatomy of Antiliberalism.* Cambridge: Harvard University Press.

Hood, John. 1992. "'96 Peers," *Reason* 24 (November): 42–44.

Hoover, Herbert. 1934. *The Challenge to Liberty.* New York: Charles Scribner's.

————. 1972. *American Ideals versus The New Deal*. Reprint, St. Clair Shores, Mich.: Scholarly Press.

Humphrey, Hubert H. 1970. *The Political Philosophy of the New Deal*. Baton Rouge: Louisiana State University Press.

Huntington, Samuel P. 1957. "Conservatism as an Ideology," *American Political Science Review* 51 (June): 454–73.

Jencks, Christopher. 1992. *Rethinking Social Policy. Race, Poverty, and the Underclass*. Cambridge: Harvard University Press.

Johnson, Paul. 1992. "Wanted: A New Imperialism," *National Review* 44 (14 December): 28–34.

Judis, John B. 1992. *Grand Illusion. Critics and Champions of the American Century*. New York: Farrar, Straus and Giroux.

Kaus, Mickey. 1992a. *The End of Equality*. New York: Basic Books.

————. 1992b. "The End of Equality," *New Republic* 206 (22 June): 21–27.

Kelman, Steven. 1987. *Making Public Policy. A Hopeful View of American Government*. New York: Basic Books.

Kemp, Jack. 1979. *An American Renaissance. A Strategy for the 1980s*. New York: Harper & Row.

————. 1990a. "A Progressive-Conservative Prescription for a New War on Poverty," 17 September. Washington, D.C.: Department of Housing and Urban Development.

————. 1990b. "Tackling Poverty. Market-Based Policies to Empower the Poor," *Policy Review*, no. 51 (Winter): 2–5.

————. 1992a. Address at the John F. Kennedy School of Government. 18 March. Washington, D.C.: Department of Housing and Urban Development.

————. 1992b. Address to U.S. Conference of Mayors. 22 June. Washington, D.C.: Department of Housing and Urban Development.

————. 1993a. "Capitalism Requires a Moral Foundation," *Human Events* 53 (17 July): 578–79.

Kemp, Jack, et al. 1992. "How the President Can Win in 1992," *Human Events* 52 (22 August): 682.

Kinder, Donald R., and D. Roderick Kiewiet. 1979. "Economic Discontent and Political Behavior: The Role of Personal Grievances and Collective Economic Judgments in Congressional Voting," *American Journal of Political Science* 23 (August): 495–527.

Kinsley, Michael. 1992. "Bias and Baloney," *New Republic* 207 (14 December): 6.

Kirk, Russell. 1953. *The Conservative Mind*. Chicago: Regnery.

————. 1974. "Burke and the Philosophy of Prescription," in *Edmund Burke*, ed. Isaac Kramnick. Englewood Cliffs, N.J.: Prentice Hall.

————. 1986. *The Conservative Mind. From Burke to Eliot*. 7th rev. ed. Chicago: Regnery.

———. 1990. "The Vision Thing," *Policy Review,* no. 52 (Spring): 24.

———. 1993. *The Politics of Prudence.* Bryn Mawr, Pa.: Intercollegiate Studies Institute.

Kirkpatrick, Jeane. 1982. *Dictatorships and Double Standards.* New York: Simon and Schuster.

———. 1984. "Law and Reciprocity," *Proceedings,* American Society of International Law, 78: 59–68.

Krauthammer, Charles. 1989. "The Curse of Legalism," *New Republic* 201 (6 November): 44–50.

Kristol, Irving. 1952. "'Civil Liberties' 1952—A Study in Confusion," *Commentary* 13 (March): 228–36.

———. 1978. *Two Cheers for Capitalism.* New York: Basic Books.

———. 1981. "Ideology & Supply-Side Economics," *Commentary* 71 (April): 48–54.

———. 1983. *Reflections of a Neoconservative. Looking Back, Looking Ahead.* New York: Basic Books.

———. 1984. "The Political Dilemma of American Jews," *Commentary* 78 (July): 23–29.

———. 1985. "Skepticism, Meliorism, and the Public Interest," *Public Interest* 81 (Fall): 31–41.

———. 1991. "The Future of American Jewry," *Commentary* 92 (August): 21–26.

———. 1992a. "The Cultural Revolution and the Capitalist Future," *American Enterprise* 3 (March/April): 42–51.

———. 1992b. "America's Mysterious Malaise," *The Times Literary Supplement,* no. 4651 (22 May): 5.

———. 1993a. "The Coming 'Conservative Century,'" *Wall Street Journal,* 1 February, A10.

———. 1993b. "My Cold War," *National Interest,* no. 31 (Spring): 141–44.

Kristol, William. 1993. "A Conservartive Looks at Liberalism," *Commentary* 96 (September): 33–36.

———. 1994. "Kristol Ball. William Kristol Looks at the Future of the GOP. An Interview with Adam Meyerson," *Policy Review,* no. 67 (Winter): 14–18.

Krugman, Paul R. 1992. "The Right, the Rich, and the Facts. Deconstructing the Income Distribution Debate," *American Prospect,* no. 11 (Fall): 19–31.

Kuttner, Robert. 1991. *The End of Laissez-Faire. National Purpose and the Global Economy After the Cold War.* New York: Knopf.

———. 1993. "Deliverance?" *American Prospect,* no. 13 (Spring): 7–8.

Laffer, William. 1993. "Proven Way to Create Jobs: Cut Regulation," *Human Events* 53 (17 April): 319.

LaHaye, Tim. 1980. *The Battle for the Mind.* Old Tappan, N.J.: Fleming H. Revell.

Layne, Christopher. 1985–86. "The Real Conservative Agenda," *Foreign Policy,* no. 61 (Winter): 73–93.

Ledeen, Michael. 1992. "Common Sense 1992," *American Spectator* 25 (June): 23–26.

Libertarian Party. 1993. "1992 National Platform," *Libertarian Party News* 8 (February): insert.

Lienesch, Michael. 1983. "The Paradoxical Politics of the Religious Right," *Soundings* 66 (Spring): 70–99.

Lind, William S., and William H. Marshner, eds. 1991. *Cultural Conservatism. Theory and Practice.* Washington, D.C.: Free Congress Foundation.

Lipkis, Jeff. 1991. "The Brainchild of Earnest Gentlemen: How Liberalism Went Left," *Reason* 22 (April): 36–40.

Lipset, Seymour Martin. 1988. "Neoconservatism: Myth and Reality," *Society* 25 (July-August): 29–37.

Lock, F.P. 1985. *Burke's Reflections on the Revolution in France.* London: Allen and Unwin.

Lockhart, Charles. 1989. *Gaining Ground. Tailoring Social Programs to American Values.* Berkeley: University of California Press.

McGovern, George. 1974. *An American Journey.* New York: Random House.

Marmor, Theodore R., Jerry L. Mashaw, and Philip L. Harvey. 1990. *America's Misunderstood Welfare State: Persistent Myths, Enduring Realities.* New York: Basic Books.

Marshall, Prince J. 1965. *The Impeachment of Warren Hastings.* London: Oxford University Press.

Marshall, Will. 1992. "The Politics of Reciprocity," *The New Democrat* 4 (July): 4–8.

Massey, William A. 1992a. "The New Fanatics: Part One," *Conservative Review* 3 (October): 28–35.

———. 1992b. "The New Fanatics: Part Two," *Conservative Review* 3 (December): 34–41.

Meyer, Charles W., and Nancy Wolff. 1993. *Social Security and Individual Equity. Evolving Standards of Equity and Adequacy.* Westport, Conn.: Greenwood Press.

Meyerson, Adam. 1989. "Adam Smith's Welfare State. Generous Government Is Consistent with a Market Economy," *Policy Review,* no. 50 (Fall): 66–67.

———. 1990. "The Vision Thing," *Policy Review,* no. 53 (Summer): 2–5.

———. 1993. "Bay State Boomer," *Policy Review,* no. 65 (Spring): 12–17.

Mill, John Stuart. 1975 (1859). *On Liberty.* Edited by David Spitz. New York: Norton.

Miller, James C., III, and Phillip Mink. 1992. "The Ink of the Octopus," *Policy Review,* no. 61 (Summer): 4–12.

Moon, J. Donald, ed. 1988. *Responsibility, Rights, and Welfare. The Theory of the Welfare State.* Boulder, Colo.: Westview Press.

Moore, Stephen. 1993. "Clinton's Dismal Scientists," *National Review* 45 (March 15): 32–39.

Moynihan, Daniel Patrick. 1986. *Family and Nation.* New York: Harcourt Brace Jovanovich.

———. 1990. *On the Law of Nations.* Cambridge: Harvard University Press.

Mueller, Dennis C. 1989. *Public Choice II.* New York: Cambridge University Press.

Muravchik, Joshua. 1991. *Exporting Democracy. Fulfilling America's Destiny.* Washington, D.C.: American Enterprise Institute Press.

Murray, Charles A. 1993a. "The Local Angle. Giving Meaning to Freedom," *Reason* 25 (October): 40–44.

———. 1993b. "The Coming White Underclass," *Wall Street Journal,* 29 October, A14.

Myers, William Starr, ed. 1934. *The State Papers and Other Public Writings of Herbert Hoover.* Garden City, N.Y.: Doubleday.

Neuhaus, Richard John, and Michael Cromartie, eds. 1987. *Piety and Politics. Evangelicals and Fundamentalists Confront the World.* Washington, D.C.: Ethics and Public Policy Center.

Newman, Bertram. 1927. *Edmund Burke.* London: Bell.

Nisbet, Robert. 1988. *The Present Age. Progress and Anarchy in Modern America.* New York: Harper & Row.

Niskanen, William A. 1988. *Reaganomics. An Insider's Account of the Policies and the People.* New York: Oxford University Press.

Oakeshott, Michael. 1948. "Contemporary British Politics," *Cambridge Journal* 1 (May): 474–90.

———. 1962. *Rationalism in Politics.* New York: Basic Books.

OECD. 1992. *Revenue Statistics of OECD Member Countries, 1965–91.*

Olson, Mancur. 1982. *The Rise and Decline of Nations. Economic Growth, Stagflation, and Social Rigidities.* New Haven: Yale University Press.

———. 1984. "Ideology and Economic Growth." In *The Legacy of Reaganomics. Prospects for Long-Term Growth,* ed. Charles R. Hulten and Isabel V. Sawhill. Washington, D.C.: Urban Institute.

O'Neill, Tip. 1987. *Man of the House. The Life and Memoirs of Speaker Tip O'Neill.* New York: Random House.

O'Rourke, P.J. 1993. "Brickbats and Broomsticks," *American Spectator* 26 (February): 20–21.

Osborne, David. 1988. *Laboratories of Democracy.* Boston: Harvard Business School Press.

Page, Benjamin I. 1983. *Who Gets What from Government.* Berkeley: University of California Press.

Pangle, Thomas L. 1992. *The Ennobling of Democracy. The Challenge of the Postmodern Era.* Baltimore: Johns Hopkins University Press.

Patterson, James T. 1986. *America's Struggle Against Poverty 1900–1985.* Cambridge: Harvard University Press.

Pearson, Robert, and Geraint Williams. 1984. *Political Thought and Public Policy in the Nineteenth Century. An Introduction.* New York: Longman.

Peters, Charles, and Phillip Keisling, eds. 1985. *A New Road for America.* New York: Madison Books.

Phillips, Kevin. 1990. *The Politics of Rich and Poor. Wealth and the American Electorate in the Reagan Aftermath.* New York: Random House.

Pilon, Roger. 1991. "The Forgotten Ninth and Tenth Amendments," *Cato Policy Report* 13 (September-October): 12.

Pines, Burton Yale. 1991. "A Primer for Conservatives," *National Interest,* no. 23 (Spring): 61–68.

———. 1992. "The Great Potomac Earthquake," *Policy Review,* no. 62 (Fall): 18–23.

Podhoretz, Norman. 1981. "The Future Danger," *Commentary* 71 (April): 29–47.

———. 1982 "Kissinger Reconsidered," *Commentary* 73 (June): 19–28.

———. 1989. "New Vistas for Neoconservatives," *Conservative Digest* 15 (January-February): 56–57.

———. 1993. "A Conservative People, A Liberal Culture," *National Review* 45 (29 March): 45–46.

*Public Papers and Addresses of Franklin D. Roosevelt (1938–50).* Compiled and collated by Samuel I. Rosenman. New York: Random House.

*Public Papers of the Presidents of the United States.* Washington, D.C.: Government Printing Office, 1960– .

Ravitch, Diane. 1990. "Multiculturalism. E Pluribus Unum," *American Scholar* 59 (Summer): 337–54.

Rawls, John. 1971. *A Theory of Justice.* Cambridge: The Belknap Press of Harvard University Press.

———. 1982. "The Basic Liberties and Their Priority." In *The Tanner Lectures on Human Values,* III, ed. Sterling M. McMurrin. Salt Lake City: University of Utah Press.

———. 1993. *Political Liberalism.* New York: Columbia University Press.

Reich, Robert B. 1983. *The Next American Frontier.* New York: Times Books.

———. 1988. *The Power of Public Ideas.* Cambridge: Ballinger.

————. 1989. *The Resurgent Liberal: And Other Unfashionable Prophecies.* New York: Times Books.

Robbins, James S. 1990. "Defining a Libertarian Foreign Policy," *Liberty* 3 (July): 53–58.

Rockwell, Llewellyn H. 1990a. "The Case for Paleo-Libertarianism," *Liberty* 3 (January): 34–38.

————. 1990b. "The Case for Paleolibertarianism" and "Realignment on the Right," *RRR Rothbard-Rockwell Report.* Burlingame, Calif.: Center for Libertarian Studies.

Rothbard, Murray N. 1978, 1985. *For A New Liberty. The Libertarian Manifesto.* New York: Libertarian Review Foundation.

————. 1992. "A Strategy for the Right," *RRR Rothbard-Rockwell Report* 3 (March): 1-16.

Rothenberg, Randall. 1984. *The Neoliberals. Creating the New American Politics.* New York: Simon and Schuster.

Rowley, Charles K., ed. 1987. *Democracy and Public Choice. Essays in Honor of Gordon Tullock.* New York: Basil Blackwell.

Rummel, Rudolph J. 1983. "Libertarianism and International Violence," *Journal of Conflict Resolution* 27 (March): 27–71.

Rusher, William A. 1993. "Forward, March," *National Review* 45 (15 February): 37–46.

Schlesinger, Arthur M., Jr. 1990. "The Liberal Opportunity," *American Prospect,* no. 1 (Spring): 10–18.

————. 1991. *The Disuniting of America.* Knoxville, Tenn.: Whittle Direct Books.

Schultze, Charles L. 1977. *The Public Use of Private Interest.* Washington, D.C.: Brookings Institution.

Schwarz, John E. 1988. *America's Hidden Success. A Reassessment of Public Policy from Kennedy to Reagan.* New York: Norton.

Sears, David O., Richard R. Lau, Tom R. Tyler, and Harris M. Allen, Jr. 1980. "Self-Interest vs. Symbolic Politics in Policy Attitudes and Presidential Voting," *American Political Science Review* 74 (September): 670–84.

Sears, John F., ed. 1991. *Franklin D. Roosevelt and the Future of Liberalism.* Hyde Park, N.Y.: Franklin and Eleanor Roosevelt Institute.

Segal, David. 1994. "The *Real* Leader of the Opposition," *Washington Monthly* 26 (March): 38–48.

Seldon, Arthur. 1990. *Capitalism.* Cambridge, Mass.: Basil Blackwell.

Shapiro, Robert J. 1991. *Paying for Progress: A Progressive Strategy for Fiscal Discipline.* Washington, D.C.: Progressive Policy Institute.

————. 1993. "Tax and Mend," *New Republic* 208 (22 March): 19–24.

Smith, Adam. 1976 (1776). *The Wealth of Nations.* Ed. Edwin Cannan. Chicago: University of Chicago Press.

Smith, Fred L., Jr. 1992. "Carnival of Dunces," *National Review* 44 (6 July): 30–32.

Smith, Tom W. 1990. "Liberal and Conservative Trends in the United States Since World War II," *Public Opinion Quarterly* 54 (Winter): 479–507.

Sobran, Joseph. 1985. "Pensées: Notes for the Reactionary of Tomorrow," *National Review* 37 (31 December): 23–58.

Solarz, Stephen J. 1992. "A Once-in-a-Lifetime Opportunity," *National Interest,* no. 27 (Spring): 24–27.

Solow, Robert, et al. 1987. "The Conservative Revolution: A Roundtable Discussion," *Economic Policy* 2 (October): 181–200.

Sørensen, Georg. 1993. *Democracy and Democratization. Processes and Prospects in a Changing World.* Boulder, Colo.: Westview Press.

Spencer, Herbert. 1898. *The Principles of Ethics.* New York: Appleton.

Starr, Paul. 1991. "Liberalism After Socialism," *American Prospect,* no. 7 (Fall): 70–80.

Stelzer, Irwin M. 1993. "Clintonism Unmasked," *Commentary* 95 (May): 32–25.

Stockman, David A. 1986. *The Triumph of Politics. How the Reagan Revolution Failed.* New York: Harper & Row.

Sullivan, William M. 1982. *Reconstructing Public Philosophy.* Berkeley: University of California Press.

Surrey, Stanley S., and Paul R. McDaniel. 1985. *Tax Expenditures.* Cambridge: Harvard University Press.

Talbott, Strobe. 1990. "Rethinking the Red Menace," *Time* 135 (1 January): 66–71.

Taylor, Arthur J. 1971. *Laissez-faire and State Intervention in Nineteenth-Century Britain.* London: Macmillan.

Taylor, Jared. 1992. *Paved With Good Intentions.* New York: Carroll and Graf.

Theroux, David J. 1984. *Politics and Tyranny. Lessons in the Pursuit of Freedom.* San Francisco: Pacific Institute for Public Policy Research.

Thurow, Lester C. 1983. "From Infancy to Senility and Back," *New York Review of Books* 30 (3 March): 9–11.

———. 1992. "Communitarian vs. Individualistic Capitalism," *Responsive Community* 2 (Fall): 24–30.

Tinder, Glenn. 1993. "Liberalism and Its Enemies," *Atlantic Monthly,* 272 (October): 116–22.

Tonsor, Stephen J. 1986. "Why I Too Am Not a Neoconservative," *National Review* 38 (20 June): 54–56.

Trilling, Lionel. 1950. *The Liberal Imagination. Essays on Literature and Society.* New York: Viking.

Tugwell, Rexford Guy. 1958. *The Art of Politics.* Garden City, N.Y.: Doubleday.

U.S. Congress. House of Representatives. Committee on Ways and Means. 1990a. *Tax Progressivity and Income Distribution.* 101st Cong., 2d sess. 26 March.

———. Senate. Subcommittee of the Committee on Appropriations. 1990b. *Hearings on H.R. 5158.* 101st Cong., 2d sess. 8 May. Part 2.

———. Joint Economic Committee. 1991. Hearings. *The War on Poverty.* 25 July, 25 September, 19 November. 102d Cong., 1st sess.

Vogel, David. 1989. *Fluctuating Fortunes. The Political Power of Business in America.* New York: Basic Books.

Waldron, Jeremy. 1986. "Welfare and the Images of Charity," *Philosophical Quarterly* 46 (October): 463–82.

Wallop, Malcolm. 1994. "Can the GOP Take America Back?" *National Review* 46 (7 February): 36–41.

Weede, Erich. 1986. "Catch-up, Distributional Coalitions, and Government as Determinants of Economic Growth or Decline in Industrialized Democracies," *British Journal of Sociology* 37 (June): 194–220.

*Weekly Compilation of Presidential Documents.* Washington, D.C.

Weidenbaum, Murray. 1992. "Return of the 'R' Word. The Regulatory Assault on the Economy," *Policy Review,* no. 59 (Winter): 40–43.

Wheeler, Jack. 1992. "A Reagan Doctrine for the Liberation of the Peoples of China," *Conservative Review* 3 (June): 25–28.

Whitaker, Robert W., ed. 1982. *The New Right Papers.* New York: St. Martin's.

Wilcox, Clyde. 1988. "The Christian Right in Twentieth Century America: Continuity and Change," *Review of Politics* 50 (Fall): 659–81.

Will, George F. 1992. *Restoration. Congress, Term Limits and the Recovery of Deliberative Democracy.* New York: Free Press.

Wilson, James Q. 1985. "The Rediscovery of Character: Private Virtue and Public Policy," *Public Interest,* no. 81 (Fall): 3–16.

———. 1990. "The James Madison Lecture," *PS* 23 (December), 558–63.

———. 1992. "The Moral Sense," *American Political Science Review* 87 (March): 1–11.

## Legal Cases

*Brown v. Board of Education of Topeka,* 347 U.S. 483 (1954).
*Brown v. Board of Education of Topeka,* 348 U.S. 294 (1955).
*Green v. School Board of New Kent County,* 391 U.S. 430 (1968).
*Plessy v. Ferguson,* 163 U.S. 537 (1896).
*Roe v. Wade,* 410 U.S. 113 (1973).
*Stamps v. Detroit Edison,* 365 F.Supp. 87 (1973).

# Index

*A remarkable tour through contemporary American ideology. As guide, Van Dyke traverses numerous forms of liberalism and conservatism with both charm and clarity. The student will meet along the way theorists John Rawls, Friedrich Hayek, Murray Rothbard, and Russell Kirk, as well as politicians FDR, LBJ, Ronald Reagan, Jack Kemp, and William Bennett, and will be introduced to debates over "fusionism," economic vs. social equality, multiculturalism, "workfare," "learnfare" and welfare, neoisolationism vs. democratic internationalism. Chapters on the nineteenth-century British background and on the ideological dimensions of public choice theory are worth special commendation. **Philip Abbott,** *Wayne State University*

*For years, I have taught students in American Political Thought classes that liberals and conservatives vary as much within as across camps, for reasons that are as deeply rooted in philosophy as in contemporary politics. They are surprised, but receptive. At last we have a book that makes that case with authority, elegance, philosophical sophistication, and persuasiveness. **Jennifer Hochschild,** *Princeton University*

*A rich mix of history, ideology, and policy. Van Dyke shows what is at stake in choices among ideologies by illustrating their political applications. His analysis of liberals' New Deal and Great Society programs is especially thorough. The public choice and libertarianism chapters are unique. The distinction between five kinds of conservatism helps explain the Republicans' "family" quarrels. Van Dyke has an engaging style that moves easily back and forth between T.H. Green and Hubert Humphrey, Thomas Aquinas and Tim LaHaye, all the while sustaining a strong argument for giving worth to liberty. **Nancy S. Love,** *Penn State University*

*Ideology and Political Choice* is a fine guide to contemporary political ideas in practice, as valuable as a scorecard at a baseball game. The book is remarkably comprehensive, conspicuously fair-minded, and everywhere marked by Van Dyke's mixture of learning and common sense. **Wilson Carey McWilliams,** *Rutgers University*

*Van Dyke has produced an excellent analysis of the "isms" and ideologies that influence the lives of every American. In addition to perceptive reviews of liberalism, libertarianism, and conservatism, his examination of public choice theory is particularly thoughtful. Students and scholars of contemporary political theory will find this a must read. **James D. Savage,** *University of Virginia*

*A lively and illuminating examination and texturing of current ideologies on the American political landscape. Its gracefully written presentation will bring students to an understanding of the ideological impulses that shape our politics and help determine the country's current direction. I look forward to using it in my classes for its intelligence, its content, and its clarity. **Joel H. Silbey,** *Cornell University*

ISBN 1-56643-017-8

**Chatham House Publishers, Inc.**
Box One, Chatham, New Jersey 07928

1-56643-017-8